Slam the Door on Employee Lawsuits

Keep Your Business Out of Court

By
Paul M. Lusky, Esq.

CAREER PRESS
3 Tice Road, P.O. Box 687
Franklin Lakes, NJ 07417
1-800-CAREER-1
201-848-0310 (NJ and outside U.S.)
Fax: 201-848-1727

Copyright © 1998 by Paul M. Lusky, Esq.

SLAM THE DOOR ON EMPLOYEE LAWSUITS
ISBN 1-56414-311-2, $15.99
Cover design by Foster & Foster
Printed in the U.S.A. by Book-mart Press

To order this title by mail, please include price as noted above, $2.50 handling per order, and $1.50 for each book ordered. Send to: Career Press, Inc., 3 Tice Road, P.O. Box 687, Franklin Lakes, NJ 07417.

Or call toll-free 1-800-CAREER-1 (NJ and Canada: 201-848-0310) to order using VISA or MasterCard, or for further information on books from Career Press.

Library of Congress Cataloging-in-Publication Data

Lusky, Paul M., 1947-
    Slam the door on employee lawsuits : keep your business out of court / by Paul M. Lusky.
        p.   cm.
    Includes index.
    ISBN 1-56414-311-2 (pbk.)
    1. Labor laws and legislation--United States--Popular works.
    2. Discrimination in employment--Law and legislation--United States--Popular works.   3. Employees--Dismissal of--Law and legislation--United States--Popular works.   4. Employment at will--United States--Popular works.   I. Title.
    KF3457.Z9L87   1997
    344.7301'133--dc21   97-43562
                                                                          CIP

Acknowledgments

This book would never have been written without the encouragement and support of my wife, Beth. She is the one who inspired the idea of writing a book. She put up with my late nights and lost weekends working on the book. For all of those things and more, I am very grateful. I want to thank my teenage sons, Brian and Evan, for their enthusiastic reaction to the idea of their father writing a book. It fueled my enthusiasm for the project.

I want to thank all the attorneys at my law firm, Kruchko & Fries, for their support of this project. In particular, I want to thank John G. Kruchko and Jay R. Fries, senior partners with the firm, for their encouragement and for allowing me the time to finish what I started. I am particularly grateful for Jay's advice as I took the first tentative steps toward getting this book published. Special thanks to attorneys Kathleen A. Talty and Joan E. Book who took time away from their legal practice with the firm to provide professional and technical assistance to me. For their contributions to the finished project, I am grateful.

Finally, I wish to thank Linda Ashdown and Diane Schisler, legal secretaries with Kruchko and Fries, for their help in preparing and editing the manuscript for this book.

—Paul M. Lusky

Contents

Employers Are Under Siege

A jury in Seattle, Wash., concludes that an employer did not discriminate against a female sales manager but nevertheless awards her $11.7 million on her claim that the company retaliated against her for bringing gender discrimination issues to the attention of management. A Pennsylvania woman is awarded $1.4 million by a jury that determines that her employer defamed her by telling her co-employees that she stole a bag of potato chips. Employees working for a Connecticut telecommunications company are awarded $14.5 million because they were required to stay at the job site while they ate lunch.

Two female office workers in Florida receive an award of $6 million on their sexual harassment claim against a plastic surgeon. A female lab technician is awarded $4.2 million in Pennsylvania after she was successful in proving that a hostile environment existed for her in her place of employment. In California, a male employee claiming sexual harassment by his female supervisor (who allegedly forced him to have intercourse with her) is awarded over $1 million by a jury.

Texaco Corporation settles a race discrimination lawsuit brought by six black employees for $176 million. Martin Marietta Corporation agrees to pay $13 million in back pay and rehire 450 older workers at an estimated cost of $171 million in order to settle an age discrimination class action lawsuit. Southern California Edison Company enters into an $11.25 million settlement with nine black plaintiffs who brought a class action alleging that the utility company had limited pay increases, career advancement, and other employment opportunities for black employees.

In today's litigious society, employers have become a key target. The Commission on the Future of Worker-Management Relations, an advisory body appointed by President Clinton, analyzed data regarding lawsuits filed in federal court during a 20-year period from 1971 to 1991. The total number of personal injury cases filed in federal court during that 20-year period increased by 17 percent. The total number of employment law disputes filed in federal court, however, increased 430 percent in that same 20 year period, a larger increase than any other classification of cases. Employment claims are rapidly becoming the "slip and fall" action for the 21st century.

These statistics, while frightening in their own right, may understate the threat faced by employers. The Commission's study ended before passage of the Civil Rights Act of 1991, the Americans with Disabilities Act, and the Family and Medical Leave Act, all of which have generated even more litigation. The Civil Rights Act of 1991 is particularly responsible for luring many new plaintiff's attorneys into the employment litigation field. This statute allows plaintiffs to receive large compensatory and punitive damage awards for violations of employment discrimination statutes. The discharged employee has become a more appealing prospective client for many lawyers who had heretofore disdained representation of discharged employees because they could only recover back wages and "make whole" relief such as medical expenses.

The Civil Rights Act of 1991 also created a jury trial right for employees claiming discrimination, a procedural change that has increased the size of damage awards. The median jury verdict in employment cases in 1995 was $184,000, up more than 40 percent from the median verdict in 1994. Juries in employment law cases are notoriously sympathetic to plaintiffs and unsympathetic to corporate defendants. Many jurors have spent their entire working lives as nonsupervisory employees; very few have held positions where they were required to make hiring or firing decisions.

In addition to discrimination actions, employers are also being sued on various "wrongful discharge" theories. The once venerable employment-at-will rule, which held that employment may be terminated by either the employer or the employee at any time, for good reason, bad reason, or no reason at all, is riddled with exceptions such as the "public policy" exception or the "covenant of good faith and fair dealing" exception. Employees who cannot dredge up a public policy violation will, nevertheless, claim that their employers breached an employment contract by discharging them. Finally, in virtually every wrongful discharge or employment discrimination action, the employee bringing the lawsuit will also state several "tort" claims such as intentional infliction of emotional distress, assault, battery, defamation, and invasion of privacy. These tort claims also allow for the recovery of punitive damages, thus increasing the potential for large damage awards against employers.

How can a business protect itself from potential jury verdicts in favor of disgruntled employees? My primary goal in writing this book is to show employers how to avoid unnecessary labor and employment law problems and stay out of court. You may be asking yourself: *What in the world does a lawyer know about keeping employers out of court?* The answer is that I have spent the last 15 years doing exactly that—helping clients avoid costly employment litigation.

10 protective principles

This book is based on 10 protective principles that I have distilled from the advice that I have given employers over the last 15 years. The principles are not magical talismans for making employment litigation disappear. Rather, each principle is intended as a reminder to employers of certain strategies that can keep them out of court.

1. Employment-at-will is a myth.

Employers can no longer afford to discharge employees for "good reason, bad reason, or no reason at all." Even if it's only unemployment compensation liability, a discharge decision that is not grounded in a valid performance-based reason will cost the employer money.

2. Disclaim everything in your handbook.

Employers will be held accountable for promises they make to employees. If a statement is not intended as a promise, the employer's intention in this regard should be made clear to employees.

3. Never fire a pregnant woman.

Some employees—no, make that many employees—hold protected status under state and federal discrimination laws. Therefore, the employer should not discharge these employees without a well-documented nondiscriminatory reason.

4. There is no such thing as a "safe" workplace romance.

Sexual harassment is the most dangerous of all employment discrimination claims. Employers cannot allow sexual harassment to exist in their workplace no matter how benign its origin.

5. Give abusive or combative employees the maximum penalty.

The incidence of abusive, aggressive, or violent behavior in the workplace is increasing. Employers should take a very hard line against workplace violence.

6. Assume that every workplace injury will be an ADA disability.

Employers must remember that any chronic physical ailment, any bizarre mental disorder, or even an asymptomatic condition may be protected by the broad definition of disability in the Americans with Disabilities Act (ADA).

7. Never assume an employee is exempt.

Employers are cautioned against being overinclusive when categorizing employees as exempt for wage and hour purposes. The "salary basis" requirement for establishing an exemption from the overtime requirements in wage and hour statutes is undoubtedly the most violated provision in the federal wage and hour regulations.

8. If they don't need to know, don't tell.

Employers should abide by the rule of confidentiality when handling personnel matters. Employees have received huge damage awards on claims that an untrue communication by their employer damaged their reputation.

9. Employee privacy is not an inalienable right.

Employee privacy need not be a primary concern for employers as they operate their business. There are laws that regulate workplace privacy issues but, in general, employers who do not create an expectation of privacy for employees by allowing them to believe that they or their possessions will be free from surveillance or searches have no reason to fear invasion of privacy claims.

10. It's never too late for union avoidance.

Employers who practice positive employee relations, which is really the basis for the first nine principles, will not be targeted by unions for organizing. However, even if an employer is confronted with the prospect of a union organizing campaign, it is never too late to defeat the union.

Goals and objectives

In writing this book, I have tried to give practical advice for avoiding problems that can lead to litigation. Each chapter starts with an introductory narrative which, although completely fictional, has its roots in actual problems that can confront employers. As you read each narrative, try and figure out what the employer is doing right or where there has been a misstep. Sometimes the result is obvious, but there also may be a surprise along the way.

I have built the legal discussion in each chapter around actual cases. Employers can take a lot of information from the case discussions in each chapter, which they can apply to their own business. I have closed each chapter with a summation section that outlines the things employers should be doing to minimize their potential for liability.

This book is intended as a practical guide for employers, human resource professionals, managers, and supervisors who want to avoid workplace problems. It is not intended to give legal advice on any specific problem where particular facts underlying the problem may recommend analysis by a competent labor and employment law attorney. This book will help managers respond effectively to day-to-day issues that arise in the workplace. The author is not soliciting an attorney-client relationship with any particular reader.

—Paul M. Lusky

Chapter 1

Employment-at-Will
Is a Myth

Susan Borden, the Human Resources Director for Ace Electronics, was sitting at her desk waiting for her phone to ring. The company had moved to dismiss a complaint by a former employee, a female who claimed her termination from employment violated public policy. Now, the judge has called both the company's attorney and the plaintiff's lawyer to his courtroom for a hearing on the motion. The company's lawyer, Paula Lionville, was confident of victory and told Susan not to worry—Alabama courts did not recognize the public policy exception to the employment-at-will rule.

Susan had transferred to Ace from its parent company in California. She constantly reminded herself, "This is Alabama not California. The employment-at-will rule still exists in this state." It was a good thing too, because the supervisor who fired the employee really did not have "good cause" to let her go. Susan was still incredulous at Frank Johnson's reason for firing Judy Scott. She remembered the day he walked into her office and said, "I had to let Judy Scott go; she's getting married."

Susan asked Frank to explain why Judy being married made a difference in the way she would be doing her job. Frank said, "It doesn't. I just told her she would be fired if she got married and now she is getting married, so she's fired." Susan replied, "Frank, you can't do that!" "Yes, I can," Frank responded resolutely. "It's already done. Just get the paperwork ready." Susan had to be careful because Frank was the plant superintendent, but she knew that she could not let his decision go unchallenged. She said, "Frank, I will have to go to Jack Davis about this." She was referring to the company president. Frank said, "Go ahead, he won't overrule me," and he walked out of her office.

It turned out that Frank was right; Jack did not overrule him. Susan tried to appeal to Jack's sense of fair play, but that was a mistake. She should have convinced Jack that the employee was good at her sales job; that business would suffer if she was fired. Jack was a "bottom-line" kind of guy and as long as his company continued to make a profit, he left all the personnel decisions to Frank.

At times like this, Susan felt totally unappreciated. "If Jack had listened to me," she thought, "Judy Scott would never have been fired and we would not have ended up in court." Susan had heard rumors that prior to her arrival at Ace, Frank Johnson had tried to date Judy Scott. There was talk that after Judy had rejected his advances, Frank had given her a hard time, directing some lewd comments her way. Still, Susan was never able to get any hard evidence about Frank's involvement with Judy. No one, not even Judy Scott, wanted to talk to her about Frank Johnson.

Of course, Judy talked plenty to her lawyer after she was discharged. She filed a sexual harassment charge with the Equal Employment Opportunity Commission, claiming her discharge was in retaliation for her rejection of Frank Johnson's sexual advances. The company denied all her allegations in a position statement to the agency and no employees came forward to support Judy's allegations.

Judy Scott did not sue for sexual harassment in court; instead, she claimed that her discharge violated public policy and sued for wrongful discharge. She argued that terminating a person's employment because of a decision to get married violated public policy because it injures the fundamental right to marry. She also sued for invasion of privacy and intentional infliction of emotional distress.

"The hearing must be taking a long time," Susan thought. Finally, Paula Lionville called—and Susan didn't like what she heard. "Well, I've got some bad news," said Paula. "Although the judge agreed with our argument that the wrongful discharge claim should be dismissed, he said that plaintiff's invasion of privacy claim has to go to trial." "I don't believe it," said Susan. "How in the world does her discharge violate her privacy rights?"

Paula tried to explain, "The judge said a reasonable jury could find that the discharge wrongfully intruded into Ms. Scott's private activities causing her mental suffering. It all goes back to Frank's admission that he fired Judy for wanting to get married."

Susan was really down now. "What do we do next?" she asked Paula. "Now we prepare for trial or we settle," replied Paula.

The employment-at-will rule

The personnel decision that has the greatest potential for triggering litigation is the employer's decision to terminate the employment relationship. Despite the fact that employment law in most states is supposed to be governed by the employment-at-will doctrine—that is, employment may be terminated by either the employer or the employee at any time, for good reason, bad reason, or no reason at all—employers often find themselves embroiled in litigation over a discharge decision.

The employment-at-will rule has been overwhelmed by exceptions to the rule. Initially, the exceptions were created by statutes. The most obvious example is Title VII of the Civil Rights Act of 1964, which holds that a terminated employee whose employment was thought to be at-will may, nevertheless, allege that his discharge was a "pretext" for unlawful discrimination. If the employee is a member of a protected category under an antidiscrimination statute, for example, sex, age, race, disability, religion, or national origin, and that employee decides to sue, the employer must be able to state a credible nondiscriminatory reason for the discharge decision. When faced with a claim that a discharge was discriminatory, it does little good to argue that the plaintiff was an employee at-will and could be discharged for any reason at all.

Other statutory exceptions to the employment-at-will rule include so-called "whistle blower" statutes. Many federal and state statutes now protect employees who report illegal or improper practices of their employer to the authorities. An example is the Whistle Blower Protection Act, which provides a remedy to federal government employees who are discharged for revealing a violation of law or regulation, gross mismanagement or abuse of authority, or substantial danger to public health and safety. Many other federal statutes addressing discrimination, health and safety, or wage and hour regulations include nonretaliation provisions that protect employees who file a claim or exercise some other right under the statute.

There are existing whistle blower statutes in some states that apply to disclosures by both government employees and private sector employees. There are also many other state statutes protecting specific disclosures by employees or prohibiting retaliation against employees for exercising their rights under state law. Obviously, a whistle blower who is protected by a statute is no longer an employee-at-will for purposes of discharging the employee for the whistle blowing. Where there is no statutory protection, an employee discharged for reporting illegal acts must look to common law protections, including the public policy exception to the employment-at-will rule.

The employment-at-will rule is also riddled by judicial exceptions. For example, almost all states now recognize that a discharge that violates a "clear mandate of public policy" is actionable in court regardless of the fact that the employment was "at-will." These public policy wrongful discharge actions are usually grounded in statements of public policy found in statutes, regulations, or state constitutional provisions. For example, a discharge because the employee wants to serve on a jury or because he or she has filed a worker's compensation claim are very common public policy claims and may subject the employer to liability for both compensatory and punitive damages. As illustrated by the fictional narrative that introduced this chapter, courts in states like Alabama that do not recognize the public policy exception will still find ways to protect the rights of discharged employees.

Employers must also avoid discharges that breach an express or implied contract with the employee. Courts have enforced promises in employee handbooks where the document does not contain a disclaimer of contractual intent. Thus, if the manual states that employees will only be discharged "for cause," employers will be expected to have a performance-related reason for the discharge decision.

A number of states also recognize the implied covenant of good faith and fair dealing as an exception to the employment-at-will rule. Courts in these states will require the employers to treat the employee "fairly" even where the employment has been held to be an employment-at-will. Some states use the covenant to prohibit an "unfair" discharge while others limit the covenant's application to ensuring that the discharged employee receives all compensation and/or benefits due him.

Other tort theories of liability have been used by discharged employees to try and circumvent the employment-at-will rule. One such theory, an action for intentional infliction of emotional distress, will be discussed in more detail at the end of this chapter. Other torts, like defamation and invasion of privacy, are also frequently used to try and get damages for an alleged wrongful discharge.

The "public policy" wrongful discharge suit

The cases recognizing a public policy exception to the employment-at-will rule are extremely varied in their reasoning. In most cases, however, the basis for a public policy wrongful discharge suit is usually grounded in one of three reasons: 1) The employee has been discharged for exercising a statutory right; 2) the employee has been discharged for refusing to commit an illegal act; or 3) the employee has been fired because he or she threatened to report or did report illegal activities of the employer. This latter category may involve a wholly internal complaint process or a disclosure to government authorities. As mentioned above, these "whistle blowers" may be protected by statutory prohibitions against retaliation, in which case the employee may have to pursue a statutory remedy because a common law suit for wrongful discharge will be foreclosed under the exclusive remedy doctrine.

There is yet no clear and concise understanding of what constitutes a "public policy." Some courts have been careful to distinguish between a discharge that burdens a public interest as opposed to one that thwarts an employee's private interest. One state supreme court described the basis for the tort as a discharge for a "socially undesirable motive." The crux of the problem for employers is that the definition of "public policy" has been left for courts to determine on a case-by-case basis. In California, where the public policy exception to the employment-at-will rule first received wide acceptance, the courts have generally held that the public policy of the state is found in its constitution, its statutes, and the decisions of its courts. Other states have expanded the sources of public policy for the purpose of protecting at-will employees. For example, Colorado courts have held that administrative regulations and the professional ethics code can serve as the basis for a public policy wrongful discharge claim. Other courts have even gone so far as to find sources of public policy in "sound morality."

The many sources of public policy

There are so many potential sources for public policy that employers cannot be certain that a discharged employee won't find a creative plaintiff's attorney to argue an after-the-fact violation of public policy in a wrongful discharge suit, despite the fact that the employee never voiced any policy concerns during his or her employment. A discussion of some of the published cases will illustrate the danger to employers in this area of the law.

In *Tameny v. Atlantic Richfield Co.*, a landmark decision in California, the plaintiff alleged that he was discharged after 15 years of service because he refused to participate in a scheme to fix retail gasoline prices in violation of antitrust laws. The California Supreme Court, while holding that the plaintiff could maintain a tort action for wrongful discharge, stated that it is against "public policy" for an employer to demand that an employee commit a criminal act to further the employer's interests. The source for the public policy in *Tameny* was the federal antitrust laws. *Tameny* represents the classic public policy wrongful discharge theory: an alleged discharge for refusing to violate the law.

An Arizona decision, however, found a violation of public policy where no law was specifically violated. Instead, the employee was discharged for reasons the court described as running "contrary to public standards of morality." While on a camping trip with her supervisor and other employees, the plaintiff refused to participate in a skit that parodied the song "Moon River" and concluded with the participants in the skit "mooning" the audience. She also refused to participate in the "Moon River" skit when it was performed twice more after the group returned to work following the camping trip. The plaintiff claimed that she was discharged for refusing to go along with the "mooning."

The plaintiff argued that the source of the public policy that was violated by her discharge was the Arizona criminal statute prohibiting indecent exposure in public. The Arizona Supreme Court said that a violation of public policy occurs even if the employer had reason to believe there would be no crime because "all the onlookers were voyeurs and would not be offended" by the display of bare buttocks. The court said, "In this situation, there might be no crime, but it would be a violation of public policy to compel the employee to do an act ordinarily proscribed by the law." The court protected the employee's refusal to moon in public by concluding that the legislature had established a clear policy that "exposure of one's anus or genitals is contrary to public standards of morality."

In a New Jersey case, a plaintiff brought a wrongful discharge action after she was fired for refusing to perform a catheterization. The plaintiff was an X-ray technician, not a licensed nurse, and thus could not legally perform the medical procedure. The New Jersey Supreme Court held that public policy prohibits the termination of an employment-at-will in retaliation for the employee's refusal to perform an illegal act. The court emphasized that "this rule is especially cogent where the subject matter is the administration of medical treatment, an area in which the public has a foremost interest and that is extensively regulated by various state agencies."

In another decision out of California, a plaintiff was able to use a Penal Code provision as the source of public policy for his wrongful discharge claim. The plaintiff was a vice president for a corporation that had as one of its divisions, a department store chain. The plaintiff and his girlfriend visited one of the department stores where, upon leaving the store, both the plaintiff and his girlfriend were forcibly detained. The plaintiff's girlfriend was accused of theft and made to enter a room where she was strip searched by security personnel. The plaintiff sued after he was fired about six months later allegedly because he complained to management that its search policy was unlawful. The court concluded that the plaintiff had stated a viable cause of action for wrongful discharge in violation of public policy where he alleged that: 1) The strip search was contrary to a California Penal Code provision; 2) he protested to management about the procedure; and 3) the company terminated him in retaliation for his protest.

In Connecticut, a court ruled that it was against public policy to discharge a movie theater projectionist who had emptied the theater at the request of police officers looking for a possible burglary suspect. On the day in question, the plaintiff was working alone in the theater. While he was selling tickets, he heard noises coming from the projection booth that made him believe there was a burglar in the booth. The plaintiff then called the police, but when they arrived, they refused to go in the theater unless the plaintiff turned on the lights. When the plaintiff turned on the lights, the entire theater emptied. The police found no burglar.

When the plaintiff was discharged, he sued for wrongful discharge. The court ruled in his favor, holding that it was a public policy of the state to protect the safety of the public at movie theaters. The court found that the plaintiff, by turning on the lights, was merely fulfilling the employer's legal duty to protect the public.

A decision by the Washington Court of Appeals demonstrates that employees may possess facts, unknown to, or at least not contemplated by the employer at the time of discharge, that can form the basis for a public policy wrongful discharge claim. If the employer, however, can demonstrate that the employee had an opportunity to raise her public policy concerns, and either failed to do so or had those concerns addressed by the employer, the employer is likely to prevail at trial.

For example, in the Washington case, a nurse was discharged for four separate work-related infractions, including not giving medications as prescribed and violating the nursing home's narcotics control procedures. After her discharge, however, the nurse sued her employer, claiming among other things, that she was discharged because she complained about alleged unsafe practices at the nursing home. The court recognized that a public policy against abuse and neglect in nursing homes existed in the state but found that the plaintiff was not able to show that the alleged complaints were the real reason for her discharge. In fact, the incidents to which the plaintiff was referring occurred sometime prior to her discharge and she did not treat them with significant concern. For example, she discovered that a door did not lock properly and she reported it to the maintenance supervisor. She found a foreign substance in a patient's ointment and she noted it on a chart distributed to the director of nursing. She allegedly found glass or plastic in another container of ointment but failed to report it to anyone.

The court of appeals rejected her retaliatory discharge claim. The court said the nurse never treated the alleged incidents of neglect and abuse "as anything other than an isolated or unintentional incident." Noting that the plaintiff had never even reported the second "ointment" incident, the court found that the plaintiff had failed to show that her employer's articulated reasons for discharge were a pretext to cover up "a conspiracy to prevent [her] from exposing abuse and neglect at the nursing home."

Some states require an evil intent or degree of malevolence on the part of the employer before they will award damages for wrongful discharge. For example, in *Monge v. Beebe Rubber Co.*, one of the first cases recognizing the public policy exception, the New Hampshire Supreme Court concluded that a retaliatory discharge of an employee for refusing to date the foreman was motivated by bad faith or hostility and was a breach of the employment contract. The court said that "the employer's interest in running his business as he sees fit must be balanced against the interest of the employee in maintaining [her] employment." The court concluded that a bad faith termination of an at-will employment "is not [in] the best interest of the economic system or the public good."

New Hampshire courts continue to require the element of bad faith before ruling that a termination is in violation of public policy or contrary to "the public good." One case that met this requirement involved the discharge of an employee for filing a tort claim against his supervisor after the supervisor's dog bit the employee's son. The company fired the plaintiff almost immediately after he had written a letter to the supervisor advising him of his liability for the dog bite. The court said the discharge violated the public policy that guarantees "unrestricted access to the courts." The court noted that the plaintiff was fired on the same day that his supervisor received the liability letter.

Finally, a wrongful discharge decision out of Virginia underscores the uncertain status of the concept of public policy and the resulting lack of clear guidance to employers regarding the exact nature of the public policy exception. In 1985, the Virginia Supreme Court recognized an exception to the employment-at-will rule in *Bowman v. State Bank of Keysville,* where the court held that ex-employees can sue for both punitive and compensatory damages when their discharge violates some "established public policy." However, the court gave no further definition to the term "public policy."

The first public policy exceptions recognized in Virginia after the *Bowman* decision were based on Virginia statutes. This reliance on statutory sources for public policy protection changed, however, when a Virginia Circuit Court Judge used federal highway regulations as a source of Virginia public policy.

The case involved a long distance truck driver who claimed that he was ordered by his supervisor to drive for a longer time than was permitted by federal regulations and to falsify his trip logs to make them appear to comply with rules governing interstate carriers. He also claimed that he was ordered to drive long distances without taking required rest periods. At first, he went along with his employer's demands but when he later refused to continue this practice, he was discharged. The judge ruled that the plaintiff had stated an actionable claim for retaliatory discharge in violation of Virginia public policy. This decision is another example of the increased judicial willingness to create expanded protections for discharged employees. If every regulation is to be a source of protection against discharge for employees, the uncertainty for employers will obviously be magnified.

Constitutional provisions as a source of public policy

There are a number of decisions that have rejected the U.S. Constitution or state constitutions as sources of public policy where such constitutional provisions prohibit only government infringement of individual rights and thus require "state action" to implicate those protections. For example, the U.S. District Court for the Eastern District of Pennsylvania has held that the right to be free from unreasonable searches and seizures under the Fourth Amendment of the U.S. Constitution cannot be the basis for public policy exceptions to the employment-at-will doctrine under Pennsylvania law.

In this case, the plaintiff worked as a sales clerk for his employer for 15 years. In January 1990, the company adopted a drug and alcohol policy requiring all employees to sign a form consenting to urinalysis screening for drug use as a precondition for continued employment. The consent form that all employees were required to execute also authorized the employer to conduct searches of employees' personal effects located on company premises. The plaintiff refused to sign the consent form and was thereafter discharged from employment.

The plaintiff sued the company for wrongful discharge, alleging that the company's actions in terminating him were in violation of public policies embodied in the First and Fourth Amendments to the Constitution. The U.S. District Court for the Eastern District of Pennsylvania rejected the plaintiff's claim and observed that the Pennsylvania Superior Court "has not recognized a wrongful discharge public policy emanating from a constitutional amendment." The court concluded that in a dispute "between private parties, where no allegation of state action has been made, the constitutional provision cited by the plaintiff should not apply."

The District Court's decision was undoubtedly correct in its analysis that constitutional provisions should not be the basis for public policy exceptions to the employment-at-will rule. The Bill of Rights to the Constitution protects against government infringement of individual rights—it does not apply to conduct by private employers. If the decision by the court had been otherwise, purely private acts of employers would be subject to the limitations of state and federal constitutions and the "state action" defense would be meaningless.

Unfortunately, there have been decisions that have used the Constitution as a source of public policy despite the fact that the Bill of Rights only prohibits government infringement of individual rights. For example, the Maryland Court of Special Appeals has held that a real estate management company that fired an apartment manager for refusing to enter the tenants' apartments and "snoop through" their private papers had wrongfully discharged the manager and could be liable for damages. Using some very loose language, the court stated that its ruling was based upon its belief that "the constitutionally protected right of privacy, the right to be free of...snooping, spying, rummaging or searching through one's personal and private papers, is such a fundamental right that no employer may require an employee to violate it as a condition of employment."

Carried to its logical extreme, the decision would require an employer to be a guarantor of constitutional rights in the workplace. One can only imagine the disharmony that will result if every employee exercised their freedom of speech rights with impunity in the workplace. Suppose a salesman disparages his employer's product. Must his supervisor refrain from disciplining him for fear of violating his First Amendment rights? Hopefully, the "public policy" exception to the employment-at-will rule will not expand to the parameters suggested by the Maryland court's decision.

....

Employer defenses

As mentioned above, a plaintiff will not have a successful public policy wrongful discharge claim unless she can establish that she was discharged either in retaliation 1) for asserting her statutory rights, 2) for her refusal to perform an illegal act at the request of her employer, or 3) because her employer directly violated a statute by dismissing her from employment. Many courts have also emphasized the requirement that, in order to state a cause of action for wrongful termination, the discharge must violate a "substantial" or "clear mandate" of public policy.

For example, in *Burgess v. Chicago Sun Times*, an Illinois court refused to allow a delivery driver to go forward with his wrongful discharge complaint where he could not show that his discharge violated public policy. The plaintiff was employed as a driver for the purpose of delivering newspapers to retail vendors. On two occasions within a week's time, the plaintiff was assaulted and robbed. He requested reassignment to another route but his request was refused. After he refused to return to the route assigned to him, he was fired.

The plaintiff sued for retaliatory discharge claiming public policy was violated by his dismissal. The court found, however, that the plaintiff had not stated a "clearly mandated public policy" but was merely seeking a remedy for violation of his own private interests. The court said that the plaintiff had not been asked to do anything illegal or improper nor was he asked to engage in activities that would be contrary to public policy. The employer simply asked the driver to perform work that had been assigned to him. The court said the driver was aware of the risks when he took the job and his decision not to return to that job because of fear and apprehension was the cause of his discharge.

In another decision by a federal court in Louisiana, the plaintiff was simply not able to fit the facts of his discharge within the categories of discharge decisions that have been found to implicate the public policy exception. The plaintiff worked on an offshore rig for an oil exploration company. While on the offshore rig, the plaintiff illegally pumped waste materials overboard at the direction of his supervisor and with the assurance that if he got caught, the company would "help him out."

After the plaintiff was transferred back to a land-base, he was interviewed by a representative of the Alabama Attorney General's Office. The company made no attempt to influence him and, in fact, he was told to "go tell the truth." Soon after the plaintiff spoke to the Attorney General, however, he was discharged for misconduct.

He sued for wrongful discharge claiming that the discharge violated public policy because his employer was trying to "cover up" the illegal dumping activity. The court said, however, that it was difficult to see how he could prove such an accusation because, by the time the plaintiff was discharged, the "cat was already out of the bag." The record also showed that the plaintiff's employer fully cooperated with the state's investigation. The court concluded that there was nothing in the record to indicate a "cover up."

Next, the plaintiff alleged that he was discharged as a "scapegoat." The court said it might be morally reprehensible to discharge lower-level personnel involved in illegal conduct while retaining higher-level personnel, but it would not violate public policy to do so. The court said, "The court is not aware of any statutorily or jurisprudentially established policy against 'scapegoatism.'"

Finally, the plaintiff claimed he was discharged in retaliation for what he told the Alabama Attorney General. The court said that if the company had discharged the employee for not lying to the Attorney General, that would have been a violation of public policy. But the plaintiff admitted that his employer made no attempt to get him to lie and, in fact, told him to tell the truth. The court concluded that he had no claim for retaliatory discharge on such facts.

The willingness of courts to find sources of public policy varies from state to state. Thus, it is not possible to state with any certainty whether a plaintiff claiming a public policy in nonstatutory sources is likely to be successful in court. As will be explained later, the best way to avoid a public policy claim is to use the termination process to eliminate any possible claim. For every court that appears to go out of its way to create public policy for the protection of employees, there are those courts that steadfastly refuse to recognize a new source of public policy despite the apparent arbitrariness of an employer's decision.

For example, in one case, a restaurant manager took a job at a hotel owned and operated by his father's management company. Everything appeared to be going along fine until the son married a Roman Catholic. The father did not like the son's chosen spouse or her religion and he told the son that he would be fired unless he divorced his wife. When he refused to divorce his wife, the son was fired.

He sued for wrongful discharge claiming that his termination violated a Pennsylvania public policy in favor of family cohesiveness. The plaintiff pointed to general policy statements in the Pennsylvania Divorce Code that provided that the family deserves protection and preservation and also the state's prohibition against testamentary attempts to destroy the family. The federal district court rejected the plaintiff's arguments, finding that the policy statements relied upon by the plaintiff were too vague to be used as a basis for the public policy exception to the employment-at-will rule.

Similarly, in another case out of Pennsylvania, a female employee working in a doctor's office was raped by her estranged husband and severely beaten with a pipe at gun point. She received medical attention and returned to work a short time later. When the doctor who employed her found out about the spousal abuse, he terminated her employment, allegedly because she had been a victim of violent crime and he was concerned for the physical and emotional danger to other employees and patients if the estranged husband came to the workplace and engaged in further violent behavior.

The plaintiff sued for wrongful discharge arguing that the discharge violated the public policy in favor of protecting an employee's right to privacy and the policy protecting victims of crime or spousal abuse. As to the first count, the court found that the doctor had not intruded on her privacy. She was the one who revealed the circumstances of her spouse's abuse to a co-worker.

With regard to the alleged policy protecting victims of crime and domestic abuse, the court found that the statutes referred to by the plaintiff (Protection from Abuse Act, Crime Victim's Compensation Board) did not create a protected employment class. Neither statute provided for employment rights or privileges to victims of crime. The court dismissed the plaintiff's claim, stating, "Plaintiff was not discharged because she refused to violate the law, because she complied with the law, or because she exercised a right or privilege granted by the law." The court concluded, therefore, that no "clear mandate" of public policy had been identified by her complaint.

Beware of discharges that implicate statutory concerns

A general rule can be divined from the published cases dealing with public policy violations. In cases where the alleged public policy is not closely connected to a statute, courts are more likely to refuse to find a cause of action for wrongful termination. Therefore, where a plaintiff can only point to an administrative regulation as the source of the alleged public policy, it may be that the public policy is not substantial enough to sustain a cause of action for wrongful discharge. This may depend upon the nature of the regulation, however. Also, the discharge of an employee for refusing to violate an administrative regulation should not be held to contravene public policy unless the impact of the statute giving birth to the implementing regulations would be severely undermined if employees were fired without recourse for following the regulations. It is not always clear, however, that a substantial public policy is undermined when an employee is discharged for refusing to violate an administrative regulation.

For example, suppose an employee is discharged for refusing to perform work on an automobile's emission control system because, although he is licensed to perform such work, his employer is not properly licensed under an administrative regulation. The "policy" behind the licensing requirement is not severely undermined by the employee's discharge. The state may require licensing to insure that emission control systems are operating properly in order to reduce pollution. Since the employee is licensed to do the work and, presumably, knows how to properly perform the work, the policy of reducing pollution is satisfied, not undermined, if the work is performed. Indeed, if the work is done, the automobile would probably produce less emissions than if the work was not done.

It is important to remember that the foregoing example is not a situation where an employee is fired for refusing to falsify emission control reports or for refusing to alter an emission control system. Nor was the employee fired for reporting to the authorities that his employer did not have a license. If an employee's complaint involved such activities, then public policy could very well be violated.

When faced with a public policy claim based on an administrative regulation, an argument can be made that only the state legislature, and not administrative agencies or the judiciary, should declare public policy. In fact, as shown by the cases discussed in this chapter, it is quite rare to find a decision where a court recognized a public policy that was not embodied in, or at least closely connected to, a legislative enactment. Although a legislature may delegate certain of its rule-making powers to various administrative agencies, it seems unlikely that the legislature can also delegate its power to declare "public policy" as well. In fact, legislators usually declare their own "public policies," leaving just the implementation of these policies to administrative agencies.

Urging the courts to allow legislatures to define public policy is a frequent argument by management attorneys in wrongful discharge actions. Unfortunately, the tremendous growth of the judicially created public policy exception to the employment-at-will rule indicates that courts have not always been very receptive to this legal argument. As with all litigation "strategies," it is the employer who pays the bill for an attorney who wants to "fight it out" in court. Sometimes litigation is necessary to vindicate the employer's rights. In the case of public policy wrongful discharge actions, it is usually better for the employer not to get involved in such actions in the first place. As will be explained later in this chapter, there is a checklist employers can use when discharging employees to ensure that no possible public policy has been violated. Also, by encouraging the use of an internal employee complaint procedure, the employer should have notice of the employee's public policy theory before it can mature into a full-fledged litigation complaint.

The conflict of remedies

As explained above, employees may be protected by whistle blower statutes and/or retaliation provisions in other protective statutes. A number of courts have ruled that if a remedy is available to the employee under a statutory provision, the employee should not be allowed to use a public policy wrongful discharge suit to recover damages. In fact, the employer may be better off forcing the employee to use the statutory remedy as many of the whistle blower statutes do not provide for punitive damages as an element of the damages award.

Two different cases with two distinctive results demonstrate the potential for conflict between statutory protections and the common law wrongful discharge action grounded in a violation of public policy. In the first case, a plaintiff in Indiana who was fired for complying with a jury duty summons failed to file a claim within 90 days as required by the state's whistle blower protection statute for service on jury duty. She instead filed a wrongful discharge case in court. The defendant moved to dismiss, arguing that the jury duty statute, with its prohibition against retaliation, was the plaintiff's exclusive remedy. The Indiana Court of Appeals disagreed and allowed the plaintiff to sue for wrongful discharge. The court said that the statute did not clearly specify its status as an exclusive remedy and therefore the plaintiff's right to serve on the jury and the selection process itself must be protected.

A slightly different result occurred in a 1988 decision out of Michigan. In that case, the plaintiff's wife received obscene phone calls, including one threatening to rape her, from an unknown individual. The calls continued for almost 18 months. The couple worked with the police to identify the caller but were unsuccessful. One day in August, however, the plaintiff and his wife heard an upper-level manager saying grace at the company picnic. The plaintiff's wife immediately recognized the manager's voice as the person who had been making the obscene calls.

After the plaintiff angrily confronted the manager at work and then refused the company's request to drop a criminal investigation against the manager, the plaintiff was discharged. He sued for wrongful discharge claiming the company was trying to prohibit him from pursuing the manager by conditioning his continued employment on an agreement to "stifle" the investigation into the criminal wrongdoing. He alleged that this conduct violated public policy.

The court agreed with the plaintiff and held that he had stated a viable public policy claim. The court allowed the plaintiff to receive damages of $152,000 despite the defendant's argument that the Michigan Whistle Blowers' Protection Act was the plaintiff's exclusive remedy. The court agreed that prior cases had held the whistle blowers' Act to be an exclusive remedy but, because the defendant's attorney had not raised the issue before the trial court, the court of appeals ruled that the issue was not properly before it. The result would undoubtedly have been different had the defendant raised the exclusive remedy argument in a timely manner.

Whistle blower statutes may be a viable alternative to the continued explosion in the courts of public policy wrongful discharge litigation. Both the statute cited in the Indiana case and the Michigan Whistle Blowers' Protection Act require that claims be brought within 90 days of discharge. The short limitations period in these statutes is obviously preferable to the statutes of limitations in most states for common law tort or contract actions. In almost all cases, the applicable statute of limitations will be at least one year and often can be five to seven years in duration. Thus, the current system for adjudicating wrongful discharge cases allows for very stale claims to be heard in court.

Although the damages available in the whistle blower statutes obviously vary from state to state, many such statutes only award actual damages to the whistle blower and do not allow punitive damages. Again, avoiding punitive damages is a distinct advantage for employers because the huge damage awards in many of these wrongful discharge suits result not from any compensatory award to the plaintiff/employee, but from the jury's desire to punish the employer.

Intentional infliction of emotional distress

Wrongful discharge suits do not come with only one theory of liability. Plaintiffs' lawyers will bring every cause of action they can to increase their chances of winning. Thus, although the complaint may allege that the discharge violated public policy, plaintiffs will also claim that the discharge was a breach of their employment agreement. If available to the plaintiff in the particular jurisdiction chosen for the suit, the complaint will undoubtedly also contain a cause of action for breach of the implied covenant of good faith and fair dealing.

Tort causes of action are a particular favorite of plaintiffs' attorneys because of the availability of punitive damages in such claims. A frequent tort claim brought by discharged employees is an action for intentional infliction of emotional distress or outrage. This cause of action, however, is not an easy one for employees to use to recover damages. Most states require proof of outrageous conduct by the employer that causes severe emotional distress to the employee. The discharge decision standing alone can usually not be the basis for an intentional infliction of emotional distress. There must be some outrageous behavior by the employer or its supervisors apart from the discharge decision. Consequently, the tort has been most successful as an adjunct to sexual harassment or racial harassment claims.

For example, a Mexican-American successfully convinced the Supreme Court of Washington that he and his wife had a viable claim for the tort of outrage where the husband was subjected to continuous humiliation and embarrassment during his employment by reason of racial jokes, slurs, and comments about him in the presence of other employees. He was also wrongfully accused of stealing property owned by the employer following his discharge. These false statements made it impossible for the employee to find other employment in the area and, according to the court, he and his wife faced "public scorn and ridicule." The court concluded that the employer's conduct went beyond "reasonable bounds of decency" and caused the plaintiff severe emotional distress.

A decision by the Maryland Court of Appeals, however, demonstrates that even where there is substantial harassment, plaintiffs will have difficulty in recovering damages under the tort theory of intentional infliction of emotional distress. In this case, a female management trainee confronted her immediate supervisor about his romance with an assistant manager at the store. Almost immediately after complaining, the trainee's boss began harassing her, ordering her to put a promotional banner on the roof without help, phoning her at home on her day off, and assigning her a substandard assistant manager. Two months later, the trainee and two other employees were ordered to take polygraphs after $1,600 was discovered missing from the store safe. Within days, the manager suspended this employee pending an investigation regarding the missing money. She was then demoted, her salary was cut by $11,000, and she was assigned to a store where she was to work for someone she had previously supervised. Two days later, the employee sought psychiatric help and was hospitalized for six months for what her psychiatrist called "severe depression and homicidal as well as suicidal thoughts, relating to her work situation."

The employee sued her employer for intentional infliction of emotional distress. A jury awarded the plaintiff $145,000 in damages, but the trial judge overturned the verdict finding no evidence that the company was aware of any emotional condition that would have made the plaintiff especially vulnerable. The Maryland Court of Appeals affirmed the trial court's decision stating, "The workplace is not always a tranquil world where civility reigns. Personality conflicts and angst over disciplinary actions can be expected. Even a certain amount of arbitrary nastiness may be encountered at all levels and all occupations; this is a fact of life we must accept as readily as we recognize that employers and employees on the job interact differently than do friends at a summer picnic. If anxiety from management decisions were deemed so severe that no reasonable person could be expected to endure it, nearly all employees would have a cause of action for intentional infliction of emotional distress."

The tort of intentional infliction of emotional distress usually requires proof of four essential elements: 1) The conduct of the defendant must be intentional or reckless; 2) the conduct of the defendant must be extreme and outrageous; 3) there must be a causal connection between the wrongful conduct of the defendant and the emotional distress; and 4) the emotional distress must be severe. Most of the published decisions have focused primarily on the second and fourth elements of the tort, that is, extreme and outrageous conduct and the severity of the emotional distress. As shown above, liability can be found only where the conduct has been "so outrageous in character, and so extreme in degree, as to go beyond all possible bounds of decency, and to be regarded as atrocious, as utterly intolerable in a civilized community." Courts have said that the law will intervene "only where the distress inflicted is so severe that no reasonable man could be expected to endure it."

This requirement of "outrageous" conduct has made the tort of intentional infliction of emotional distress largely ineffective as a remedy for wrongful discharge. For example, even in those cases already reviewed in this chapter, where the employer clearly acted in an arbitrary and perhaps even malicious fashion, the courts dismissed the plaintiff's tort claims. For example, in the case of the father who discharged his son because he would not divorce his wife, the court said, "While we do not endorse the [father's] alleged conduct, we cannot conclude that it was so outrageous as to be "utterly intolerable in a civilized society." In the case of the doctor who discharged a female employee as soon as he heard she had been the victim of spousal abuse, the court said, "Although any involuntary discharge from employment is unpleasant, defendant's conduct was not so outrageous in character or extreme in degree as to exceed all bounds of decency."

In the case of the delivery driver who had been twice "mugged" on his route, yet was told by his employer that he had to return to his route, the plaintiff claimed that the defendant's conduct has caused him to suffer from "acute post-traumatic stress and other psychotherapeutic disorders." The court dismissed his intentional infliction of emotional distress claim, however, stating, "It is clear that defendant's employment policy with respect to drivers cannot be characterized as so outrageous, so atrocious and so utterly intolerable that a person of ordinary sensibilities could not reasonably be expected to endure it.... In essence, defendants actions did not reach that extreme level of outrageousness and severity 'beyond all possible bounds of decency' so as to give rise to a cause of action for intentional infliction of emotional distress."

Some recent decisions, however, appear to be willing to relax the requirements of the cause of action for intentional infliction of emotional distress to allow certain especially vulnerable employees/plaintiffs to recover substantial damages. The trend appears to be one that gives substantial consideration to the weakened emotional condition of the plaintiff during the time period when the alleged conduct creating the emotional distress occurred. The courts also require the defendant/employer to have had knowledge of plaintiff's vulnerable emotional condition.

For example, a jury in the District of Columbia awarded $425,000 against an employer and $10,000 against an individual defendant on an employee's claim that the defendant had intentionally inflicted emotional distress on her. The plaintiff presented evidence that the chairman of the board of a credit union engaged in harassing conduct toward her after she broke off an extra-marital affair with him.

The chairman "yelled" at her for talking to a member of the board about an automobile repossession; "yelled" at her for "going behind his back" and talking with another member of the board about the minutes of an August meeting; threatened to do his own evaluation of her performance in which he vowed he would "get her"; threatened to tell lies about her because she refused to sleep with him; threatened to tell the board that it would have to choose between the two of them if she complained about him; "yelled" at her in front of the board for passing out documents at a meeting; berated her in front of the board about supposed deficiencies in the credit union newsletter; and threw a heavy box of documents at her feet, commanding her to carry it to the credit union even though he was aware that she was physically unable to do so.

The court said that the effects on the plaintiff from the chairman's actions were not "trivial." The court said she was in a fragile psychological state due to her marital problems and the effects of medication she was taking for a chronic pulmonary disease. The court concluded that the chairman's actions "pushed her over the edge and she sank into a deep depression." In making its ruling, the court declared its reluctance to treat conduct growing out of the tensions of a business as actionable, but nevertheless found that the chairman's previous sexual relationship with the plaintiff and his awareness of her fragile emotional and physical state differentiated the case from the "garden variety bickering or hostility" that is often commonplace in the workplace, but that is not actionable.

It should be obvious by now that the employment-at-will rule is largely a myth. It is riddled with exceptions, both statutory and judicial. Thus, it is foolish for an employer to rely on the doctrine as a potential defense to a wrongful discharge suit.

Preparing for the public policy argument

Employers must train their supervisors to recognize situations that are likely to give rise to potential public policy claims. For example, employees who seem to complain about every minor safety or environmental issue in the workplace may be able to claim retaliation if they are discharged for other reasons later. Employees who have filed a worker's compensation claim or have just returned from a worker's compensation leave carry with them a protected status because any discharge soon after the filing or the return from leave will likely be characterized as retaliatory. Government contractors are particularly vulnerable to employees who, after discharge, may allege that it was their intent to "blow the whistle" on practices by the contractor in violation of federal law.

For these reasons, supervisors must take the following actions to protect their employer against wrongful discharge claims:

- Supervisors must know the whistle blower, antidiscrimination, and antiretaliation statutes that govern the company's conduct and make sure that none of these statutory protections are implicated by a potential discharge decision.

- Supervisors must show respect and consideration to all employees who complain about workplace conditions or the employer's practices or policies. Even though the complaint may seem to be minor, the supervisor should document the complaint and the response to demonstrate the appropriateness of the supervisor's response to the complaint in later proceedings.

- Supervisors should urge employees who seem to have a serious problem with a policy, procedure, or practice of the employer to file a formal complaint with management, using the employer's complaint procedure. In that way, a potential public policy claim and its resolution can be documented. If the complaint has validity, it can be remedied by management. If the complaint is frivolous, its existence in writing will be valuable for impeachment of the employee if he brings a litigation claim. A sample employee complaint procedure is included in the Appendix on page 274.

- Employers should consider using an employee complaint procedure that allows appeal to an internal adjustment panel that will provide a "hearing" to the complaining employee. The hearing procedure can be limited to suspension or discharge situations. The employee must be required to put the complaint in writing and all "testimony" by the employee at the hearing should be reduced to a written "transcript" by a secretary who has excellent shorthand skills. No lawyers should be at this proceeding to make the employee more loquacious about the facts underlying his or her claim.

- A hearing serves several purposes: 1) A written complaint signed by the employee and a documented "record" of the employee's testimony of the hearing limits the employee's ability to expand on his theories during any subsequent litigation; 2) the employer will have notice of a potential "public policy" claim; 3) the employee may perceive that he or she got a "fair hearing" and not pursue the complaint further; and 4) if the appeal panel is truly neutral, the appeal procedure may establish a legal "exhaustion" requirement for ex-employees who wish to sue the company. If an employer want to preserve its discretion to overrule an internal panel's decisio the procedure will still provide a deliberate process by which discharge decisions can be reviewed.

The termination decision

If a discharge is unavoidable, the employer must make certain that the reason for discharge is grounded in poor performance or a violation of a known conduct rule. To protect against a wrongful discharge suit, an employer should demand that every supervisor who proposes to terminate an employee under their direction, first ask themselves a series of questions prior to making any final discharge decision. If all questions are answered "yes," then the employer should be on firm ground for the discharge. The questions were developed more than 30 years ago by arbitrator Carroll R. Daugherty for use in labor arbitration proceedings. As modified below, these questions should help employers avoid wrongful discharge liability.

Did the company give the employee prior warning of the possible disciplinary consequences of the employee's conduct?

Most employees understand that certain behavior is inappropriate in the workplace. Nevertheless, all policies and conduct provisions should be published and made available to employees for their review. Also, an employee's evaluation of the seriousness of an infraction generally differs from that of the employer. A termination may seem "unfair" to a judge or jury if the employee had no idea that a violation of the rule would lead to termination. For this reason, many employers use warning notices that specifically state the level of discipline (warning, suspension, or discharge) to which the employee will be subjected if he continues to engage in misconduct. The warning notice should have a clause that requires the employee to acknowledge by his signature that both the warning and the consequences of continued misconduct were discussed with the employee. If the employee refuses to sign the form, the supervisor should note on the warning notice that "this warning and the consequences of future misconduct were discussed with [employee name] but he refused to sign." The notice should be dated and witnessed.

Was the company's rule or the supervisor's order reasonably related to the orderly, efficient, and safe operation of the business?

Everyone would agree that a rule prohibiting excessive personal telephone calls during working hours is reasonably related to the efficient operation of a business. However, a blanket rule that prohibits employees from receiving even an emergency personal telephone call while on the job would not be considered reasonable. Employers should audit their conduct rules for "reasonableness" by consulting with employees as to the practical implications of a rule or policy.

Also, if a supervisor's instructions were not followed by an employee and this is the trigger for the discharge decision, the employer should make certain that the supervisor's instructions were not ambiguous. Sometimes, supervisors are not clear on the time frame for finishing a task. If an employee had good reason to misunderstand the instructions given by the supervisor or the immediacy of a command, discipline may have to be mitigated. Also, if the supervisor's time frame for completing a task is arbitrary (not related to efficiency or business necessity), a jury is not likely to find the discharge to be reasonable.

Did the company make an effort to discover whether the employee actually violated or disobeyed a rule or an order of management?

All employers know the risks of disciplining an employee on a suspicion that a violation occurred. Not only is such action almost impossible to defend in the courtroom, it also causes significant employee relations problems. For example, supervisors often will claim "insubordination" when employees criticize or protest an order vehemently yet proceed to do what the supervisor requested. An employer cannot simply take the supervisor's word as "gospel" when it comes to an insubordination charge. "Insubordination" is the deliberate refusal by an employee to follow the reasonable directions of a supervisor. Employers must be able to distinguish insubordination from grumbling, griping, and criticizing of a supervisor by a subordinate. None is particularly appropriate in the workplace, but only insubordination is likely to support termination from employment, and then only after the employee realizes the risk of losing his or her job for not obeying the supervisor's order.

Was the company's investigation conducted objectively?

Although the employee's supervisor may be the best person to know whether a violation of company policy occurred, an investigation should be conducted by an individual who was not directly involved in the incident. This is probably best handled by a human resources professional with training in credibility resolution. Supervisors should realize that they may have an irrational emotional investment in a discharge decision and seek the advice of other management officials.

In the investigation, did management obtain sufficient evidence that the employee actually violated a rule or engaged in misconduct?

In gathering evidence, written statements from witnesses may be of significant assistance in defending the company's decision. As time passes, witnesses may forget the details of the incident or have a change of heart about testifying against a co-worker. The employee facing discipline should have a chance to tell his or her side of the story *before* any decision is made on the appropriateness of discipline or the level of severity of the discipline that will be given for the misconduct. It is a serious mistake to have the discharge papers written up before the employer has heard the employee's side of the story.

Did the company apply its rules without discrimination?

If an employee can demonstrate that he or she has been treated more severely than others with regard to enforcement of a particular rule or the level of discipline chosen by management, the company will be hard-pressed to justify its decision to discipline or discharge. The discharge decision is then subject to attack as a "pretext" for a more sinister reason for the discharge, perhaps discrimination or a public policy violation. Also, the assignment of onerous tasks or ostracism by the supervisor and co-employees should never be an adjunct to a progressive discipline system. In that way, claims of intentional infliction of emotional distress can be avoided.

Was the discipline administered by the company reasonable related to the seriousness of the offense and the employee's past work record?

Judges and juries will often consider the "equity" of the punishment applied in a particular situation. For example, an employer may have a rule that if employees do not report an absence, even for one day, they will be considered to have voluntarily terminated their employment. Although an employer would probably not be faulted for terminating an employee who is on probation for previously violating this rule, terminating an employee who has 18 years of unblemished service with the company upon a first violation will probably be considered unfair.

Although there is no foolproof method to ensure that termination decisions will not be challenged, consistent application of well-defined rules and thorough investigations of any rule violation will assist in the defense of such decisions.

....

Chapter 2

Disclaim Everything in Your Handbook

Phil Mitchell was on the stand, trying to convince the jury that he had been discharged without good cause in violation of his employment agreement with TMS Corporation. He also claimed that he was owed $128,000 in commissions on business he had brought to the company. His lawyer, Peter Greencastle, was throwing him "softball" questions so that Phil could tell his story in a way that would appeal to the jury. "What kind of promises did TMS make to you to get you to come to work for them?"

Phil Mitchell answered his lawyer's question, "Well, it was more than one interview. I met with Dave Timson, the COO for TMS, on several occasions. We met once at TMS corporate headquarters and then a couple of times over dinner."

"What did he offer you?" asked Phil Mitchell's attorney, trying to move his client's story along. Phil Mitchell answered, "I told him about these contracts but he wanted me to guarantee that I could deliver each of them to TMS. I told him that no one could do that, but if anyone was in a position to deliver these contracts, it would be me. There was a lot more talk about the details of these contracts and he could tell I knew what I was talking about. Finally, at one of the dinner meetings—I think it was the second one—he offered me $70,000 a year to do marketing and program development for TMS. As an incentive, he also offered to pay me 1 percent of the gross revenue accruing to TMS from any contracts I brought to the company."

Phil Mitchell hesitated and then said, "I told Timson that his offer sounded pretty good but that I was still worried about leaving my job at Electromatics. I was doing very well there. I explained to him that I would have to relocate my family and that I was worried about the fiscal stability of TMS.

"How did Mr. Timson respond?" Greencastle asked his client. Phil Mitchell replied quickly, "He told me the offer was for a 'permanent' position—that I had his word that I would not be terminated. Well, with that kind of assurance, I took the job."

Bill Bognell, the company's attorney, had heard this all before—during the plaintiff's deposition. He listened to the testimony but he knew Phil Mitchell's story. Mitchell said all he had to do was give the name of the contract opportunity in writing to Dave Timson, and once the company got the contract, he was owed 1 percent of the revenue for the life of the contract. Dave Timson had told Bognell that the 1 percent commission was only to be paid on the four specific contract opportunities that Mr. Mitchell identified to him when Mitchell first approached him for a job. Unfortunately, the offer letter sent to Mr. Mitchell stated the bonus program in more general terms, providing that Mr. Mitchell would receive a "1 percent bonus on all revenue accruing to TMS from contracts brought to TMS by Mr. Mitchell." As to the "permanent position" offer, Dave Timson said that Phil Mitchell was "lying through his teeth."

"Mr. Mitchell," Mr. Bognell began his cross examination, "you admit, do you not, that during your meetings with Mr. Timson, you identified four specific contract opportunities that you described as 'high probabilities' for developing into contracts for TMS. Isn't that right?" asked Mr. Bognell. "I don't think I ever said 'high probabilities,' said Phil Mitchell. "I believe I said those contracts were 'probabilities.' But I never guaranteed anything."

"Now, those were the only four contract opportunities that you identified and documented prior to becoming employed with TMS. Isn't that correct?" asked Mr. Bognell. Mr. Mitchell nodded in agreement. Mr. Mitchell also admitted that none of the four contract opportunities he originally mentioned ever came to fruition. "But that didn't matter," said Mr. Mitchell, "Mr. Timson's offer letter said 1 percent on any contracts that I might obtain for the company." Mr. Bognell quickly corrected the plaintiff, "Mr. Mitchell, if you would look at the offer letter, I believe you will notice that it says '1 percent of all contract opportunities brought to TMS by Mr. Mitchell.' Isn't that correct?" "Yes, that's correct," said Mr. Mitchell. "Can you also see that the offer letter uses the word 'brought' to describe the contract opportunities on which you are eligible to receive commission?" asked Mr. Bognell. "Yes, I see that," admitted Mr. Mitchell.

Mr. Bognell continued, "Your interpretation of your commission agreement with TMS is that, at any time during your employment with TMS, you could write a contract opportunity on a scrap of paper, even a napkin, hand it to Dave Timson and then if TMS got the contract, *you would be entitled a 1 percent commission on all gross revenue accruing to the TMS."*

"That's right," said Phil Mitchell. "That's all I had to do. My job was to find a contract opportunity."

"Mr. Mitchell, would you agree with me that information such as the date when a contract with the government is up for renewal is a matter of public knowledge?" asked Bill Bognell. "You and others would have had access to that information, isn't that correct?" "Yeah, that's true," said Phil Mitchell.

"In fact, it is generally known in the industry when contracts are up for renewal, isn't that true?" Phil Mitchell replied, "Well, I guess some people know, but not everybody." "Mr. Mitchell," Mr. Bognell persisted, "doesn't the Commerce Business Daily list contracts coming up for renewal?" "Yes, it does," said Mr. Mitchell. "And can anybody in the industry get a copy of that paper?" asked Mr. Bognell. "Yes," said Mr. Mitchell resignedly. "Well, getting back to your theory about this offer letter," said Mr. Bognell, "you say all you needed to do was to identify and document possible contract opportunities. Under your theory, you could have simply made a list from the Commerce Business Daily of all the contracts coming up for renewal and labeled them as opportunities; isn't that right?" "I guess so," said Mr. Mitchell. "Then if TMS contracted with any one of these agencies on your list, you believe you would be entitled to a 1 percent commission. Isn't that right?" asked Mr. Bognell. "Well, I suppose so." said Phil.

"Mr. Mitchell, did you ever tell anyone at TMS that you had a contract for 'permanent' employment?"

"No, I didn't," said the plaintiff, "I didn't want to get anyone upset because I didn't think they had the same deal."

"No further questions, your honor," said Mr. Bognell.

Mr. Bognell was satisfied with his cross-examination. He thought Mr. Mitchell's story would not be believed by the jury. He felt even better after Mr. Timson testified. Dave Timson was convincing when he told the jury that he would never had made such a bad deal for TMS. He pointed out that Phil Mitchell was paid a generous salary for marketing and it would make no sense to offer him a 1 percent commission to do the very things he was supposed to do for his $70,000 salary.

After the plaintiff's attorney gave his closing rebuttal, the jury retired to try to reach a verdict. Mr. Bognell and Mr. Timson decided to go have dinner. Over dinner, Mr. Timson thanked Mr. Bognell for his efforts during the trial, expressing his confidence that the jury would find for TMS. "I think we won, don't you?" said Mr. Timson. "I can't believe they would find for him—Mitchell's claims are so ridiculous."

Mr. Bognell responded optimistically but with a word of caution, "You are certainly right about his claims but I've seen juries do some strange things." Inwardly, Bill Bognell was worried that the jury had already been out for an hour and a half and had not reached a verdict.

After three hours of waiting, the jury sent a message to the judge, asking whether they had to award damages on every contract opportunity identified by the plaintiff or if they could just award a commission on one contract. Mr. Bognell knew TMS would lose on the contract claim. He was right—half an hour later the jury came in with its verdict awarding $67,000 to Mr. Mitchell on his claim for a commission on the NAVCO contract. The fact that the jury rejected Mr. Mitchell's "permanent" employment claim and awarded him nothing on the Soledad contract was little consolation to Mr. Timson and TMS.

Introduction

Employers are increasingly faced with the dilemma of how to attract competent employees without making promises that may later be enforceable as part of an oral employment contract. Courts are willing to find an exception to the traditional employment-at-will rule when an employer makes unambiguous promises to a candidate for employment in order to induce that applicant to join the employer's work force. Discharged employees continue to bring lawsuits alleging employment contracts for a definite term on grounds that their former employer had promised them "permanent" employment or that they would be discharged only for "just cause."

In addition to breach of contract suits based on oral promises, employees will also seek to enforce written promises made in employee handbooks or personnel policy manuals. Thus, where a disciplinary procedure requires that employees be terminated only for "just cause" or only after a specific number of warnings, the discharged employee will seek to hold the employer to the letter of the policy.

In this chapter, we will review the various "contract" theories, the "evidence" used by employees to support these theories, and the steps employers should take to prevent an employment contract from being formed. Also, additional theories for recovering damages in the absence of a valid contract, like promissory estoppel and misrepresentation, will also be addressed.

Finally, this chapter also covers another important exception to the employment-at-will rule: the implied covenant of good faith and fair dealing. Although not widely accepted in many states, this theory of liability for employers appears to be gaining renewed popularity in some states. Although not strictly a "contract" doctrine, some courts have said that the covenant exists in all employment agreements, even where it is conceded that the plaintiff was an at-will employee.

The theory of contract formation

An employer's right to terminate an employment-at-will has never been absolute. Employers have always been limited in their discretion by the agreed-upon terms of the relationship, whether the terms are the result of express promises to the employee or the product of implied-in-fact promises. Stated very simply—if you hire someone to paint a fence for $50 and he completes the job, you owe that individual $50. A problem may arise if you hire someone to paint the fences around your business and agree to pay him $50 but the individual is so slow at the job, you terminate him after he has completed only one side of the fence. You pay him $25 but the employee claims you hired him to paint only one side of the fence and he demands the other $25. Someone has to decide what was meant by the contractual term "painting the fence."

Similarly, you may decide to hire a painter for your factory. You like the appearance of your competitor's factory, so you hire away his painter for $15 an hour. The painter quits his job and comes to work for you but after 60 days you decide you don't like the painter's "attitude," so you fire him. The painter sues you, claiming he could only be fired for "good cause" because you made him sign an agreement that required him to work for you for at least one year. He also says you promised him he would always have a job as long as he didn't get any paint on your floors, and as he was a very careful painter, you cannot produce evidence of any spills. He also claims you promised him two weeks vacation a year, effective as soon as he began work. He also says you promised him severance pay amounting to one month's salary. You don't have any written personnel policies, but all the other employees get two weeks vacation and you have paid severance to each and every employee you ever fired.

In the first scenario, a court could decide that a reasonable construction of the term "paint the fence" is that only the outside of the fence was to be painted because that was the "intent of the parties to the agreement." The court reaches that conclusion because it is clear from the evidence that only the outside of the fence has ever been painted and when you described the job to the painter, you walked around the perimeter of the property pointing to graffiti on the fence that you said was "embarrassing to the company in the eyes of the public." You owe the painter $25. The court has construed the terms of your agreement against you even though you insist it was always your intention to have the fence painted on both sides.

In the second scenario, if the painter can produce the written agreement or can prove you said "he would always have a job," you may owe damages to him for breach of contract because your reason for firing him is not job-related. His "attitude" problem consisted only of his failure to say "hello" to you each morning as you passed under his ladder on your way to your office. It turns out the painter was just hard of hearing and not deliberately rude. You may also owe him severance pay and vacation pay regardless of whether he was an at-will employee. Your alleged express promises may support the painter's claims or the promise of vacation pay and severance pay may be implied-in-fact from your habit of always providing vacation pay and severance pay to every other employee.

The point is that contract law has always provided a remedy to employees when they can present sufficient evidence of an enforceable promise to rebut the presumption of at-will employment. All contracts, even in an at-will employment context, are the result of at least one promise that has a legal consequence. The requirements of an enforceable contract are most often stated as an offer, an acceptance, and consideration. Thus, a contract is formed, even with an at-will employee, when an employer offers an applicant employment, the individual accepts the offer by beginning employment, and provides "consideration" for the payment of wages by performing the duties of the position.

In a wrongful discharge suit, there is never a dispute about whether a contract existed, only whether one of the terms of such an agreement was termination only upon "good cause." Courts will imply a promise to terminate only for cause where there is a fixed term of the employment agreement. Moreover, even if the employer retains the discretion to discharge at any time for any reason, the employee's performance may be adequate consideration for the payment of wages, benefits, or a commission.

In other words, an employer cannot rely on the employment-at-will rule if the employee expressly promises an applicant continued employment as long as he continues to perform in a satisfactory manner. The contract becomes enforceable when the would-be employee accepts the offer of employment and performs satisfactorily. Similarly, an employer becomes obligated to pay a commission when the employee provides sufficient performance (the consideration) to earn the commission. The problem arises not so much in cases seeking the enforcement of express promises (although factual disputes over the exact nature of the promise are quite common), but rather where courts are willing to imply promises from other circumstances of employment like longevity of service of the employee, the personnel policies and practices of the employer, other related communications and conduct of the employer, or the practice in the industry. Employers must guard against the creation of circumstances that promote the tendency of some courts to find implied-in-fact promises.

Oral employment contracts

As explained earlier, courts will enforce express contracts, whether oral or written, when an employer makes unambiguous promises to applicants or employees. The question of whether an employment was "at-will" or an employment for a definite term is an issue of fact for resolution by a jury. As a result, discharged employees have great incentive to bring lawsuits alleging employment contracts for a definite term. Juries are likely to be very receptive to an ex-employee's allegations against her employer.

Decisions dealing with alleged oral employment contracts continue to be in conflict. For example, a jury in Richmond, Va., awarded more than $160,000 to a discharged sales executive who claimed that his employer breached an oral employment contract by terminating him. In this case, the discharged employee claimed that his supervisor induced him to transfer to a new position with the promise that he would retain the new job as long as he "did a good job." However, eight months after moving into the new position, the employee was discharged. The employer argued that the employee was an employee-at-will and that, additionally, he had done a poor job. The jury's verdict in favor of the employee demonstrates the danger in making promises to applicants or current employees that the employer may not be able to keep and that may later become terms of a binding contract.

Maryland courts have ruled that an employer's statements or provisions in personnel policy manuals can create contractual rights for employees. For example, in *Dahl v. Brunswick Corp.*, the Maryland Court of Appeals held that vacation and severance pay provisions in a policy directive or even an unwritten general practice could be binding contractual promises if employees knew about the provisions or practice and relied on them in starting or continuing employment. In this case, one of the employer's divisions was to be sold to another corporation. The employee affected by this sale were employed by the successor corporation in same positions, the same salaries, and with the same or better bene

The defendant employer had a written severance pay policy that provided for severance pay to any employee involuntarily terminated "when no other suitable opening [was] available." The court construed the phrase "no other suitable opening" to mean positions with the defendant employer and ruled that the employees could recover severance even though they immediately began employment with the successor employer.

Further, the court of appeals said that the defendant employer's general unwritten practice of providing two weeks' pay in lieu of two weeks' notice of termination would be binding on the employer if the employees relied on this practice in accepting or continuing employment. The court described the practice as "an offer of a unilateral contract that the employees accepted by continuing to work for [the employer] in reliance on it."

Courts are not universal in their willingness to enforce oral employment contracts. In another Virginia decision, the U.S. District Court at Alexandria held that even though an employer orally promised a security guard that he would have his job as long as he did not violate standards of conduct in the employee handbook, this oral contract was unenforceable under the Virginia statute of frauds because it was incapable of being performed within one year. The "statute of frauds" makes oral contracts that are intended to last more than one year unenforceable, unless there is a "writing" to evidence the terms of the contract. The District Court conceded that the employee's "just cause" oral employment contract was one that could be breached within one year if the employee did not perform adequately. The court said, however, that breaching the contract within a year is not the same as demonstrating that the contract could have been satisfactorily performed within a year. The court concluded, therefore, that the contract could not be performed within one year and, being an oral contract, violated the statute of frauds and was unenforceable.

This decision is at odds with many other decisions that have held that oral employment contracts are not unenforceable under the statute of frauds because the employee could conclude the performance of the contract within one year. For example, the U.S. Court of Appeals for the District of Columbia ruled that the District of Columbia's statute of frauds did not bar a discharged employee's action for breach of an oral contract for permanent employment because the contract possibly could have been performed in one year if the employee died or retired. Similarly, a 51-year-old employee's breach of contract claim was found to be outside the statute of frauds by a New York court because the employee could have retired within a year. Because of the judicial conflict on this issue, it is unwise to rely on the statute of frauds as a defense to an oral contract claim.

Courts appear to be more willing to enforce claims for specific compensation or benefits than oral contracts for permanent or continued employment. Many courts have held that written disclaimers that recite the employee's at-will status, or an employee's written acknowledgment of his or her at-will status, cannot be defeated by a contrary assertion of an oral promise that termination would only be for "just cause." Similarly, promises that are too general or ambiguous will not overcome the presumption of at-will employment.

For example, an employee who was told by her employer that they would "do everything possible to avoid discharging [her]" and that "everything looked fine for rehire next year" did not state a sufficiently definite promise to support her contract claim. In another case, a Florida court ruled that promises of "permanent" employment or employment "so long as evaluations of performance were satisfactory" did not create a contract for a specific term requiring termination only for good cause. "Vague utterances" about job security by management employees like "the company will take care of you" cannot modify a written agreement for termination upon 60 days notice. Oral assurances about employment "for life" or "until retirement" were also ruled to be too vague to create a contract for a definite term.

Although decisions that reject claims for breach of contract based on vague or casual comments regarding the permanency of employment are gratifying to the specific employer involved in the decision reaching such a conclusion, other employers cannot be confident that a particular judge will find similar oral statements to be unenforceable in their case. There are just too many judges willing to create an employment contract so that the employee can recover damages.

A perfect example is a case out of Oregon where the trial court found that a manager's statement at a workers' compensation hearing that a light duty job was available to the claimant created a lifetime employment contract terminable only for cause. The plaintiff suffered a lower-back injury while unloading furniture for the employer. When he received only a 25-percent disability award for the injury, the plaintiff appealed the determination. At the workers' compensation hearing, a production manager testified that a light-duty job was available for the plaintiff that he believed the plaintiff could perform. On cross-examination, the manager said the job was available and permanent "so long as [the company] had production to run."

....

After the plaintiff returned to work, he was terminated two months later for refusing to perform assigned tasks and because of co-workers' complaints. The plaintiff sued for breach of a lifetime employment contract premised on the production manager's testimony at the hearing. The court affirmed a jury verdict for the plaintiff, stating that the production manager's testimony could be understood to mean that the parties intended to enter into an employment contract that was not terminable at-will.

The court said the jury's conclusion "may not have been the most reasonable conclusion," but it refused to overturn the verdict. It is hard to believe that the production manager intended that his testimony at the compensation hearing would bind his employer to a lifetime agreement with the plaintiff. This case demonstrates the lengths judges and juries will go to provide contractual protection to employees.

Offer letters

One area where employers have frequently experienced difficulties is in the writing of "offer" letters or "hiring" letters. Employers who specify the compensation to be paid to the prospective employee in terms that reflect an intent to keep him employed for at least a year may find themselves bound by a contractual promise. A court may conclude that the prospective employee was offered a contract for a definite term that can only be terminated for just cause.

For example, an Arkansas employer drafted a letter that reviewed a financial agreement reached with its new regional director. The letter stated that the employee would receive a $2,500 monthly subsidy for the first 36 months of employment. The employee argued that the letter guaranteed him a minimum of three years of employment. The court agreed and said the letter was definite enough to create a three-year contract. The court said, "Because the parties' initial financial agreement was exclusively contained in that letter and revolved around a three-year period, we believe the...[employer] contracted to pay [the plaintiff] over a three-year period."

An Illinois court held that a hiring letter stating that an employee would be paid "a guaranteed salary for 12 months at $750.00 per week ($39K per annum)" was an enforceable contract for a specific one-year term. When the employer fired the employee for poor sales performance, he sued claiming he had a "guaranteed" contract. The court agreed, granting summary judgment to plaintiff and damages in the amount of

$15,000. The court said the hiring letter that was sent to the plaintiff guaranteed him employment for 12 months regardless of whether his performance was "good, bad, or indifferent."

It should not surprise employers that courts are willing to declare an offer letter to be an enforceable contract. Frequently, these letters contain all the traditional elements of a contract. They are couched in terms like "we are pleased to *offer* you employment" and often request the prospective employee to indicate his or her "acceptance" of the employment offer by signing and returning the letter to the employer. If the employer additionally inserts language in the offer letter that indicates a definite term of employment, what more would the court require to find an enforceable contract? If employers want to state the terms of the prospective employment in specific terms in an offer letter, they should insert an "employment-at-will" clause or expect that the employee will attempt to bind the employer to express or implied promises contained in the letter. These hiring documents must be used with care.

Implied contracts of employment

As mentioned above, sometimes the circumstances of a particular employment and, especially the conduct of the employer, can create a contract for continued employment that can only be terminated for good cause. At the very least, the conduct may serve as evidence to support an inference that the employer did promise the employee certain employment benefits. If the employment-at-will doctrine is to retain any vitality (and that remains doubtful because of the ever-expanding statutory remedies for employees), employers must use express disclaimers of contractual intent to prevent the judicial creation of implied-in-fact contracts. Otherwise, employers must be prepared to discharge all employees only for good cause.

There are many states that have recognized implied contracts of employment as exceptions to the employment-at-will rule. One of the most expansive applications of the implied-in-fact contract theory occurred in *Pugh v. Sees Candies, Inc.*, a California decision recognizing a limitation on the right of the employer to terminate at-will. The plaintiff in the *Pugh* decision was an employee with 32 years of service but with no fixed term of employment. The court nevertheless said that there was sufficient evidence for a jury to find an implied-in-fact promise not to terminate without good cause. The court gave particular emphasis to the employee's longevity with his employer and the policies of the defendant. Moreover·

the court allowed a very broad inquiry by the jury for determining the existence of an implied-in-fact promise to terminate only for good cause that embraced the totality of the employment relationship including promotions, commendations, and lack of criticism of the employee during his long tenure with the employer.

In another case, *Staggs v. Blue Cross of Maryland*, the Maryland Court of Special Appeals held that policy statements in employee handbooks might transform an at-will employment relationship into an enforceable contract. In Staggs, the court ruled that the traditional employment-at-will rule does not apply if "an employer communicates personnel policy statements to its employees that...limit the employer's discretion to terminate an indefinite employment or that set forth a required procedure for termination of such employment." The *Staggs* decision concluded that provisions in the Blue Cross employee handbook could be enforceable promises where the handbook set forth a required procedure for termination that required at least two formal counseling sessions prior to dismissal.

Some courts will even allow handbook provisions providing for discharge only upon good cause to override other inconsistent writings between the employer and the employee. For example, in a Virginia case, a Circuit Court judge held that a company violated the provisions of its employee handbook by failing to follow the progressive discipline provisions in its handbook in dismissing an employee without cause. The plaintiff in this case had received a copy of the handbook at the time he was hired. A provision of the employee handbook prohibited the discharge of employees without cause and also required, with the exception of certain specified misconduct, for the issuance of at least one written warning before discharge. A few days after the plaintiff received the handbook, however, he signed a letter of hire that described the employment relationship between him and the company as "at-will" and provided that employment could be terminated by either party at any time.

Following his discharge from employment, the plaintiff sued the company, alleging a breach of contract. The court rejected the company's argument that the document signed by the employee created an employment-at-will that could be terminated at any time. Because a conflict existed between the letter of hire and the employee handbook with regard to the employment relationship, the court ruled that the two documents had to be construed together. When read together, the court found that the at-will language contained in the letter of hire referred to the employer's

30-day probationary period set forth in the handbook, during which all employees were terminable at-will.

The court's decision underscores the importance of following the provisions of existing employee handbooks and eliminating ambiguities in conflicting documents. Documents containing ambiguities or conflicting provisions will be construed against the employer. It is imperative that employers carefully review all employment-related documents such as employment applications, offer letters, personnel policies and manuals, and employee handbooks to ensure that language describing the employment relationship is consistent.

Disclaimers of contractual intent

Employers have attempted to counter claims for breach of contract premised on the reasoning of decisions like *Pugh* and *Staggs* by placing language in their handbooks that disclaim any intent to establish an enforceable contract. For example, in *Castiglione v. Johns Hopkins Hospital*, the Maryland Court of Special Appeals affirmed a trial court's decision that a discharged employee could not have justifiably relied on policy provisions in the hospital's handbook where the handbook contained the following express disclaimer: "Finally, this handbook does not constitute an express or implied contract. The employee may separate from his/her employment at any time; the Hospital reserves the right to do the same."

Other employers have used disclaimer language on their application forms to give added protection against claims from employees that they could not be terminated at-will. For example, in a Colorado decision, a court of appeals concluded that a disclaimer placed in a new version of an employee handbook defeated the plaintiff's breach of implied contract claim. The disclaimer language read in part: "IMPORTANT. This Hand book is not a contract but merely a condensation of various Company policies, procedures, and employee benefits.... Management has the right to change the policies and benefits of the Company in accordance with the needs of the business without notice."

The court found that this disclaimer language was sufficiently clear and conspicuous so as to notify employees that the company did not intend to be bound by the provisions in the handbook. In particular, the court noted that the disclaimer was on the first page of the handbook and it was labeled "IMPORTANT." The plaintiff had also signed an acknow ledgment that she had received and read a copy of the handbook.

Relying on judicial decisions giving preclusive effect to disclaim language, employers became confident that if they inserted disclaimers their handbooks or on their application forms, the so-called "implied contract of employment" as an outgrowth of handbook provisions and other personnel documents would not be a threat to their company's financial security. There are still decisions, however, that find ways to transform handbook provisions into enforceable contracts despite the existence of disclaimers.

For example, in several California decisions, courts have refused to dismiss a cause of action for breach of an implied contract even though the employers had at-will disclaimer language in their handbooks. The courts ruled that the employers had not reduced the at-will employment relationship to an integrated written agreement, signed by the employee, and therefore, the handbook language was not effective as a bar to the creation of an implied-in-fact agreement to terminate only for good cause.

A 1994 decision by the New Jersey Supreme Court stated additional requirements for making a handbook disclaimer completely effective in preventing the creation of an implied contract premised on the handbook's provisions. In this case, the employer had issued an employee manual that was 160 pages long and that included a disciplinary procedure section that was 11 pages in length. Within the introductory section of the handbook, the employer had inserted the following disclaimer:

> This manual contains statements of [the employer's] Human Resource policies and procedures....The terms and procedures contained therein are not contractual and are subject to change and interpretation at the sole discretion of the Company and without prior notice or consideration to any employee.

Relying on language from prior decisions of the New Jersey Supreme Court that required disclaimer language to be put in a "very prominent" place in the handbook and be stated in terms "such that no one could reasonably have thought [the manual] was intended to create legally binding obligations," the court held that the disclaimer did not prevent the creation of an implied contract based on the employer's manual. The court said that the disclaimer did not meet the "prominence" requirement because it was not "highlighted, underscored, capitalized, or presented in any other way to make it likely that it would come to the attention of an employee reviewing it." Further, the court said that the disclaimer language was not an "appropriate statement" because it contained "confusing legalese" such as the terms "not contractual," "subject to...interpretation" and "consideration." The court found the disclaimer ineffective because it used "language that a lawyer would understand" but not language that an employee would understand to mean that the company, despite the lengthy discipline and termination provisions in the manual, reserved the "absolute power to fire anyone with or without cause."

Decisions such as this one demonstrate that both the location of disclaimer provisions in a handbook and the clarity of the disclaimer language are important in preventing employees from utilizing the handbook as a contractual shield against discharge. Employers should have language underscoring the at-will nature of employment in both their handbooks and on their application forms. The disclaimer language in the handbook should be placed in a separate section marked "Important" or "Important Notice" and it is probably best located at either the start or the end of the handbook. The employer should also use a separate acknowledgment page where the employees can specifically acknowledge in writing their understanding that the handbook is not intended to set forth contractual obligations of the employer and, further, that their employment is at-will. By placing the disclaimer language in a separate section of the handbook, there is not likely to be confusion with other handbook provisions. To be safe, however, employers may also want to add disclaimer language into the progressive discipline section of the handbook. Finally, all signed acknowledgments should be placed in each employee's personnel file.

If employers are to escape jury trials on the issue of whether the discharged employee could have justifiably relied on policy provisions in a handbook, the disclaimer provisions must be written in very clear language so as to allow the court to make a finding that reliance on the handbook as a contract would be unreasonable as a matter of law. Also, the conspicuous nature of the disclaimer must be apparent to the court so that it cannot seize on another issue to avoid the effectiveness of the disclaimer language as a bar to an implied contract action.

For example, in a decision dealing with a less-than-conspicuous disclaimer, an employer revised its policy and procedure manual and included a disclaimer in the introduction that stated: "This manual does not contain all terms and conditions of employment nor constitute an express or implied employment contract." This disclaimer changed the employment relationship from an implied contract that continued employment until "good cause for termination exist[ed]" to an at-will employment relationship.

Instead of highlighting the disclaimer, however, the employer issued the revised manual to all employees with a memorandum that explained that the new manual, "while similar in content to the old one, has been restructured to make it easier to use and update." The court noted that the memorandum given to employees did not contain any notice that the manual modification also changed the nature of the employment relationship. The court said that because the memorandum indicated that the changes in the manual went to procedure and not to substance, employees "would not be likely to review the manual to ascertain whether important changes to the very nature of their employment relationship had been made." Thus, although the disclaimer was clear, the court found that it was not conspicuous and may not have placed employees on notice that the employment relationship had changed.

Individual employment contracts may not be the answer

Some employers have found that individual employment contracts with selected employees can be useful in memorializing certain aspects of the employment relationship. For example, individual employment contracts have routinely been used to restrict competition by employees after the employment relationship has ended. Similarly, individual employment agreements can be used to protect trade secrets against unfair appropriation by employees and/or competitors. In recent years, executives of many companies have been provided with significant payout provisions in their employment contracts that become activated by a change in control of the company. These so called "golden parachute" provisions provide for specific cash payments upon termination of the executive after the company is taken over by another corporation.

Individual employment contracts have also gained increased popularity because of the erosion of the employment-at-will doctrine. Employers faced with claims of breach of implied contract or wrongful termination suits, despite having made no written promises to their employees, have sought refuge in individual employment agreements with employees that spell out the conditions of employment including wages and benefits, the duration of the contract, and "cause for discharge" provisions. Where the written employment contract is carefully drafted, a provision setting forth the employment-at-will status of an employee can provide a substantial measure of protection for the employer against a wrongful discharge action. If the agreement is hastily drafted and significant provisions are omitted, it may engender more disputes with the employee rather than operate as an effective dispute resolution mechanism.

One mistake that often occurs in drafting individual employment agreements is the assumption by employers that even if they provide a measure of employment security to employees by drafting an agreement for a fixed term, once the term of the written agreement expires, the employee's status will revert to at-will and the employer will be free thereafter to terminate the employee for any reason at any time. Unfortunately, such an assumption is not accurate. A contract of employment that provides for a definite term and that expires without any attempt by the employer to discharge the employee is presumed to be renewed upon the same terms if the employee continues to render the same services. For example, in a Massachusetts decision, an employer attempted to terminate an employee after the expiration of a contract of employment that was to run for 18 months and "for such additional periods as may be mutually acceptable." The court ruled that because the employer had taken no action to terminate the employee at the end of the term, the employment agreement was presumed to be renewed for an additional 12 months. To avoid automatic renewal of a contract, a contrary intention must clearly be evidenced by some action taken by the employer or the contract of employment must clearly state that the employee's status is to be "at-will" following expiration of the contract term.

If an employer wants to fully protect itself in its contractual relationships with individual employees, all important terms of the employment relationships must be spelled out. An employer cannot assume that they will retain the right to discharge an at-will employee if it enters into an agreement for a specific term but omits the "reasons for discharge" provision from the individual employment agreement. In reality, the exact opposite is true. When a contract provides for a definite term of employment, the contract is no longer terminable at-will and the employee can only be discharged for "good cause." Thus, express written assurances of continued employment lead to difficulties if the employer attempts to discharge the employee for other than good cause during the term of the agreement. Often, this issue arises because the employer was haphazard in creating an employment for a definite term and simply did not realize that it was entering into an enforceable employment agreement terminable only upon good cause.

For example, in one decision, an owner of an office building entered into an agreement with an individual to provide janitorial services. The janitor signed a contract bearing the heading "1/84-12/84." The written agreement also provided for annual compensation that was stated in the agreement. The contract contained no provision for discharge, because the employer assumed the janitor was a subcontractor, not an employee. The court ruled otherwise, however, saying that the janitor was, in fact, an employee who had a contract for a definite term that could only be terminated upon good cause.

If employees are to be hired for a definite period of time and a written agreement is used to cover certain aspects of their compensation, it is very important to spell out the reasons for discharge. If the employer intends to retain its discretion to discharge the employee for any reason or no reason at all, such discretion must be clearly specified in the agreement. If the employee is to be employed for as long as the employee's performance remains satisfactory to the employer, that discretion must also be expressly set forth in the agreement. The contract must clearly state that the employer is the ultimate judge of "satisfactory performance." Even with such language, courts will likely imply a "reasonableness" requirement into any clause giving the employer the right to determine "satisfactory performance." Where the employee is afforded the right to be discharged only for good cause, the term "good cause" should be specifically defined in the agreement. An employer can define "good cause" in any manner it desires as long as the definition provides a clear understanding to both parties as to the deficiency in performance that will result in the discharge of the employee.

Finally, even if the individual employment agreement adequately sets forth the at-will status of the employee, or if the employee is discharged for reasons that are clearly within the good cause definition in the agreement, the employee may still bring a breach of contract action to enforce specific rights under the contract. Thus, it is important to clearly define the wages and benefits to be received by the employee in the contract itself. Also, if the employee is to receive severance pay or other benefits upon termination, the total amount of such benefits should also be specified in the contract of employment.

Individual employment contracts can be very useful in reducing an employer's potential liability in breach of contract or wrongful discharge suits. Such contracts should not be hastily drafted, however, and they should be reviewed carefully by the employer and/or his legal representative prior to execution by the employer and employee. Although good draftsmanship cannot anticipate every problem that can arise during an employment relationship, proper protective language can limit liability when and if the unexpected happens.

Misrepresentation or fraud

Employers who are careful to avoid the creation of contracts for a definite term may still find themselves in hot water if they make other exaggerated representations about the company to induce people to accept employment. For example, if the plaintiff can convince a jury that the employer's representations were untrue when communicated to him and the employer never intended to make good on promises, the employer will be liable for fraud or intentional misrepresentation, allowing the plaintiff to recover compensatory and punitive damages. Similarly, an employee who is promised "permanent" employment and then is discharged soon after starting employment at the new job, will undoubtedly have changed his position (e.g., terminated his prior employment, sold his house, relocated) in reliance on the promises made to him and will naturally be upset that the promised job security was illusory. Even though the individual may not have a contract action, he can still sue for misrepresentation or fraud, claiming the assurance of "permanent" employment was a misrepresentation that the employer knew was untrue.

Misrepresentation claims will either be brought as an adjunct to a contract claim in an attempt to get punitive damages or as a "stand alone" cause of action that attempts to circumvent facts that would otherwise establish that no binding agreement was ever reached between the parties.

Although fraud and misrepresentation claims are most often associated with promises or representations made to prospective employees, such claims can arise from statements made to employees during employment. For example, in a case decided by the Virginia Supreme Court, a female sales representative received a $125,000 jury award on her claims for breach of contract and fraud. The plaintiff alleged that she was induced to resign her sales representative position by a promise from her employer that she could have another position that would involve less travel. She was told, however, that she had to actually tender her resignation before her employer would "officially" say that she had the other position. The plaintiff resigned on a Friday and her supervisor announced that she would be taking a job in another division. Unfortunately, when the plaintiff reported to work on Monday and tried to assume her new position, she was told she could not have the job. The plaintiff tried to withdraw her resignation, but the company said it was too late to retract the letter of resignation.

On appeal to the Virginia Supreme Court, the employer argued that its offer of another position was a statement or promise relating to future events and thus could not be the basis for a fraud action. The court acknowledged that, ordinarily, a plaintiff bringing a fraud action must prove a misrepresentation of present or preexisting facts and cannot bas the claim on promises that relate to future events. The court affirmed the jury award, however, stating: "[T]here is much authority to the effect that an action in tort for deceit and fraud may sometimes be predicated on promises that are made with a present intention not to perform them."

In most states, the general rule of pleading for a fraud action continues to be that the plaintiff must show a misrepresentation of a material, existing fact. In other words, the claim cannot be based on predictions, projections, opinions as to future events, or statements of expectation. The exception is, as illustrated by the Virginia Supreme Court decision, that a misrepresentation cause of action will be allowed where there is definite promise made regarding future employment and the plaintiff is able to establish the employer's "present intent" not to fulfill the promise. Thus, an employer might state projected earnings to an applicant or even promise a base salary and a specific commission schedule. If the employer changes its commission schedule soon after the new employee begins work, there is no actionable misrepresentation unless the employer knew the change in commission would occur but nevertheless promised the applicant the rate schedule anyway.

In another decision involving a promise to do a specific act in the future, a federal court of appeals reversed the dismissal of a plaintiff's claim that his employer had committed fraud by offering to purchase his home as an inducement to get him to move to California. The plaintiff alleged that he relied on the promise and moved to California. After five months, the plaintiff still had not been able to sell his home in Illinois. He asked his employer to purchase his home, appraising its value at about $195,000. Soon after making the request, the plaintiff was fired.

The federal district court dismissed the plaintiff's fraud claim concluding there was not sufficient evidence to establish that the employer had promised to purchase the plaintiff's home. On appeal, the court of appeals disagreed, pointing to evidence that a vice-president told the plaintiff the employer would purchase his home. The court of appeals also rejected the employer's argument that the promise could not give rise to an actionable fraud claim because it was a promise to do something in the future. The court said, "It is well settled that a promise made with no intention of performing it is actionable fraud where the other party relies upon it as an inducement to enter into an agreement."

Plaintiffs are less successful in fraud claims dealing with promises of permanent employment. For example, in a case out of Indiana, a state police captain applied for the position of corporate security manager for a private company. During the interview, he told his prospective employer that he would not consider leaving his state police position unless he was offered a "permanent" position with the company. The captain had 25 years of service with the police and claimed that his position with the force was one of "permanent employment." The plaintiff said that the interviewer told him that if he came to work for the company, he would have "such permanent employment."

The police captain took the private sector job but, after five years of work, was terminated. He sued on the promise of permanent employment, claiming breach of contract, fraud, and negligent misrepresentation. The court dismissed his claim holding that the promise of permanent employment was a promise to do some act in the future and it did not support the fraud or negligent misrepresentation action. The court followed the general rule that a fraud claim must be based on a misrepresentation of existing facts and not a prediction as to future events.

Lies about existing facts relating to a potential employment can also be the basis for a fraud claim. For example, in a case out of South Dakota, two painters were each awarded $17,000 in punitive damages after the owner of a corporation misrepresented the conditions of employment so as to induce the painters to take a job painting window frames in a sugar refinery in California. The plaintiffs were told that they would not have to paint at heights greater than 40 feet, that ladders, stack scaffolding, and a boom truck would be on site, and that available campground accommodations would be available for them close to the work site at a rate of not more than $40 per week.

Upon arriving at the job site, however, the painters found the working conditions were not as promised. The campground was situated on a polluted lake, the showers and toilets did not work, and there were no 110 volt electrical outlets. The plaintiffs could not find room accommodations nearby and were forced to stay at a motel in another town at a cost of $85 per week. The motel rooms were filthy and infested with cockroaches. There was no stack scaffolding, boom trucks, or ladders at the job site and none were ever provided. Also, their repeated requests for safety lines went unheeded. After three days on the job, the painters quit when their employer accused them of wrecking a company truck that had actually broken down on its own accord.

The South Dakota Supreme Court approved an award of punitive damages to the plaintiffs, finding that the award properly punished the defendants for their wrongful conduct. The court said, "[The defendants] needed brush painters at their job site in California. They were willing to say almost anything to induce [the plaintiffs] to travel to California. It appears from the transcript that nearly every promise made to these two men was a lie."

These fraud and misrepresentation cases demonstrate that employers who lie about material conditions of employment can be liable for damages regardless of the fact that they may have successfully preserved their discretion to terminate at-will. Employers who make exaggerated promises about wages and benefits associated with a job offer also run the risk that the plaintiff will be able to prove that the employer knew such assurances were false when it communicated the "facts" of the employment to the plaintiff. Fortunately, a written disclaimer that disavows the authority of management officials to make binding oral promises to potential employees will be effective in avoiding a fraud claim just as it is effective in blunting a contract claim. A plaintiff cannot claim he reasonably relied on oral representations of agents of the company where he has signed a document acknowledging his understanding that the officials have no authority to make such binding representations. Obviously, individuals who are interviewing a potential candidate for employment must be careful to qualify any statement regarding job requirements, workplace conditions, or future wages and benefits with phrases like "I believe," "I think," "we anticipate," "we hope," or "possible" and "potentially." In that way, candidates cannot claim a reasonable reliance on the interviewer's statements.

Where a condition or requirement for beginning employment is subject to misinterpretation or attempted avoidance by the candidate for employment, an employer may want to notify the applicant that no final offer of employment is valid unless it is communicated to the candidate in writing by a designated management official. The plaintiff will not be able to establish that he reasonably relied on any oral assurances made to him by the employer regarding the finality of the job offer if he has been notified in writing that an offer of employment remains contingent until he receives subsequent written notice from his prospective employer that the condition or contingency has been fulfilled. This procedure may seem overly cautious but it can be very useful where candidates are subject to drug testing, medical examination, or criminal background checks. Also, many government contractors assemble contingent work forces in anticipation that they will be awarded a contract. If the contract award does not come through, the contractor will have no work for the contingent candidates for employment. These employers must protect themselves with contingent or conditional offer letters that authorize a final or non-contingent offer of employment only upon written notice to each candidate.

Promissory estoppel—when all else fails

The last refuge for the employee/plaintiff who cannot establish a legally binding employment agreement and cannot prove that the employer misrepresented the facts of the employment is a cause of action for promissory estoppel. Promissory estoppel is a method by which courts can bind an employer to a promise that otherwise would not be enforceable under contract law. Although not widely accepted in the employment context—probably because it is viewed as an attempt to circumvent the employment-at-will rule and accepted principles of contract formation—there are some states that have recognized the doctrine as necessary to avoid injustice. It is most often used to provide a remedy for plaintiffs who change their position in reliance on an offer of employment and then are told the position is no longer available.

The elements of a promissory estoppel claim are: 1) a promise; 2) that the promisor should reasonably have expected to induce action or forbearance to act on the part of the promisee; 3) which in fact did produce such action or forbearance by the promisee; and 4) under such circumstances that the promise must be enforced if injustice is to be avoided. It is essential in a promissory estoppel action that the promise be clear and definite. It must be a promise that one would reasonably expect would induce reliance on the part of the individual receiving the promise.

For example, in a case arising in Connecticut, the state supreme court ruled that promises to a teacher that "everything looked fine for her rehire for the next year," that "she would have a teaching contract for the next year," and that the defendants "would do everything possible to avoid discharging teachers" were not "sufficiently promissory" nor "sufficiently definite" to support liability. The court said that, at most, the statements were "representations concerning the expectation of a future contract" but not a "definite promise of employment on which she could reasonably relied."

In a contrasting decision out of Michigan, the court concluded that a promise could be enforced under a theory of promissory estoppel. The plaintiff alleged he was offered a salary of $40,000 plus a 20 percent ownership interest in the business to leave his job as a buyer for a department store in Green Bay, Wis., and establish a clothing store in Detroit

The court said, "One could say that this promise should reasonably have induced action on plaintiff's part to accept defendants' offer. Plaintiff left his former employment as a buyer, moved himself and his family to the Detroit area, set up and then, subsequently, ran defendants' clothing store, hence it reasonable to believe that, in fact, the promise 'produced reliance' on plaintiff's part." The court concluded that, if the facts as alleged were true, the promise "must be enforced if injustice is to be avoided." The appellate court remanded the case to the trial court for reconsideration of the plaintiff's claim that he was owed a 20 percent interest in the defendant corporation.

The doctrine of promissory estoppel is most often applied in situations where although there has been no agreement between the employer and the employee, there has been no "bargained-for exchange" or, if there was a "meeting of the minds" on a particular employment provision, it is unenforceable by operation of law, but to allow the employer to avoid the promise would be particularly unjust. Thus, in situations like the case involving the relocated clothing store entrepreneur where there has been a definite promise, reasonable reliance by the employee, and the employer reneged on the promise under circumstances evidencing bad faith, the court will use the doctrine of promissory estoppel to remedy the situation.

Again, disclaimers of contractual intent and reservations of authority to bind the employer will prevent the plaintiff from reasonably relying on alleged representations of agents of the employer. For example, in a decision arising in Colorado, an employee brought a claim for promissory estoppel alleging that her discharge was in violation of promises made to her in the company's employee handbook. The handbook had a conspicuous disclaimer that stated it was not a contract and that the company reserved the right to change its provisions without notice. There was no provision regarding "just cause" for discharge and it did not require progressive discipline in all cases. The court said that the absence of such provisions and the presence of the disclaimer defeated her claims. The court concluded that the company "made no promise in the...handbook on which plaintiff could base an implied contract or promissory estoppel claim."

The covenant of good faith and fair dealing

As has been discussed, theories of recovery in breach of contract suits are usually premised on express promises by the employer or some conduct by the employer that gives rise to implied-in-fact promises. There is one covenant, however, that is implied into employment agreements, not because of any conduct engaged in by the employer, but because courts believe employers should conduct themselves fairly and in good faith when dealing with employees. This "covenant of good faith and fair dealing" is implied into the employment relationship by the operation of law. Since it is not based on facts, the employer cannot disclaim its existence.

Fortunately, there are only about 15 states that have recognized this exception to the employment-at-will rule in some form. In some states, the concept cannot really be called an exception to the at-will rule because it is applied only to guarantee the enjoyment of certain employment benefits by "non-at-will" employees. Other courts recognize the covenant of good faith and fair dealing in an at-will employment context but only where employees are trying to recover specific benefits due them like bonuses or commissions. These courts will not recognize the covenant as a limitation on the employer's right to discharge the employee at-will. For example, in Illinois, courts do not recognize the breach of the covenant of good faith and fair dealing as an independent cause of action. Instead, the courts regard it as a "derivative principle" to be used by courts to interpret the scope of other specific contractual obligations. Thus, the obligation to act in good faith will be implied into the parties' employment relationship because to do otherwise would prevent the employee from enjoying a bargained-for benefit.

In New Jersey, the courts have refused to infer an implied covenant of good faith and fair dealing into an at-will employment relationship to limit an employer's discretion to make discharge decisions. The Appellate Division of the New Jersey Supreme Court qualified this principle, however, in cases interpreting a written compensation contract that purported to give the employer an absolute right to alter sales quotas and thereby manipulate the employee's right to commission. The court acknowledged that in New Jersey an employer can discharge an at-will employee for any reason, but said, "This does not mean that an implied obligation of good faith is inapplicable to those aspects of the employer-employee relationship that are governed by some contractual terms, regardless of whether that relationship is characterized generally as being 'at-will.' As to such aspects, there can be no doubt that they are subject to the implied covenant of good faith and fair dealing extant in all contracts." The court held that the employer's power to alter sales quotes and commissions "must be exercised in good faith and for legitimate business reasons so as not to deprive an employee of the fairly agreed benefits of his labors."

Undoubtedly, the broadest application of the implied covenant of good faith and fair dealing concept is an outgrowth of cases like *Cleary v.*

American Airlines, Inc., a California decision that held that an employee could sue for wrongful discharge using the implied covenant of good faith and fair dealing that the court said "exists in every contract." The court found a breach of the covenant because the company had allegedly terminated a long-standing employee without legal cause. The court in *Cleary* said that the plaintiff's length of employment (18 years) along with the policies and procedures adopted by the employer for adjudicating employee problems, created a "form of estoppel, precluding any discharge...without good cause." The *Cleary* decision appeared to indicate that an absence of good cause is enough to establish a breach of the implied covenant of good faith and fair dealing. Other courts applying the covenant have required an additional element of wrongfulness, that is, a showing that the employer acted in bad faith in discharging the plaintiff.

For example, in a Massachusetts decision, *Fortune v. National Cash Register Co.*, the Massachusetts Supreme Judicial Court held that a written "salesman's contract" did contain an implied covenant of good faith and fair dealing. The court affirmed a jury verdict in favor of the discharged employee and based its conclusion on facts that it believed demonstrated that the employer had acted in bad faith in terminating the plaintiff. The court held that a "bad faith" termination would constitute a breach of contract. The court said that "where the principal seeks to deprive the agent of all compensation by terminating the contractual relationship when the agent is on the brink of successfully completing the sale, the principal has acted in bad faith."

Until recently, Pennsylvania courts were split on the issue of whether an implied covenant of good faith and fair dealing exists in at-will employment contracts. Although a 1992 Superior Court decision had recognized the existence of the covenant, the majority trend appeared to be clearly in favor of rejecting any further erosion of the employment-at-will rule. For example, the Superior Court said in a subsequent decision: "It is well settled that no such cause of action [for the breach of the covenant of good faith and fair dealing] is recognized in Pennsylvania."

Pennsylvania courts now seem to be moving the opposite way toward recognition of this dangerous exception to the employment-at-will rule. In a 1995 decision, the U.S. District Court for the Eastern District of Pennsylvania held that a discharged employee claiming race discrimination could also assert a claim for breach of the covenant of good faith and fair dealing even if he was unsuccessful in proving race discrimination. Citing a prior decision, the federal court said, "The duty to perform contractual obligations in good faith does not evaporate merely because the contract is an employment contract and the employee has been held to be an employee at-will." In January 1997, a federal district court ruled that both the federal courts in Pennsylvania and the Pennsylvania state courts recognize a cause of action for the breach of the covenant of good faith and fair dealing.

If the law in Pennsylvania continues to develop along the lines suggested by recent cases, all Pennsylvania employers will be expected to adhere strictly to the discipline and discharge procedures set forth in their handbooks, regardless of any disclaimers of contractual intent that may be included in the handbooks. Courts in other states that have recognized the covenant of good faith and fair dealing have held that the covenant cannot be avoided by a disclaimer.

In states that have recognized the covenant of good faith and fair dealing, the "good faith" or "reasonableness" of an employer's actions is almost always determined by a jury. This is not a desirable outcome because employers will not be able to use the summary judgment procedure to avoid trial. Win or lose, the cost of litigation will escalate dramatically in any state where the covenant of good faith and fair dealing becomes an exception to the employment-at-will rule.

What should an employer do?

There are many things employers can do to minimize their exposure to breach of contract and misrepresentation lawsuits. In many respects, the employer can control the hiring process and communications to employees once they are hired so as to limit the possibility that an express or implied contract for termination only upon good cause will be created. Employers should routinely take the following steps:

♦ Carefully instruct anyone who might have any contact with the person being considered for employment not to promise "job security," a "long and successful career," or "steady," "lifelong," or "permanent" employment, and to avoid suggesting that the person will not be terminated unless he or she deserves it or does a poor job.

♦ Do not allow employees to oversell the company to the extent that the employer becomes liable for negligent misrepresentation or fraud. Recruiters should use qualifying language like "possibly" or "potentially." If the recruiter does not know an answer to an applicant's question, he or she should simply admit that.

- All writings sent to applicants must be carefully reviewed by a Human Resources representative and/or legal counsel.

- If an employment offer is made in writing, be very sure that you have left yourself the "discretion" to terminate the employment upon short notice or for reasons acceptable to management. If the employment is to be at-will, put that fact in the offer letter.

- Review and revise as necessary all personnel manuals, application forms, employee handbooks, and notices to employees to ensure that employees cannot legitimately read these documents, in isolation or together, as guaranteeing them that they will only be discharged "for cause," that certain designated disciplinary procedures will necessarily precede a discharge action, or that their wage/benefits package will never be adjusted downward.

- Place conspicuous disclaimers on employee application forms (have them signed even by applicants who send full resumes) and in the employee handbook. The disclaimer should confirm the employment-at-will status and state that the document is not to be construed as a contract of employment, that policies and practices may change without notice and that nobody is authorized to enter into any contract or make any inducements to any applicant or employee except the president or CEO and then only expressly and in writing to a specifically named person. Have employees sign an acknowledgment form that affirms their understanding that the handbook is not a contract and they can be terminated at-will. A sample disclaimer for handbooks and for application forms is included in the Appendix on page 274.

- Consider revising a potentially binding employee handbook at the same time that a new benefit is introduced so that it can be argued that current employees accepted the change to at-will status in exchange for a new benefit.

- Be careful that statements made to the employees when introducing a new policy or benefit do not suggest that the policy or benefit may not be changed except by mutual agreement or after notice to the employee.

- Add language after the probationary period provision in the handbook that states: "Completion of the probationary period does not guarantee your continuing employment with the Company. Your status as an at-will employee does not change."

- Add language to the progressive discipline section of the handbook that states: "The Company reserves the right to depart from any of the progressive discipline steps in this policy and discharge without notice and for reasons other than those listed in this section. The progressive discipline policy does not alter your status as an employee-at-will."

- Very few handbooks contain language that puts employees on notice that their benefits as listed in the handbook can be changed by the company. Add appropriate disclaimer language to the handbook to preserve discretion to change an employment benefit without notice. The disclaimer should also provide that the summary plan description (SPD) or plan document itself shall govern in all cases of contradiction between the language in the handbook and language in the plan documents.

- Excessive detail in the handbook's description of group medical plan provisions may conflict with provisions in the SPD for the medical plan because the plan is changed more often than the handbook. Limit the handbook description to a general discussion of medical benefits. Designate the description to be a general overview of benefits and refer employees to the SPD for more information.

How about a release agreement?

One other option available to employers for avoiding breach of contract liability is the use of severance agreements that include a general release of claims. Many employers have started to require employees to sign a release of claims before they will be given a severance benefit. These severance agreements require the employee to waive legal claims against the employer, in exchange for the severance benefit. When the employee to be discharged has stated a potential claim against the company and management knows it is on shaky ground with respect to the grounds for discharge, it may be necessary to agree to pay a larger severance benefit in order to convince the departing employee to sign the release agreement. Release agreements can provide a cost-effective method of avoiding litigation especially where the employer's potential liability for damages is substantial.

Chapter 3

Never Fire a Pregnant Woman

The Director of Engineering, Bob Foley, was pacing in his office. He dreaded what he was about to do. His boss, Phil Gabbel, had instructed him to remove Sally Finkelstein from her management position. Gabbel said he was very upset about the way Sally had handled a personnel problem on the SRX project. "Gabbel is right," thought Bob. "Sally did botch the promotion decision." Still—he wasn't sure demotion to a nonmanagement spot was necessary.

As a department manager for the company, Sally Finkelstein was responsible for overseeing various projects and supervising various project managers working for the company. Despite the fact that she was more than seven months pregnant, she put in long hours and kept on top of all projects she was supervising.

"Sally's approach to management is very confrontational," thought Bob. He remembered how often she was abrupt and abrasive with subordinates who did not perform in the manner she believed necessary. Similarly, if she did not get timely assistance from support staff, she would get highly agitated about what she perceived to be a lack of support for her projects. "All in all," he thought, "she is one of the hardest working managers we have."

The problem arose after Sally was assigned the task of evaluating candidates for the SRX project manager position. She had been asked to interview Pat Rist and Joy Fonce and choose the appropriate candidate. Instead of choosing one candidate to be the project manager, however, Sally decided to appoint both Ms. Rist and Ms. Fonce as co-managers. Each woman was furious that she had not been given full responsibility for the project. The client was also very confused about the arrangement.

Sally's handling of the promotion decision was brought to the attention of Phil Gabbel. Now he was dumping the problem in Foley's lap. "Fix it!" Gabbel had told him. "And get Finkelstein out of that Department Manager spot. I'm tired of hearing complaints about her."

When Sally Finkelstein entered his office, Bob Foley knew the next few minutes would be difficult. He told Sally that she was being removed as a department manager. He discussed her handling of the SRX promotion decision. As the decision to remove Ms. Finkelstein from her position came without warning to her, Bob felt extremely awkward in discussing the reasons for senior management's decision to replace her as a department manager. He said, "Sally, you just don't fit the corporate culture for managers. There are a number of people here who are disenchanted with your management style."

Sally said, "Bob, what the hell are you talking about? I manage just like you do." Bob replied, "Look, Sally, there's nothing I can do. You won't lose your salary, you just won't be a manager." Sally didn't look up. Bob continued, "You know, we can tell everyone that because of your pregnancy, you want to slow down a little. They don't ever have to know you were demoted. Why don't you take tomorrow off and I will announce that you are stepping down."

That was the last time Bob saw Sally. Sally took her accrued vacation and then requested maternity leave. Bob told everyone that he would be "filling in" for Sally while she was on leave. He never let on that management had asked her to step down. Unfortunately, it didn't take long for the word to get out.

About four weeks later, Bob Foley was called into Phil Gabbel's office. Gabbel did not look happy. He immediately confronted Foley. "Did you tell Sally Finkelstein that her management style was not in tune with the company's corporate culture?" asked Phil. Bob Foley hesitated. "Yeah, I think so," said Bob. "I was referring to the abrasive manner in which she supervised her staff. Why do you ask?" "Well, it seems her lawyer believes you used the term 'corporate culture' as a reference to her pregnancy. In fact, she's suing us for discrimination," said Phil.

Bob quickly defended himself saying, "When I talked to her about the demotion, her pregnancy never entered into my mind." Phil immediately replied, "That's not what her lawyer says. He claims you told her that she needed to slow down because of her pregnancy and that the demotion would accomplish that. He said you told her that her emotional outbursts were probably the result of the pregnancy."

"That's not true." said Bob. "I only said we could use the pregnancy as a 'cover story' to explain why she was leaving the department manager post. That way people wouldn't know she had been demoted."

"What about the 'emotional outburst' comment?" asked Phil. Bob hesitated and then said, "I talked to her about her emotional outbursts

but I don't think I tied it to the pregnancy. I think we had a discussion about three weeks before her demotion concerning the fact that she wasn't getting enough sleep and that maybe that was why she was more irritable. She brought that up, not me. In fact, she is the one that said she thought the pregnancy was keeping her from sleeping. I just agreed with her and said something like, "It's probably all those hormones running through your system.'"

Phil Gabbel stopped him then, saying, "I've heard enough. We're going to have to get the lawyers involved with this. I think we're going to pay through the nose for this one."

Ever-expanding discrimination protections

Over the years, employers have been lectured frequently about their obligation to refrain from discrimination on the basis of race, sex, age, religion, and national origin. Despite years of exposure to Title VII of the Civil Rights Act of 1964 (Title VII), employers are more vulnerable today than ever. More and more claims are being filed with discrimination agencies and class actions on behalf of protected classes have suddenly become the rage again.

The rapid growth of protected classes has been accomplished by the passage of new federal and state statutes as well as by judicial expansion of the scope of existing statutes. For example, since the passage of Title VII, Congress has passed the Age Discrimination in Employment Act of 1967 (ADEA), making it unlawful for an employer to discriminate against any individual because of such individual's age; the Pregnancy Discrimination Act of 1968, which provided additional protections to pregnant women; and the Rehabilitation Act of 1973, which requires contractors with the federal government to refrain from discrimination against qualified handicapped individuals. More recently, Congress decided to increase the penalties for discrimination and enacted the Civil Rights Act of 1991. The Americans with Disabilities Act was passed in 1992 to extend protection to the physically and mentally infirm. After that, came the Family and Medical Leave Act, which guaranteed that those with temporary disabilities would not lose their jobs while they were out on sick leave.

State governments have been even more generous in affording protection to employees. Almost all states now have fair employment practice. Employers who do business in a number of states may find themselves bound not only by the conventional prohibitions of federal discrimination law but by less traditional categories of discrimination protection under state law. Additionally, these laws are by no means uniform from state to state. In addition to race, color, sex, religion, national origin, age, and disability, states have extended protection to employees who have been discriminated against because of their marital status (many states); arrest records (many states); child bearing capacity (Connecticut); parenthood (Alaska); family responsibilities (District of Columbia); familial status (Kentucky, Michigan, Pennsylvania); family relationship (Oregon); status with regard to public assistance (Minnesota, North Dakota); source of income (District of Columbia); sexual preference or orientation (Wisconsin, District of Columbia, Illinois, Hawaii, California, Connecticut, Maine, Massachusetts, Minnesota, New Hampshire, New Jersey, Rhode Island, Vermont); matriculation (District of Columbia); sickle cell trait (Louisiana, North Carolina, New Jersey); height (Michigan); weight (Michigan); personal appearance (District of Columbia); social position (Puerto Rico); political affiliation (District of Columbia, Maine, South Dakota); unfavorable discharge from the military (Illinois); place of birth (Vermont); genetic test results (Arizona, Texas); history of mental disorder (Connecticut); or mental retardation (Texas).

It should be recognized that these protective statutes have no doubt corrected some historic injustices. Still, the broad protections in these discrimination statutes make them vulnerable to abuse. Further, what is often overlooked is that the protection afforded one employee often burdens another employee. It is usually the quiet, hard-working employee who bears the brunt of the accommodations provided to the "protected" employee, whether it be in hiring, discipline, promotion, or layoff decisions.

The changing face of discrimination law

Two recent legislative enactments have significantly altered the litigation playing field for employees who believe they have been adversely treated by their employers. First, the Civil Rights Act of 1991 created new penalties for discrimination, including compensatory and punitive damages. The 1991 Civil Rights Act also provided a jury trial for employees claiming discrimination, a procedural change that has contributed to an increase in the size of damage awards. As the statute enhances the opportunity for plaintiff's lawyers to recover their fees and other litigation expenses if they are successful on behalf of their clients, it was inevitable that many attorneys would seek to get such claims out of the Equal Employment Opportunity Commission (EEOC) and into the courts as quickly as possible.

The Americans with Disabilities Act (ADA) created a new protected class of potential claimants with disabled employees now able to allege discrimination under a statute with a very broad definition of the term "disability." Protection was extended to persons with either mental or physical infirmities. It was predicted that the ADA would quickly over-burden the EEOC with not only an increased number of claims, but also with a type of claim that would take much longer to investigate.

The consequences for those who must adjudicate discrimination cases has been substantial. The predicted increase in discrimination charges has occurred and the EEOC is having difficulty coping with the new in-flux of claims. The shift away from agency resolution of these claims to judicial determination of discrimination charges has begun in earnest. Many plaintiffs' attorneys are not even waiting for an agency investiga tion of their clients' discrimination claims, but instead are asking for a "right to sue" letter from the EEOC. And, because the agency can hon-estly say that it will probably not be able to investigate the claim within the 180 day statutory waiting period for issuance of the letter, these claims go right to court. The result is a more expensive process for adju-dication of such cases.

The investigatory procedures of the EEOC that were effective in weeding out meritless claims now do not touch many of these unsub-stantiated charges. Further, those claims that have merit are no longer subject to the conciliation process of the EEOC where employee and em-ployer might come to an amicable resolution of their dispute. Instead, lawyers with an eye on the ultimate prize, a large damage award from a jury sympathetic to their clients' claims, resolutely refuse to compromise their clients' demands and instead push more and more of these cases into the litigation morass.

The employee's burden of proof

The ultimate inquiry in an employment discrimination case is whether the employer intentionally discriminated against the employee by treating the individual less favorably than others because of his or her protected status. There are many peculiarities to the various discrimina-tion protections (as will be discussed later in this chapter), but in general, an employer should prevail in any discrimination case if it can show documented, performance-related reasons for the discharge, demotion, or decision not to hire a job applicant and consistency in its application of performance standards.

Slam the Door on Employee Lawsuits

In a 1993 decision by the Supreme Court, *St. Mary's Honor Center v. Hicks*, the Court clarified the burden of proof for plaintiffs claiming discrimination and, in so doing, appeared to make it somewhat more difficult for plaintiffs to establish a case of intentional discrimination. In *Hicks*, the Supreme Court held that discrimination cannot be proven simply by demonstrating that the employer's stated reason for discharging the employee was a "pretext" for discrimination. The Court rejected an argument by the Justice Department that an employee claiming discrimination should be entitled to judgment as a matter of law once he establishes a *prima facie* case and proves that all the permissible reasons for discharge advanced by the employer are not credible. The Court said, "We have no authority to impose liability upon an employer for alleged discriminatory employment practices unless an appropriate fact finder determines...that the employer has unlawfully discriminated."

The *Hicks* ruling means that plaintiffs will have to prove not only that the employer's reason for discharging or not hiring them was false but also that discrimination was the real reason. The decision was attacked by civil rights attorneys as a "major setback" that will make it more difficult for employees to prevail in discrimination litigation. Arguably, however, existing precedents dealing with the burden of proof in Title VII cases have always required the plaintiff to establish the employer's discriminatory motivation with either direct or circumstantial evidence of bias. Justice Scalia was therefore correct when he stated, "Nothing in law would permit us to substitute for the required finding that the employer's action was the product of unlawful discrimination, the much different (and much lesser) finding that the employer's explanation of its actions was not believable."

The *Hicks* decision is not as restrictive as plaintiffs' attorneys would claim. There indeed may be that occasional case where the trier of fact does not believe the employer's proffered reason for discharge (for example, poor performance), but also concludes that discrimination was not the motive either. In most cases, however, where the employer's witnesses are not credible, the jury will find other evidence to establish a discriminatory motive (for example, the timing of the discharge, incriminating statements of supervisors, or comparable performance by non-minorities who were not discharged). *Hicks* may serve as a reminder to triers of fact that they have an obligation to find evidence of an illegal motive before ruling in the plaintiff's favor but it certainly is not a panacea for employers beleaguered by discrimination claims.

As more and more classes of employees receive protection under discrimination statutes, it becomes even more paramount that employers have sufficient documentation of performance deficiencies before terminating an employee who has protected status under a discrimination statute. As will be shown below, there are idiosyncracies to the various types of discrimination claims. Nevertheless, the ultimate inquiry in each case usually involves a determination as to the "fairness" of the discharge decision. Juries care little about "burdens of proof"; they will not return a verdict for the employer unless they are satisfied that the company acted in good faith and was "fair" in its dealings with the employee/plaintiff.

Sex discrimination

Today, women comprise more than 48 percent of the nation's work force. It should not be surprising, therefore, that claims involving sexual discrimination protections contribute significantly to the increase in employment litigation. Sexual harassment claims have received the most publicity in recent years and this variation of sexual discrimination will be discussed in detail in Chapter 4. There are other gender-based claims dealing with pay, promotion, and discharge, however, that invoke the more general sexual discrimination protections of Title VII.

Pay disparity

Despite increased employment in management positions in recent years, statistics show that women managers are earning only about 70 percent of what males in management positions are making. For female employees alleging pay disparity in the workplace, the law provides two avenues of relief, a Title VII claim for discrimination in the payment of wages, or an Equal Pay Act claim.

In a Title VII wage discrimination case, the plaintiff can present direct evidence of discrimination in pay or that the employer had adopted an objective system of determining wages based on an evaluation of the job, but that the employer has set the wage rate for job classifications held by women at a level less than the objective evaluation would indicate as proper. Obviously, to the extent that a female employee can establish that her employer has deliberately assigned her a lower pay rate because of her gender, she can prevail in a disparate treatment claim under Title VII.

If the pay disparity involves positions with substantially equal duties and responsibilities, the female employee may also have a cause of action under the Equal Pay Act. The Equal Pay Act requires employers to pay equal compensation to women who perform equal work unless the difference in pay is based on factors other than sex. The Act lists several affirmative defenses for employers to utilize in avoiding an Equal Pay Act claim. For example, if the pay difference is based on seniority, a merit system, a compensation system that measures quantity or quality of production, or "any other factor other than sex," the employer will not be liable.

Some employers make it easy for plaintiffs to establish pay disparity liability under Title IV or the Equal Pay Act. For example, in a well-publicized case involving a national restaurant chain, a federal judge found that the company had paid the plaintiff, a recruiter for the restaurant chain, less money than male employees who had identical duties and responsibilities. The plaintiff had been hired at $28,000 per year with a bonus potential of $8,000. Her male predecessor in the position had earned $38,000 with a potential bonus of $10,000.

Even if the employer had a potential defense to the pay disparity claim based on the experience of the male predecessor, the plaintiff's supervisor destroyed any chance of defending the pay disparity by his comments to the plaintiff when she asked about the disparity. The supervisor allegedly told plaintiff that the difference in pay was justified because she was not the "bread-winner" in her family; that she did not need to make as much money as a man because her salary was only a "second income." Plaintiff claimed that the supervisor also said that he had hired her because he had seen her "in a halter top and shorts." Under such circumstances, it is easy to see why the court found the employer liable on the pay disparity claim.

Sexual stereotyping

In a 1989 decision, the U.S. Supreme Court confirmed that employment decisions based in part on sexual stereotyping are discriminatory unless the employer can prove by a preponderance of the evidence that it would have made the same decision even if it had not taken the employee's gender into account. In *Price Waterhouse v. Hopkins*, the Court examined whether sexism tainted the partnership selection process of a national accounting firm. The plaintiff, an associate with Price Waterhouse, was nominated for partnership in 1982 after four years as a senior manager in the firm's Washington, D.C., office. She was the only woman among 88 candidates for partnership that year. Although the plaintiff presented evidence that she had generated more new business and logged more billable hours than any other candidate for partnership, the accounting firm determined she lacked proper interpersonal skills and her nomination was placed on hold.

The plaintiff claimed she was denied a partnership because her colleagues believed her to be too "macho" and unladylike. There was testimony that several partners, including some of her supporters, said she was overly aggressive, sometimes arrogant to co-workers, and generally displayed a "somewhat masculine" attitude on the job. A partner who supported the plaintiff for the partnership reportedly advised her to "walk more femininely, talk more femininely, wear makeup, have her hair styled, and wear jewelry." The plaintiff left Price Waterhouse in 1984 after she was not renominated for partner.

In the *Price Waterhouse* decision, a severely divided Court decided that once an employee shows by competent evidence that sexual stereotyping was a "substantial" or "motivating" factor in a decision to deny a promotion, the burden falls on the employer to *prove* by the preponderance of the evidence that it would have taken the same action regardless of the improper stereotyping. The Court said that an employer could avoid liability in a mixed motive case if it could establish that the nondiscriminatory reason actually motivated the employment decision.

A provision of the Civil Rights Act of 1991 modified the Supreme Court's holding in *Price Waterhouse v. Hopkins* by providing that a Title VII violation will still be established when a plaintiff proves that race, color, religion, sex, or national origin was a motivating factor for the adverse employment decision even though other nondiscriminatory factors may have also motivated the decision. The Act allows the plaintiff in mixed motive cases to recover declaratory and injunctive relief but not reinstatement, back pay, compensation, or punitive damages. Thus, the employer can avoid monetary liability if it proves its other nondiscriminatory motivation would have produced the same result: discharge.

Although the parameters of mixed motive cases have yet to be completely established, it is clear that prudent employers must not make personnel decisions adversely affecting women, minorities, and older workers in a manner that allows plaintiffs to force the employer to prove that an alleged improper motive did not determine the personnel decision. We all know that it is much more difficult to prove that something did not occur than it is to merely assert the nonexistence of a fact and force the other side to prove you wrong. The *Price Waterhouse* decision makes

....
73

clear that employers who allow supervisors to use "loose talk" and make public remarks that a protected group might find offensive or stereotypical, will be placed in a much more difficult position to defend themselves in lawsuits. Never allow decision-makers to give written statements or evaluations that contain sexist, racist, or similar remarks. The decision-makers must be sensitized to avoid making "suspicious," albeit innocent, remarks that could later be construed as having a secondary, discriminatory meaning. Like Bob Foley's "corporate culture" remark in the introductory narrative, a "catch-phrase" can have more than one meaning.

The glass ceiling problem

In 1995, the Glass Ceiling Commission found that women held less than 5 percent of top corporate positions. The term "glass ceiling" refers to the concept that there is an invisible barrier that prevents women from progressing to the highest positions in management within a given organization. The idea is that either intentionally or unintentionally certain written or unwritten employment practices and policies prevent individuals in protected classes from advancing within the organization.

The Civil Rights Act of 1991 created the Glass Ceiling Commission to study and prepare recommendations for Congress on this issue. Faced with this obvious infringement on its bureaucratic turf, the Office of Federal Contract Compliance Programs (OFCCP), the agency that enforces federal affirmative action requirements, began a series of glass ceiling audits of federal contractors to determine whether such a ceiling exists and what remedies are effective to combat it. The OFCCP has conducted glass ceiling audits not only in traditional manufacturing firms, but also in other industries such as law firms, hospitals, and universities. The agency uses the audit to determine whether a barrier exists not only for women but also for minority employees.

The OFCCP has also prepared guidelines discussing the issues to be investigated in a glass ceiling audit. One key focus of the audit is a careful study of how upper-level management positions are filled. The agency will look carefully at external hires around and above the level where minorities/female participation declines. The agency will pay particular attention to patterns of hiring from outside the organization when there are internal minority and women candidates with similar qualifications available.

Although the focus of the glass ceiling audit is on entry-level to upper-level management, the audit also investigates the treatment of women and minorities who obtain upper-level jobs. The agency will carefully review the compensation of women and minorities in management positions to determine whether they are compensated in a manner similar to other management officials who are not in the protected classes. This investigation considers not only salary, but bonuses, stock awards, stock options and other perquisites.

Currently, the glass ceiling issue most directly affects contractors with the federal government who are subject to the jurisdiction of the OFCCP. However, the report of the Glass Ceiling Commission may prompt Congress to draft further employment legislation extending glass ceiling audits to noncontractors. Also, "glass ceiling" allegations and analysis are likely to become a regular part of individual sex discrimination actions dealing with promotion decisions. For example, in a 1995 federal court decision out of New York, a female assistant vice president was awarded $150,000 in compensatory damages and $300,000 in punitive damages after her employer failed to promote her to vice president and eliminated her position in a reduction in force. During trial, the plaintiff produced statistical evidence of a glass ceiling at the company and a disparity in pay. The plaintiff showed that despite the fact that more than 80 percent of the company's field offices were run by female branch managers, there were no female vice presidents or senior vice presidents in the office services field organization. Rather, virtually all the senior management positions at the corporate headquarters were held by males. The Second Circuit Court of Appeals affirmed the trial court's decision holding that the statistical data showing a glass ceiling was properly admitted into evidence because it was probative of the company's discriminatory intent.

Discharge actions involving sex discrimination allegations

Claims involving discharge continue to be the most frequent type of discrimination charge brought by women. Obviously, a discharge leaves the ex-employee with more incentive to sue her former employer. In fact, discharge is the motivation for most claims filed with federal and state discrimination agencies. For example, during 1995, discharge cases constituted approximately 47 percent of all charges filed with the EEOC.

Individual discharge claims are almost always brought using a disparate treatment theory. If the female employee can establish that she was treated differently than her male counterparts, particularly with respect to the application of discipline or the severity of discipline imposed, she should prevail. Although women bringing sex discrimination lawsuits lose more often than they win, those plaintiffs who can establish proof of a discriminatory discharge can recover considerable damages. For example, in November, 1996, a real estate saleswoman received a $6.5 million jury award after she brought a complaint in a New Jersey state court alleging that her employer had fired her because of her gender. The plaintiff claimed her employer had excluded her from sales meetings, insurance advisory councils, and business lunches attended by male employees. She claimed she was fired when she refused to back down on her complaints.

This case illustrates an important point. Although punitive damage awards are capped at $300,000 in Title VII actions, there is no such limitation in many state discrimination statutes. Thus, employers can expect that plaintiffs will bring discrimination claims under statutes that maximize their opportunity for punitive damages. Plaintiffs will also combine their discrimination claims with tort actions such as defamation or intentional infliction of emotional distress that are not limited by a damages cap.

Pregnancy discrimination

Since the passage of the Pregnancy Discrimination Act in 1978 (the Pregnancy Act), employers have been prohibited from making distinctions in employment policy on the basis of pregnancy unless such distinctions can be justified by certain judicially recognized defenses to discrimination claims under Title VII. The basic principle of the Pregnancy Act is that pregnant women must be treated the same as other employees. A woman is protected against being fired or refused a promotion or a job merely because she is pregnant. Additionally, she cannot be forced to go on leave of absence as long as she can still work.

When the Pregnancy Act was passed, employers were clearly put on notice that they were forbidden from discriminating on the basis of pregnancy. Unfortunately, charges of pregnancy discrimination are still being litigated, often with expensive consequences for employers. Employers must not use a maternity leave as a convenient excuse for replacing a female employee who is not performing as well as the company might like. If the woman is having performance problems, those deficiencies must be confronted honestly by the employee's supervisor. The performance problems or misconduct should be documented right away and not after a woman has announced her pregnancy or gone on maternity leave.

Employees who allege that they were discharged because of pregnancy make very sympathetic plaintiffs. Discrimination agencies appear to be very receptive to these types of claims. Also, judges and juries often want to "do right" by pregnant employees. It is always a struggle to establish the validity of an employer's pressing need to terminate a female employee who is either expecting a baby or has just given birth. The pitfalls in such a case are so abundant that I have been tempted to frame a blanket rule for employers: "Never fire a pregnant woman!"

Employers continue to experience the hazards of terminating a female employee protected by the Pregnancy Act. In a 1995 federal court decision in Maryland, a jury awarded a former employee of a utility company $750,000 in damages after she was terminated by the company while on maternity leave. The plaintiff had worked for the company for 14 years and, just prior to announcing her pregnancy, she was told she would be given a promotion. After going on maternity leave, however, the plaintiff found out that her employer had announced cutbacks in the work force.

When she initially called the company to see if her position was eliminated, she was allegedly assured that she still had a job with the company. Subsequently, however, her job was eliminated but she was told she could apply for a senior analyst position. When the job was not posted right away, the plaintiff filed a charge of discrimination with the EEOC. The EEOC recommended that the company reinstate the plaintiff. When she was not reinstated, the plaintiff sued her employer in the federal district court and was awarded $750,000.

Although the employer appealed the jury's damage award and got it reduced to $300,000 and then ultimately convinced a court of appeals to reverse the jury verdict, the case is illustrative of the evidentiary problems that can arise in a discrimination case.

Abortion decisions find protection

The Pregnancy Act will also be applied to abortion decisions. When the Act was passed in 1978, it did not specifically address the question of whether abortion is a medical condition related to pregnancy or childbirth that would be covered under the Act. In its regulations construing the Pregnancy Act, the EEOC states unequivocally that "an employer cannot discriminate in its employment practices against a woman who has had an abortion." Despite this pronouncement, there have been very few cases that have applied the Act to the decision to have an abortion. A decision by a federal court in Michigan found a violation of the Pregnancy

Act, however, after a pregnant employee was discharged following her announcement that she was considering an abortion.

In the decision, the federal court awarded a 19-year-old ex-employee $9,400 in back pay, $50,000 in compensatory damages and $30,000 in punitive damages, finding that the employee would not have been discharged from employment at a hotel but for her disclosure that she was thinking about having an abortion. Concluding that abortion is "a medical aspect of pregnancy," the court said that the Pregnancy Act forbids an employer from "treating an employee differently on the basis of her consideration or use of an abortion."

The employer defended its discharge decision on grounds that the employee's discussion of her abortion decision agitated other employees. The hotel's food and beverage director testified that the "very Christian" restaurant staff was "very offended" by the employee's consideration of an abortion. Nevertheless, the employer said that it merely warned the plaintiff that she should no longer discuss her abortion decision at work. The hotel maintained that the plaintiff was fired for performance problems relating to her failure to make sure the coffee urn was full during the morning hours. The court concluded, however, that the plaintiff's abortion decision was the real reason for her discharge because the decision to discharge came one week after she received the written warning for discussing abortion in the workplace.

It has become clear that regardless of an employer's ethical, moral, or religious objections to an employee's conduct, it is risky to ground a discharge decision on such motivation. For most employers the safest course to take is to ground all discharge decisions in performance-related reasons and not in its opposition to the morals or opinions of its employees.

Race discrimination

Race discrimination claims continue to be the most prevalent of all charges filed with the EEOC. In 1996, approximately 34 percent of the agency's docket was devoted to race allegations. Although African-Americans have been assisted in their employment progress by programs implemented by various interest groups, Title VII litigation remains a particularly effective method for remedying individual cases of discrimination in the workplace. As illustrated by two recent lawsuits, however, black plaintiffs also continue to be successful as a class.

On November 15, 1996, Texaco Corporation settled a race discrimination lawsuit brought by six black employees alleging that the company had denied jobs and promotions to blacks. The tentative agreement, whereby Texaco will spend $176 million in affirmative relief, came soon after it was reported that several high-ranking company executives had made racially insensitive and derogatory comments about minorities. The company faced the prospect of an economic boycott led by the NAACP and other unfavorable publicity. Texaco agreed to pay $115 million in damages, $26.1 million in pay increases to black employees, and $35 million in program changes throughout the company to further equal opportunity efforts. The EEOC also reached its own conciliation agreement with Texaco that had requirements beyond those agreed to by the oil company and the attorneys for the six plaintiffs.

Also, in 1996, the EEOC was party to an $11.25 million settlement between Southern California Edison Company and nine African-American plaintiffs who brought a class action alleging that the utility company had limited pay increases, career advancement, and other employment opportunities for black employees. The settlement also included provisions whereby Southern California Edison agreed to provide "diversity training" to all employees and implement mechanisms for addressing and resolving employment discrimination complaints. The money is to be paid to African-American employees who worked for the company between 1989 and 1996. Edison will set aside $8.15 million to resolve back pay claims and $3.1 million for emotional distress claims.

Racism and technology

Recent events demonstrate that the modern workplace with its computer technology is still afflicted with an old problem: racial bias. A number of national corporations have been sued by black employees for discrimination that they allege was the result of messages sent by electronic mail (e-mail). For example, a suit filed in January, 1997, alleged that an electronic message containing racist jokes had been disseminated through the computer system at an investment banking firm. The two black plaintiffs claim that they were professionally isolated and denied promotions after they objected to the e-mail messages. The investment firm claimed the e-mail was transmitted only among a small group of employees and that those involved were severely disciplined. Nevertheless, the plaintiffs asked for $5 million in compensation damages and $25 million in punitive damages.

The use of e-mail is increasing at a very rapid pace. Whether it is a false sense of security regarding the privacy of the communication or a

....

feeling that one's identity can be disguised on the e-mail system, employees seem to be more willing to communicate racist and sexist comments through the computer. If employers don't monitor and regulate e-mail communications, they can be liable for any hostile environment that develops for minorities and women in the workplace.

Dealing with racial animus

Unfortunately, racial discrimination in employment is not likely to subside without continued training of supervisors in all aspects of discrimination protections. Despite extensive experience with diverse workplace populations, many employers tend to concentrate training in areas like sexual harassment, which has received extensive publicity over the last few years. Employers must continue to be conscious of potential racial animus, however, as black and Hispanic employees strive to get ahead in the workplace and compete with white employees trying to hold onto their career path.

Employers must confront supervisors who exhibit racial animus. Obviously, a supervisor who ridicules a subordinate because of the employee's race should be severely disciplined. Managers must not run "scared," however, and avoid confronting minority employees who exhibit performance problems. A recent decision by a federal appellate court demonstrates that an employer's failure to discipline an employee because of concern that the employee would claim discrimination can be used as actual evidence of discrimination when the employee is subsequently terminated. The U.S. Court of Appeals for the Fifth Circuit held that withholding criticism or counseling from a black employee was discriminatory even though the employer was actually treating the employee more leniently than other employees.

The plaintiff in this case worked as a contract analyst. The plaintiff's supervisor criticized her for her low volume of work and the excessive number of visitors to her office. When the plaintiff complained to the manager of her department about the supervisor's criticism, the manager, in an effort to avoid charges of racial discrimination, directed plaintiff's supervisor not to confront the plaintiff in the future about her work. For the next two years, neither the supervisor nor the manager gave the plaintiff any criticism of her work. During this period, the plaintiff received satisfactory written evaluations and a merit salary increase. Later, in an attempt to reduce costs, the company fired the plaintiff, who by that time, was believed to be one of the two poorest performers in the department.

The plaintiff filed suit under Title VII alleging race discrimination. The Court of Appeals for the Fifth Circuit concluded that race played a part in the plaintiff's employment relationship with the company. The court held that in neither criticizing the plaintiff when her work was unsatisfactory nor counseling her on how to improve, the company treated the plaintiff differently because she was black. As a result, the company did not afford the plaintiff the same opportunity to improve her performance as it did its white employees.

The court's decision is significant because it illustrates the consequences of treating a minority differently than other employees. It should serve as a warning to employers that they cannot make exceptions to their regular disciplinary policies for particular employees and then discharge them without adequate documentation of the poor performance.

Age discrimination

In recent years, claims of age discrimination have been one of the most frequently brought charges against employers. Age discrimination litigation is likely to continue to increase as more and more "baby boomers" enter their 50s and 60s. Often, age discrimination claims arise out of reductions in force by employers. This is especially so where the layoff results in an inordinately high number of older employees being laid off in favor of younger employees. Further, as older employees often find it more difficult to land another position following their termination from employment, they are more inclined to seek an economic remedy in court.

In the past, employers were successful in insulating themselves from liability for age discrimination by replacing the older laid off employee with another individual who was older than 40 years of age. The Age Discrimination in Employment Act of 1967 (ADEA), the primary statutory vehicle for claims of age bias in employment decisions, provides protection to individuals who are older than 40. It was assumed by employers, and many courts agreed, that an age discrimination claim must fail where the employee who was retained in employment over the older employee was himself older than 40 and thus within the protected class under the ADEA.

The U.S. Supreme Court has ruled that an employee claiming age discrimination need not show that he was replaced by someone younger than 40 in order to establish a *prima facie* claim of discrimination. In *O'Connor v. Consolidated Coin Caterers Corp.*, the Court ruled that all that is required for a *prima facie* showing of age discrimination is for the plaintiff to establish that he was replaced by a younger person. The Court said, "The fact that one person in the protected class has lost out to another person in the protected class is thus irrelevant, as long as he has lost out *because of his age.*"

All employers should carefully analyze layoff decisions to make certain that age is not a determining factor in choosing employees for layoff. Further, supervisors should be cautioned against making off-hand remarks about age to their employees. The most innocent joke about an employee's age can be transformed into substantive evidence of age discrimination in an age suit. For example, in one case, a 53-year old vice president successfully supported his age discrimination claim with evidence that his supervisor commented on his age and baldness and asked about his retirement intentions. In another case, a court found that an employer discriminated against a veteran shoe saleswoman by discharging her for slapping an argumentative, young co-worker across the face. The court found substantial evidence that the 56-year old plaintiff, the oldest and most senior employee in the shoe department of a large department store, was subjected to age-related insults by the employee she eventually slapped. There was evidence in the record that a 25-year old salesman at the store had subjected the older employee to repeated harassment, calling her a "senile old woman" and a "crazy old woman."

Constructive discharge and age discrimination

Many companies that experience financial difficulties resulting from higher operating costs often decide to undergo a restructuring of their operations and a complete realignment of their staff. Although such changes can be good business practice, they present unique personnel problems. Many times the position being eliminated or restructured is staffed by a long-term employee; an older employee who has risen from the ranks into a supervisory or executive position. This older worker is dedicated and dependable and probably has consistently been evaluated as above-average on performance appraisals.

When facing this situation, the employer is caught in a dilemma with no easy resolution. If the employee is terminated without being offered another position, the employee may sue the employer for age discrimination. On the other hand, if the employee is transferred to a position that does not carry the same prestige or status, the employee still might sue the employer for age discrimination, this time claiming a constructive discharge, arguing that the working conditions are so difficult or unpleasant that a reasonable person would feel compelled to quit.

In one case dealing with a constructive discharge claim, the plaintiff sued his employer for age discrimination, alleging that he was constructively discharged because he was demoted to a position of lesser supervisory responsibilities, asked to accept a 12 percent pay cut and required to work for a supervisor who was half his age.

The plaintiff had worked for his employer for approximately 16 years. He had received excellent performance appraisals and had been promoted to director of design on a government contract. As the contract moved from the design stage to production, the need for his services decreased. On several occasions, the company offered to transfer him to other positions but the plaintiff refused.

At the conclusion of the design portion of the contract, the company offered the plaintiff three options: work another month until he was eligible for retirement, accept a 12 percent pay cut and work for another supervisor, or transfer to the company's Canadian division. The plaintiff claimed that working for the 33-year-old supervisor would be an "insult," and the Canadian position fell through, so he retired.

The court found no evidence of age discrimination, noting that the plaintiff was not asked to train his successor, nor was he asked constantly whether he was going to retire. The mere fact that he would be supervised by a younger worker was insufficient to establish age discrimination. Further, the court concluded that the decrease in pay and the slight decrease in supervisory responsibility were not so onerous as to create a constructive discharge.

Employers run the risk of age discrimination litigation whenever an employment decision bears negatively upon a worker who is in the protected age category. However, as the previous case demonstrates, as long as performance standards, policies, and procedures are reasonable and uniformly applied, an employer can successfully defend such challenges. There are "unreasonable" demotions, however, that can produce liability.

In a 1996 decision, the U.S. Court of Appeals for the Fifth Circuit affirmed a jury verdict of nearly $3 million in punitive damages to a company executive who was assigned janitorial duties. The plaintiff had a college degree and 30 years of experience in the paper industry. After working as a vice president and assistant to the president for a paper company, the plaintiff was assigned to an entry-level supervisory position requiring no more than one year's experience in the paper business. Upon assuming his new position, the plaintiff was placed in charge of housekeeping. With no employees to assist him in the housekeeping duties, however, the plaintiff was forced to sweep the floors and clean up the employee cafeteria, duties that occupied 75 percent of his working time. As a result, the former executive experienced serious emotional and psychological problems for which he was eventually hospitalized.

The plaintiff sued the company for age discrimination and intentional infliction of emotional distress. The plaintiff claimed that the degrading and humiliating manner in which the company stripped him of his duties and demoted him from executive manager to an entry level warehouse supervisor with menial and demeaning duties constituted extreme and outrageous conduct.

The Fifth Circuit held that the company's actions were sufficiently extreme and outrageous to warrant a jury verdict in favor of the plaintiff. The court noted that the plaintiff had been a long-time executive at the company. Moreover, he had been responsible for the largest project in the company's history and had completed the project on time and within budget. Yet, when transferred to the warehouse, the plaintiff's primary duty became housekeeping chores around the warehouse.

Although it found the company's actions in attempting to force the plaintiff to resign to be deplorable, the court was mindful of the implications that its ruling might have. The court cautioned, "We are cognizant that the work culture in some situations may contemplate a degree of teasing and taunting that in other circumstances might be considered cruel and outrageous. We further recognize that to properly manage its business, every employer must on occasion review, criticize, demote, transfer, and discipline employees. We also acknowledge that it is not unusual for an employer, instead of directly discharging an employee, to create unpleasant and onerous work conditions designed to force an employee to quit, i.e., 'constructively' to discharge the employee." Nevertheless, the company's actions, in the court's opinion, overstepped the bounds of permissible conduct and constituted "extreme and outrageous" behavior.

National origin discrimination

Although the term "national origin" is not defined in Title VII, it has been given a broad interpretation to protect not only employees who originally came from a particular country, but also employees whose forefathers or parents came from another country. In other words, national origin has come to mean "the country of one's ancestry."

National origin protections have been used most frequently by Hispanic employees, but the definition is broad enough to reach employees of

....

almost any ancestral heritage. The discrimination protections have even been applied to countries that no longer exist as a nationality. The defenses available to employers in racial discrimination actions remain applicable in a national origin discrimination suit. If the employer can state a nondiscriminatory reason for discharge that cannot be shown to be a pretext for national origin bias, the employer will prevail.

For example, in a 1990 case involving the National Labor Relations Board (NLRB), a federal court ruled that the NLRB had lawfully terminated a Hispanic law clerk where the NLRB proved that the law clerk's performance was the reason for his discharge. The plaintiff had inadequate writing abilities and he was unable to investigate and research cases thoroughly. In addition to the evidence of poor performance, the NLRB was able to show that the Regional Office implicated by the charge of discrimination had given excellent appraisals to other Hispanic employees and many Hispanic employees had been promoted to higher positions within the organization.

A unique situation involving national origin protections occurs when employers attempt to invoke English-only rules. The EEOC will presume that such rules violate the national origin protections of Title VII and closely scrutinize any application of such rules. Some courts have disagreed with the EEOC's position that English-only rules are presumptively unlawful and have allowed such rules where safety concerns or other business concerns justify implementation of the English-only rule. For example, in a 1993 decision by the Ninth Circuit Court of Appeals, an employer's English-only rule in its meat processing plant was held not to be in violation of Title VII. Hispanic employees working in the plant challenged the rule arguing that it prevented them from speaking Spanish, thus denying them the right to "cultural expression" and preventing them from being "comfortable" in the workplace because they could not easily make "small talk" with other employees.

The employer implemented the English-only rule after receiving complaints that some Hispanic employees were using Spanish to insult other workers in a language they could not understand. The employer argued that its rule promoted racial harmony and workplace safety because employees would not be distracted while operating machinery by the co-workers' use of Spanish. The employer also argued that employees who were not bilingual would not be able to understand if a product-related concern was raised in Spanish.

The Ninth Circuit held that the bilingual employees had not raised a triable issue of fact as to the disparate impact of their employer's

English-only rule where the rule does not have a significant impact but merely inconveniences the Hispanic employees. The court said, "Title VII is not meant to protect against rules that merely inconvenience some employees, even if the inconvenience falls regularly on a protected class." As to the plaintiffs' "cultural identity" argument, the court of appeals said, "There is nothing in Title VII that requires an employer to allow employees to express their cultural identity." The court refused to grant summary judgment for the employer on the issue of the rule's impact on one employee who could speak no English, concluding that the rule might have an adverse impact on her.

Religious discrimination

Section 703(a) of Title VII of the Civil Rights Act of 1964 prohibits employment discrimination based upon religion. The term religion is defined to include "all aspects of religious observance and practice, as well as belief, unless the employer demonstrates that he is unable to reasonably accommodate an employee's or prospective employee's religious observance and practice without undue hardship on the conduct of the employer's business."

In 1980, the EEOC issued religious discrimination guidelines that gave a very broad reading to the term "religious practice." The guidelines state that the agency will define religious practices to include "moral or ethical beliefs as to what is right and wrong which are sincerely held with the strength of traditional religious views." The fact that no religious group espouses the professed religious belief of the employee will not be determinative.

A case out of Virginia also illustrates the protections that will be afforded employees claiming a "sincere" religious belief. A Navy employee who was fired after she assaulted a fellow worker was nevertheless given an opportunity to argue in court that the firing was due to illegal religious bias. The incident that triggered the employee's discharge was described as "hunting down a fellow worker with a hammer, hitting him on the head with a purse, and choking him." The employee, a born-again Christian, claimed that the other worker was a satanist who provoked the incident by putting a curse on her. She claimed that when she put her hands around his throat she was merely "praying" for him.

The Virginia district court said that it was not clear whether the Navy had attempted to reasonably accommodate the employee's "religious-based idiosyncrasies." The court said that there was some dispute as to whether the "choking" incident was actually a "praying" incident. Thus, the court denied the employer's request for dismissal.

In 1996, the EEOC ruled that an Orange County, Calif., transit authority failed to reasonably accommodate a bus driver's vegetarian beliefs by firing him for refusing to hand out coupons for free hamburgers. The employee did not eat animal products and refused to wear clothes made from animals. The transit authority notified all drivers in advance of the hamburger coupon promotion. Nevertheless, the vegetarian bus driver did not tell his supervisors of his opposition to the promotion until five minutes before he was scheduled to begin driving on the day that coupons were to be passed out. He was fired for insubordination.

The bus driver filed a religious discrimination claim with the EEOC and also filed suit in Orange County Superior Court. The EEOC ruled in a Determination issued by its regional office in San Diego that the transit authority had failed to accommodate the bus driver's "strongly held moral and ethical beliefs" by requiring him to hand out the hamburger coupons. The EEOC concluded therefore that the transit authority violated Title VII by firing the bus driver for refusing to pass out the hamburger coupons as instructed.

These cases demonstrate that the EEOC and the courts will often be very protective of the professed "religious" beliefs of employees. It is therefore necessary for all employers to proceed cautiously when confronted with claims of religious discrimination and not assume that they will not have an obligation to accommodate the employee's religious belief even though the religious belief may seem to be extremely bizarre.

Religious freedom in the workplace

Employers are sometimes faced with claims by employees that they cannot work on a particular day of the week because it is their Sabbath. The question most often raised by employers is how far they must go in accommodating an employee's desire to observe his or her Sabbath. For example, must an employer find a substitute employee to work in order to accommodate the employee who wishes to exercise his religious freedom? Must the employee be permanently transferred to another position or another shift that would not require work on his or her Sabbath?

Although it is generally agreed that, in the absence of a demonstrable undue hardship, an employer is under a duty to accommodate the religious preferences of its employees, the concept of "undue hardship" remains ill-defined. In *Trans World Airlines v. Hardison*, the Supreme Court held that employers are not required to accommodate religious beliefs where the accommodation would impose more than a *de minimus* financial burden upon them. Guidelines issued by the EEOC provide that employers faced with the need to accommodate religious beliefs must at least explore the following alternatives: procuring voluntary substitutes; flexible scheduling to permit employees to work the required number of hours without violating their religious beliefs; and transferring an employee to a comparable job that he or she can perform without violating his or her religious beliefs. The guidelines further provide that the available alternative that least disadvantages the individual requiring accommodation must be adopted.

Federal courts appear to be adhering to the *de minimus* standard, however, in evaluating the employer's accommodation burden. In a recent case, a Seventh Day Adventist charged his employer with religious discrimination after he was discharged for refusing to work on Saturdays because of his religious belief. The plaintiff was a welder who did not tell his employer that he could not work on Saturdays until after he was hired. The company, however, had informed the plaintiff that it operated seven days a week.

The court said that the plaintiff's absence on Saturdays would result in a loss of production. The company had argued that hiring an additional welder to replace the plaintiff on Saturdays would cause a loss of production and underutilization of its assets and equipment. The court concluded that the loss of production was more than a *de minimus* burden and therefore granted summary judgment in favor of the employer.

There are cases, however, that demonstrate the danger in not accomodating an employee's religious beliefs. For example, in a 1997 decision out of Virginia, a federal court awarded $20,475 to a mine worker who was fired for missing work after being bitten by a snake during a church service. The plaintiff, a Pentecostal Holiness believer, handled deadly snakes during church services as a commandment of his religion. The plaintiff did not seek medical treatment for the snake bite, believing that God would take care of him. As a result, the plaintiff could not deliver a note to his employer stating that he was under a doctor's care.

The EEOC filed suit on behalf of the employee contending that the employer failed to accommodate the plaintiff's religious beliefs. The EEOC argued that the absence was a "mere inconvenience" to the employer and presented evidence that the company had treated other violations of the attendance policy more leniently. The jury awarded $20,475 in back pay to the plaintiff but refused to impose punitive damages. Although the plaintiff had alleged that other employees had harassed him calling him "copperhead" and "snakeman," the employer had rehired the plaintiff after the litigation began.

Harassment—not just a sexual thing

Very few issues have grabbed the public's attention in the way that sexual harassment has. Allegations of gender-based harassment seem to be continuously on the front pages of the nation's newspapers. Sexual harassment and the potential liability for employers for allowing such harassment to continue unchecked in the workplace will be explored in detail in Chapter 4. Harassment claims, however, have spread beyond those based on gender.

Racial harassment. Evidence of racial harassment has been frequently used in the past to demonstrate discriminatory motivation leading to a discharge, demotion, or other adverse employment decision. Recently, however, the courts have seen an increase in the number of "hostile environment" racial harassment cases in which the employee alleges the existence of an atmosphere of racial discrimination, typically demonstrated by racially offensive comments, cartoons, or pictures, that is alleged to unreasonably interfere with the work performance of minority employees or to create an intimidating, hostile, or offensive work environment. The legal principles applicable to these racial harassment claims are virtually identical to those of the "hostile environment" sexual harassment cases.

A racial harassment claim requires a showing that there was a "concerted pattern of racial harassment" or harassment that is "so excessive and opprobrious" as to constitute an unlawful employment practice under Title VII. In order to make out a hostile environment racial discrimination claim, the harassment must be severe and pervasive, just as in sexual harassment cases. For example, plaintiffs established their hostile environment discrimination claim in one case where their supervisor routinely used racial slurs, routinely replaced terminated black employees with white employees, assigned black employees almost exclusively to a less desirable night shift and assigned them menial duties that were not performed by white employees. In another case, however, the black plaintiff did not prove that a racially hostile work environment existed for her by pointing to an e-mail message addressing her as "Brown Sugar," by alleging that she heard from another employee that her supervisor had on one occasion made reference to her using a racial epithet, and by the fact that co-workers teased her about her alleged extramarital affair with a white employee referring to her as the Whitney Houston character in the film *The Bodyguard*, a film that depicts an interracial love affair.

Religious and national origin harassment. Claims of religious harassment in the workplace are also on the rise as employees with strong religious beliefs feel obligated to "witness" to those beliefs in the workplace. Issues of religious harassment are complicated, however, because of the obligations placed on employers by discrimination laws to "reasonably accommodate" the employee's religious beliefs unless doing so would cause an undue hardship to the business. If an employee's religious beliefs compel him to proselytize, how far must an employer accommodate those beliefs before it creates a work environment that is hostile or offensive to other employees? The courts are still wrestling with this issue.

With an increase in the diversity of the composition of the workforce, claims of national origin harassment have also increased. The EEOC regulations concerning this are almost identical to the sexual harassment regulations and make it clear that ethnic slurs and other verbal or physical conduct related to an individual's national origin may constitute harassment if they create a hostile or offensive work environment.

In 1997, a Muslim who claimed that an airline employer fired him for complaining about harassment because of his religion and national origin was awarded $2.99 million dollars by a jury in Alameda County, Calif. The plaintiff complained that flight attendants said he fit the profile of a terrorist. The plaintiff alleged that these same workers accused him of stealing wine and drinking on the job. The plaintiff was a Muslim and therefore did not drink. He said he complained to management who "brushed off" his complaint. His employer maintained that the plaintiff had never complained about harassment.

Harassment and the Americans with Disabilities Act. The discrimination protections offered by the ADA are reviewed extensively in Chapter 6 of this book. Claims of harassment, however, are also viable under the ADA. For example, in a recent Maryland federal court case, an employee with multiple sclerosis alleged that her supervisor mimicked and ridiculed her speech and her walk, both traits that resulted from her disability. She also alleged that the supervisor created an atmosphere of resentment and pity among her co-workers. Based on these allegations, the court refused to grant summary judgment to the employer on the allegations of disability harassment although the court did dismiss the employee's supervisor from the case. The court specifically found that the plaintiff had set forth sufficient facts to support a claim for unlawful harassment based on the Americans with Disabilities Act.

Some nonconventional protected classes

As mentioned previously, many states have passed fair employment practice acts that add to the original protections of Title VII and provide protection for some new and rather unconventional protected classes.

Marital status discrimination. Marital status discrimination prohibitions are becoming so prevalent that it may be time to stop calling this category unconventional. At least 25 states now provide some kind of marital status protection. Nevertheless, the boundaries of this discrimination claim are still not fixed.

The prohibition against discrimination because of marital status came about because various courts refused to extend Title VII's sex discrimination protections to employees who received adverse treatment because of their marital status. Only in cases where an employer's rule restricted the employment of married employees of only one sex and not the other, did courts find that Title VII's protections against sex discrimination extended to such practices. For example, in *Sprogis v. United Airlines, Inc.*, the court held that the airline's no-marriage rule for female flight attendants was sex discrimination. The court found that male flight personnel, including male flight cabin attendants, had not been subject to the rule. In *Stroud v. Delta Airlines*, however, the Fifth Circuit upheld a no-marriage rule for flight attendants because Delta hired no men for the job and thus there was no sex discrimination under Title VII.

Marital status discrimination statutes, on the other hand, will invalidate an employer's no-marriage rule regardless of its impact on either sex unless the employer can show a business justification for the rule. For example, in *Ross v. Stouffer Hotel Company*, the Hawaii Supreme Court ruled that the Hawaii statute forbidding marital status discrimination would prohibit an employer from forcing a married couple to choose between one spouse giving up his or her employment or getting a divorce and living together so that both individuals could continue employment. The court also held that terminating persons who marry other persons in the same department would violate the state's ban on marital status discrimination.

Sexual orientation protections. Almost all courts have held that Title VII does not prohibit employment discrimination by private employers against homosexuals or transsexuals. It remains for advocates of "sexual preference" or "sexual orientation" protection to lobby for legislative help in securing new discrimination laws. Only limited progress has been made in securing such legislation. Only 13 states have passed measures that provide protection for a private sector employee's sexual orientation.

Efforts to amend Title VII to protect sexual orientation continue to be pressed in Congress. The Employment Non-Discrimination Act would prohibit discrimination based on sexual orientation. It has been introduced in both Houses of Congress and President Clinton has expressed his support for the legislation. The Senate failed to pass a similar measure in 1996 by one vote. It appears clear that eventually some type of protection for sexual orientation will become federal law.

Genetic testing. A number of states are now enacting prohibitions against genetic testing by employers or statutes that bar discrimination by employers on the basis of genetic test results. For example, in June 1997, the Governor of Texas signed a law prohibiting both health plans and employers from discriminating against individuals because of genetic information. The law also specifically prohibits discrimination against an employee for refusing to submit to genetic tests. Several other states, including Arizona, New Hampshire, Oregon, and Wisconsin, have either banned genetic testing or prohibit discrimination on the basis of test results.

What is an employer to do?

Faced with this growing panoply of potential discrimination claims, employers should take steps to reduce their exposure. Many employers have already adopted strong policies prohibiting discrimination. The best insurance against discrimination claims is for employers to implement progressive discipline procedures and educate supervisors as to the statutory and judicial protections provided to employees under their supervision. Employers should audit their discharge decisions to determine whether the discharged employee has a potential claim for discrimination. Employers should assume that the employee to be discharged is a member of a protected category and be prepared to state a credible nondiscriminatory reason for the discharge decision.

Avoiding prohibited inquiries during the hiring process

The first step in avoiding discrimination under federal and state laws is to train those individuals who will be recruiting and interviewing applicants for positions with the employer regarding the questions or inquiries that are considered "prohibited" by the EEOC. Prohibited inquiries will obviously be viewed as evidence of discrimination in failure-to-hire discrimination suits. Further, even if an applicant is hired, any attempt to gain prohibited information during the application and interviewing process can be used as evidence of a discriminatory motive if the employee is later discharged and claims discrimination. The EEOC will assume that each inquiry on the application form and every question asked during the interview had a purpose. If the employer cannot show that the question was job-related, the EEOC will assume it had a discriminatory purpose.

A baseline requirement for assessing the permissibility of questions asked during the applicant screening process is the job-relatedness of the inquiry. As stated by the EEOC in its guidelines on preemployment inquiries: "The law...prohibits the use of all preemployment inquiries that disproportionately screen out members of minority groups or members of one sex and are not valid predictors of successful job performance or cannot be justified by 'business necessity.' " In the event an applicant challenges the validity of any question asked on an application form and shows that the question has an adverse effect on minorities or other protected groups, the burden will be on the employer to show that the question is justified by business necessity or that it is job-related.

The following inquiries are prohibited and should be avoided during the hiring process.

Race and sex. There is no legitimate reason to inquire about the applicant's race on the application form or during a telephone screening process. If it is necessary for an employer to identify the racial composition of the workforce for its Affirmative Action Program (AAP), this information should be solicited after the applicant is employed or on a voluntary disclosure form that is kept separate from the application and resume of the applicant. Also, reliance on sex as the reason to hire or not to hire an applicant will almost always run afoul of Title VII. The use of sex as a basis for a hiring decision can only be justified if the employer establishes that sex is a bona fide occupational qualification (BFOQ). The BFOQ defense is narrowly interpreted, and in the overwhelming number of cases, employers have been unsuccessful in arguing that sex is a valid BFOQ for employment. Again, data on the sex of employees in the workforce for AAP purposes should be compiled after the start of employment or on a voluntary disclosure form.

Age or date of birth. The EEOC has concluded that "because the request that an applicant state his age may tend to deter older applicants or otherwise indicate discrimination based on age, employment application forms that request such information will be closely scrutinized to assure that the request is for a permissible purpose and not for purposes proscribed by the Act." Although the EEOC suggests that age may be mentioned on the application if a lengthy statement of nondiscrimination policy is included, it is better to simply avoid asking questions regarding a person's age. The omission will help avoid any litigation risk, however frivolous, and would not prevent the company from acquiring such information later after hiring.

Height and weight. The U.S. Supreme Court held that Title VII forbids the use of employment tests or standards that are discriminatory in *effect* unless the employer meets the burden of showing that the requirement has a "manifest relationship" to the employment. Federal courts have taken notice of the fact that height and weight requirements tend to exclude some minority group members and women. For example, a fire department's height requirement of 5 feet 7 inches was found to have a disparate impact on Mexican-American applicants. The burden of proving that height or weight is a bona fide occupational qualification, or is sufficiently related to job duties, is a difficult one. It is unlikely that an employer would prevail if these factors were challenged. Also, height or weight has been ruled to be a protected category under some state fair employment statutes. Therefore, questions dealing with height and weight should be avoided.

Place of birth. Preemployment inquiries concerning an applicant's place of birth could constitute evidence of national origin discrimination if challenged by a rejected applicant. An applicant's place of birth could also divulge racial or ethnic information. This question should be avoided.

Citizenship. The Immigration Reform and Control Act of 1986 makes it an unlawful employment practice to discriminate against any individual, other than an unauthorized alien, on the basis of national origin or citizenship. Further, even though the Supreme Court has held that discrimination on the basis of citizenship is not prohibited by the Civil Rights Act of 1964, it is clear that aliens *are* protected against any discrimination under the Act, including discrimination on the basis of national origin. The EEOC has noted that discrimination on the basis of citizenship may have the effect of discriminating on the basis of national origin. Therefore, only the following question should be posed to applicants for employment: "Are you legally eligible for employment in the United States?"

Employment of relatives. If an inquiry into relatives of the applicant working for a company is pursuant to a policy whereby relatives of incumbent employees are given preferences in employment, the question should be avoided. On the other hand, if the inquiry is to permit the uniform enforcement of a policy against hiring spouses or relatives, the question is defensible, although a litigation risk exists. The EEOC's *Guide for Preemployment Inquiries* states that information about relatives working for an employer "is not relevant to an applicant's competence." The EEOC takes the position that the request for such information may be unlawful if it indicates preference for the relatives of present employees and "the composition of the present workforce is such that this preference would reduce or eliminate opportunities for women or minority group members." Conversely, the EEOC simultaneously takes the position that the question may indicate an unlawful preference if the employer's policy prohibits or limits the employment of a relative, and such a practice has an adverse impact on women or men as a group.

Referral Source. Questions about the applicant's "referral source" should be avoided. The EEOC and the courts have found that the practice of relying on referrals by a predominantly white workforce rather than seeking new employees in the marketplace for jobs is discriminatory. Thus, it has been held that having friends or relatives working for an employer is not relevant to an applicant's competence to perform.

Education and dates of graduation. An employer may inquire into an applicant's educational background as long as it can show that the educational requirements are job-related or a business necessity. However, the U.S. Supreme Court has held that an employer's requirement of a high school education was discriminatory on the basis of race where statistics showed that such a requirement was not significantly related to successful job performance. Inquiries into graduation dates may provide a rough approximation of the applicant's age. Thus, unless such information is very significant is assessing candidates for a particular position, it is best to avoid this question because it carries with it some degree of risk during an age discrimination proceeding.

....

Convictions. An employer may lawfully solicit information from an applicant concerning criminal convictions. However, both the EEOC and the courts have held that an employer may not lawfully deny employment to an applicant because of a criminal conviction unless the conviction can be shown to be related to the job applied for. Furthermore, even if the conviction is job-related, the employer must consider certain other factors in making the decision as to hire the applicant, such as 1) the nature and number of the offenses; 2) the circumstances of the convictions; 3) the length of time intervening between the conviction and the employment decision; 4) the applicant's employment history; and 5) the applicant's efforts at rehabilitation. The EEOC recommends that inquiries into criminal convictions on employment application forms contain the statement that a "yes" answer will not disqualify an applicant from consideration for employment. This statement should be added to application forms.

Medical inquiries. Preemployment inquiries (before an offer of employment) into an applicant's medical condition are prohibited under the ADA. Although this topic will be explored in depth in Chapter 6, the basic rules are that an employer cannot require an applicant to submit to a medical examination or make medical inquiries before an offer of employment has been made, and an employer cannot ask an applicant whether he or she has a disability or the extent or severity of a disability. An employer can ask the applicant if he or she is able to perform the job-related functions of the position for which the applicant has applied.

Avoiding discrimination during employment

Although discrimination litigation is usually triggered by the discharge decision, evidence to support a discrimination claim is also culled from the course of dealing between an employee and management during the individual's employment with the company. Therefore, it is extremely important to implement procedures to minimize the chance for discriminatory conduct by supervisors during the employment relationship.

The EEO statement and problem-solving procedure

At the start of employment, new employees should be introduced to the employer's philosophy against discrimination by an equal employment opportunity policy statement in the company handbook. (A sample policy statement is included in the Appendix on page 274.) Also, employees should be asked to read and sign a separate policy statement that reviews the employee complaint procedure or problem-solving procedure. This policy statement should strongly encourage employees to voice any concern about discrimination to a designated member of management, preferably a human resources executive. Assurances against retaliation should also be included in the policy statement.

It is imperative that the employee complaint procedure be an effective vehicle by which complaints of discrimination, harassment, or even inappropriate language can be brought to management's attention, and that insures an immediate and thorough investigation of these complaints. Once a complaint has been made, the employer must completely investigate the claim. The employer has a legal obligation to insure that the investigation is thorough and complete.

The importance of thorough documentation in defending an employment discrimination action cannot be overemphasized. Every complaint should be put in writing, and every step of the investigation, including all witness interviews, should be documented to the extent possible. Such documentation will prove invaluable in subsequent litigation to demonstrate that the employer conducted a thorough investigation and to memorialize the facts uncovered in that investigation. Only through prompt and thorough action can an employer be in a position to defend against these types of claims.

Supervisory training

Supervisors must be trained to avoid saying or doing things that might imply discrimination. This is an enormous task but it should be undertaken in earnest. Although it is now very popular for radio and television commentators to rail against "political correctness," employers cannot afford to be arbitrary or rebellious in their approach to this issue. Every attempt should be made to "neuter" workplace language. I use this term in the broadest sense possible; supervisors must eliminate words from their vocabulary that might be used to show bias in a future discrimination matter. As mentioned above, references to gender, age, race, or national origin should be avoided, even in casual discussions between supervisors and their employees. The EEOC and other discrimination agencies will construe words like "girl," "gal," "honey," "baby," "boy," "old man," "gramps," or "pops" to mean the supervisor has a hidden bias.

Job posting

Employers should also adopt a job-bidding procedure that includes posting of available positions to handle promotions and transfers to available positions. Experience has shown that employees prefer job-bidding systems in which vacancies are announced throughout the facility and where employees are encouraged to bid for specific jobs. From the employees' standpoint, this system gives them a greater degree of control over their career paths. If the jobs are advertised throughout the workforce, employees become aware of them, and are able to let management know if they are interested in a position. Obviously, a well-publicized posting system prevents employees from arguing that they were never given an opportunity for promotion and places the burden on individual employees to show their initiative and interest in a particular position.

Apart from the value of a formal job-bidding system in improving overall employee relations, it is also not as vulnerable to attack under Title VII. Courts have frequently found promotion systems in which vacancies are not posted and in which management is free to exercise a great deal of subjectivity in selecting employees to be unlawful employment practices under Title VII. For example, an employer's failure to post job openings, coupled with a system permitting managers who are mostly male to exercise substantial discretion in choosing the candidates to be interviewed for a position, can have an adverse effect on females within the workforce.

EEO audit during annual evaluations

Supervisors should be charged with inquiring into equal employment opportunity (EEO) issues during each individual's annual performance evaluation. Employees should be asked whether they have any EEO concerns. Their responses should be documented on the evaluation form. If an employee has a substantial EEO concern, the employee should be urged to file a written complaint with the Human Resources department using the employee complaint procedure. Even if the employee does not want to pursue a formal complaint, the supervisor should consult with Human Resources.

A progressive discipline system

The adoption and maintenance of a formal system of progressive discipline is required to ensure that supervisors treat similarly situated employees alike. A progressive discipline system is a necessity to protect against charges under Title VII and other antidiscrimination laws. Evidence of disparate treatment of similarly situated employees may also be used in breach of employment contract litigation to show that a particular discharge was arbitrary, capricious, and lacking in just cause.

The progressive discipline system should provide for increasingly more severe punishments as unacceptable conduct is repeated. For example, an initial verbal warning can progress to written warning to suspension to discharge. Of course, some forms of misconduct are so serious as to warrant immediate discharge or suspension. In addition, at each level of discipline the employee should be warned of the consequences of continued misconduct. All levels of discipline should be documented and preserved in the employee's personnel file. As to written warnings, the supervisor may request the employee to sign the written warning to acknowledge receipt.

This formal disciplinary procedure serves two purposes. First, it provides the employer with an accurate record of the past disciplinary history of the employee. Second, it provides written evidence that the employee was given an adequate warning of the possibility of an opportunity to rehabilitate himself. This warning and "second chance" will go far to impress a jury with the fairness of the employer's disciplinary action.

Of course, no system of progressive discipline, however well-written, can be more effective than the manner in which it is enforced by front-line supervision. Therefore, supervisors must be trained in the contents of the discipline system and how it is to be applied. If properly applied and monitored, the progressive discipline system should eliminate instances in which employees are terminated for offenses without sufficient warning and opportunity to correct their behavior. The system should also guarantee that all similarly situated employees are treated consistently and without favoritism.

Investigating and making the discharge decision

Employers should take precautions when making a discharge decision to avoid even the appearance of discrimination. The following guidelines can help employers reduce the threat of litigation. Although these three strategies are grounded in common sense, most lawsuits and large jury verdicts for employees occur when one of these steps is not followed.

Document the investigation. The most important part of any employment decision is the first phase of the process. The key to discouraging and defending discrimination lawsuits is creating a "paper-trail" documenting the employer's investigation that in turn supports the rationale for the employer's decision. Employers should keep in mind the following guidelines: 1) interview all those who have information relevant to the decision to be made (for example, in the case of discipline or discharge, witnesses to the wrongdoing); 2) review all relevant documents; and 3) prepare documentation of the investigation with the goal of discouraging and/or defeating future litigation. An important part of the investigation is an interview with the employee who faces discipline or discharge. The employee must be made to feel that his or her side of the story is being given careful consideration. Although the immediate supervisor can participate in the interview, it may seem more fair to the employee to have a Human Resources professional in charge of the investigation or at least present when the employee is given a chance to tell his or her side of the story.

Analyze the information. An important strategy for avoiding discrimination litigation is to ensure that whatever decision is made appears fair to all those affected. An employer can never please everyone. Nevertheless, a thorough analysis of the evidence justifying discharge will help convince a judge or jury of the employer's unbiased approach to the problem. Consequently, after gathering the necessary information from the investigation, the employer should analyze the data to ensure its consistency with past practice. The key to this analysis is to compare the decision under consideration to similar situations in the past involving other employees who were similarly-situated to the employee in question. Inconsistent decision-making, especially in the application of policies and practices, is at the heart of all discrimination claims.

Communicate the decision. After the decision is made, the manner in which it is communicated can be essential to avoiding a legal challenge. Even if a decision is well-supported by the facts and properly documented, an employee who perceives the decision to be unfair will still bring a lawsuit. Employers should therefore carefully choose how the decision is communicated and ensure that the decision is communicated to all those affected. For example, in the context of discipline, the supervisor should communicate the discipline or discharge decision in person and clearly set out the expectations for correcting the problem that caused the discipline. The employee should be reminded of the right to appeal a discipline or discharge decision. Employees should also be allowed to state their reaction to the discipline decision. Encourage them to put their thoughts in writing so that a review by a more senior management official is made more efficient. Employees facing discharge may say things that will be helpful later on if litigation does occur. Also, writings tend to be self-limiting. A plaintiff who does not mention an important fact in a letter protesting a discharge decision can be impeached if he tries to raise the issue later during litigation.

....

Chapter 4

There Is No Such Thing as a "Safe" Workplace Romance

Janet Bingham, the Human Resources manager for ARX Lighting, was worried. Harry Simpson, in sales, was being promoted to Department Manager. Janet knew that Harry had been dating another salesperson in the department for the past six months. The woman, Sally Stone, had only recently broken off the relationship with Harry. Now, Harry would be her supervisor.

Ms. Bingham took her concerns to her boss, Joe Potter, the vice president of Human Resources. He listened but seemed unimpressed by Janet's fear that a difficult situation could arise because Harry would now be Sally Stone's immediate supervisor. He told her, "Janet, you worry too much. We can't deny a promotion to Harry simply because there is a potential for harassment. Has Sally complained at all?"

Janet had to admit that Sally Stone had not registered a protest of any kind. Janet nevertheless persuaded Mr. Potter that she should talk to both Harry and Sally about the promotion. She met with Sally first and was surprised to learn that Sally had no concerns about having Harry as her supervisor. She even downplayed her previous relationship with Harry calling it a "brief encounter."

When Janet talked to Harry Simpson, his attitude was also reassuring. In response to Janet's questions, Harry said, "Sally and I are good friends, nothing more. I understand your concerns, but believe me, Janet, I will have no problem supervising Sally and she will not have any problems with me. Don't worry about a thing."

Over the next seven months, everything seemed to be going fine in the sales department. Harry spent a lot of time talking to Sally in her cubicle, but Janet was aware that Harry and Sally had been given a major marketing project by the CEO. Harry also gave Sally an excellent evaluation and recommended her for a raise. Although Harry had been seen walking Sally to her car on a number of evenings, this did not seem unusual to Janet because many male employees had begun accompanying female employees to the parking garage because of several muggings that had occurred in or near the garage area. All outward appearances indicated that there was no tension between Harry and Sally.

Several weeks later, Sally Stone called Janet and told her she had to see her. When Sally arrived, she appeared agitated and her eyes were red as if she had been crying. Sally immediately demanded that Harry Simpson be transferred to another department, saying: "I can't take it anymore. Either Harry goes or I quit! The man won't leave me alone!" She then broke down crying.

Sally claimed that Harry was "obsessed" with her and continually asked her out on dates. She always refused to go out with him but Harry was not dissuaded. "He puts little notes on my desk. He brings me flowers. He insists on walking me to my car. I've told him to stop, but he won't!" she said. Sally also said that he never got angry when she refused his invitations. "Oh, he's always very polite," said Sally. "He is so damn cheerful, it's sickening!"

Janet probed further, "Has he threatened you at all?" Sally admitted that Harry had never made any threats. "Has he made any promises to you to get you to go out with him?" asked Janet. "No, nothing like that." said Sally.

"Is there anything else you want to tell me?" Janet asked. Sally hesitated a minute and said, "He is always touching my hand or my arm. Sometimes he leans his arm on my shoulder when I am working at my computer or he will place his hand lightly on my back as he stands behind me. He has offered to massage my neck while I'm working, too."

Ms. Bingham was becoming alarmed now. "What do you do when he touches you?" she asked. "I move away," Sally replied. "I tell him I don't need a massage, but he always says 'Oh, Sally, I'm just trying to help; I don't mean anything by it.'" Sally seemed ready to cry again and said quietly, "He stops for a while, but he always starts up again."

Janet asked Sally to wait while she went down the hall to see Mr. Potter. When Joe Potter heard the story he was not very concerned. "It sounds to me like Harry may be flirting with her a little bit, but he hasn't threatened Sally and he hasn't promised her special privileges. Sure, he probably asked her out but she apparently tells him 'no' and that doesn't upset him."

"What about the touching?" asked Janet, becoming exasperated. Mr. Potter replied, "I have some concerns about that, but the touching really isn't sexual in nature. Still, he should knock it off. Call Harry and arrange a meeting for tomorrow. If this stuff is true, we'll just tell him to cut it out. But, listen Janet, I don't think we need to make a big deal out of this."

The next day Janet and Joe Potter met with Harry Simpson. Harry was angered by Sally's accusations and acted incredulous when confronted with specific claims. "I asked her to go to dinner, that's all, when we were working late. It was nothing. I bring flowers to lots of the women in the department. I would also like to see these 'notes' she's talking about. Did she save any of these notes?" asked Harry. "She has never once told me to stop walking her to the garage," he continued. "In fact, she said she was scared to walk there alone."

"Do you touch her?" asked Janet. "That's ridiculous!" exclaimed Harry. "I touch people on the shoulder to get their attention. I pat them on the back when they do a good job. I may have rubbed her neck once when we were working late but she asked me to do it. I never once touched her in a sexual way."

Mr. Potter took charge of the meeting then. "Listen, Harry. I believe you didn't mean any harm. But something you did set her off and she doesn't like it. Just do your job and stay away from her. Don't ask her to dinner, don't put flowers on her desk, and don't walk her to her car." Harry responded, "That's fine. But I better not be disciplined for this; I did nothing wrong!" Mr. Potter assured Harry that he would not be disciplined.

After Harry left, Janet called Sally to let her know that Harry promised to limit his contacts with her to business matters only. Janet told her that Harry would still need to interact with her on sales issues but that contact of a purely personal nature should not occur. Sally said, "This is not going to work. He may stop for a while, but sooner or later he will be breathing down my neck again." Janet replied: "If he does, you call me."

Over the next several weeks, Janet did not hear from Sally. Janet noted, however, that Sally had been absent quite a bit and was often late for work. Harry Simpson had even begun progressive discipline of Sally as her absenteeism and tardiness had triggered the penalty provisions of the company's no-fault policy. Janet wanted to go and talk to Sally but Joe Potter told her not to interfere.

Janet was determined, however. The next day she marched into Joe Potter's office and said, "We need to talk about Harry Simpson." Joe responded, "It doesn't really matter now; take a look at this." It was a letter from an attorney who claimed to represent Sally Stone. She

*was resigning her employment. The attorney threatened to bring causes
of action for discrimination, harassment, assault, battery, and intentional infliction of emotional distress.*

*The attorney demanded $500,000 to settle the claims, promising
that he would ask for more than $5 million in compensatory and puni-
tive damages if he had to litigate the case in court. The attorney
claimed that Harry Simpson had "stalked" Sally for months, made obscene calls to her home, touched her sexually at work, and threatened
her with discharge if she said anything to management. Janet slumped
down in the chair next to Joe Potter's desk as Mr. Potter dialed the
telephone number of the company's employment lawyer.*

Sexual harassment: the most dangerous employee complaint

The sexual harassment lawsuit with its potential for large compensatory and punitive damages awards has made it a very appealing cause of
action for plaintiffs' attorneys. Employers have been ordered to pay staggering amounts in damages to employees who are victims of on-the-job
sexual harassment. As a result, employers should be very wary of con-
doning romantic relationships in the workplace. This is especially true of
romances between supervisors and their subordinates. A company opens
itself up to charges of discrimination if one of its supervisors evaluates a
paramour higher than other employees under his supervision without
objective reasons for doing so. A promotion given to the romantic partner
of a supervisor is always subject to criticism and speculation as to the real
reasons for the employee's advancement.

If the relationship between the supervisor and the subordinate becomes estranged, the supervisor may find it difficult to discipline the subordinate employee without raising questions of retaliation. Many cases of
sexual harassment have arisen after the consensual relationship has
ended and the employee rejects any further advances of the supervisor.
Conduct that was welcomed by an employee at one point in the relationship may legitimately be deemed unwelcome at a later time. Friendly
banter and innocent flirting can evolve into exchanges that demean and
demoralize the more vulnerable employee.

Employers have other legitimate reasons for discouraging romance in
the workplace: A romantic relationship can be sexually charged and disconcerting for both employees; they may have trouble keeping their minds
on their work while they are around each other, resulting in increased
errors or reduced productivity.

A written sexual harassment policy with training for employees in permitted behavior under the policy should be effective in controlling the consequences of romantic relationships gone sour or the "rejected suitor" syndrome. Even the most comprehensive sexual harassment policy can be rendered ineffective, however, if employees do not feel encouraged to come forward with harassment complaints and those investigating the complaint do not make a prompt and thorough evaluation of the alleged harassment. A company cannot expect to avoid liability if it does not take effective corrective action in response to a harassment claim.

Defining sexual harassment

Both the courts and the Equal Employment Opportunity Commission (EEOC) consider sexual harassment a form of sex discrimination that constitutes an unlawful employment practice in violation of Title VII of the Civil Rights Act of 1964. Sexual harassment has been defined in federal regulations as "unwelcome sexual advances, requests for sexual favors, and other verbal or physical conduct of a sexual nature that has the purpose or effect of unreasonably interfering with an individual's work performance or creating an intimidating, hostile, or offensive work environment." Unwelcome sexual words, jokes, teasing, pictures, questions, gestures, threats, acts, or advances in an employment context may constitute unlawful sexual harassment for which the employer will be liable.

In a case involving posters, pictures, and other graphic displays, the United States District Court for the Middle District of Florida held that a company that condoned and encouraged the display of sexually-oriented pictures of women in the workplace engaged in sexual harassment. The female plaintiff worked as a welder for a company that operated a shipyard. During the course of her work, the plaintiff came into regular contact with work rooms where pictures depicting nude or partially nude women were posted. Other forms of harassing behavior pervaded the workplace, including sexually demeaning remarks and jokes by male workers.

The Florida district court held that the sexually-explicit posters constituted behavior that was disproportionately more offensive or demeaning to one sex. The court said, "The pictures themselves...[constitute] behavior that did not originate with the intent of offending women in the workplace...but clearly has a disproportionately demeaning impact on the women now working at [the company]." The court noted that the presence of the pictures, even if not directed at a particular female employee, sexualizes the work environment to the detriment of all female employees. The court stated, "[This] behavior...creates a barrier to the progress of women in the workplace because it conveys the message that they do not belong, that they are welcome in the workplace only if they will subvert their identities to the sexual stereotypes prevalent in that environment."

Types of sexual harassment

Sexual harassment charges fall into two categories: *quid pro quo* harassment, the traditional demand for sexual favors in exchange for some job benefit; and "hostile environment" harassment, unwelcome conduct based on sex that is sufficiently severe or pervasive so as to interfere with an individual's job performance. In *quid pro quo* harassment, a single sexual advance may constitute harassment if it is linked to the grant or denial of employment benefits. In contrast, a "hostile environment" claim generally requires a showing of a pattern of offensive conduct.

A 1986 decision by the U.S. Supreme Court defined the parameters of an actionable hostile sexual harassment claim under Title VII. In *Meritor Savings Bank v. Vinson*, the Court stated that for sexual harassment to be actionable, it must be sufficiently severe or pervasive to "alter the conditions of [the victim's] employment and create an abusive working environment." The Court held that employers are not always automatically liable for sexual harassment by their supervisors. The Supreme Court suggested that lower courts look to general agency principles in assessing employer liability. The Court warned that the mere existence of a grievance procedure and a stated policy against discrimination, coupled with an employee's failure to invoke that procedure, does not insulate an employer from liability. The Court suggested, however, that a properly drafted grievance procedure and sexual harassment policy that was "calculated to encourage victims of harassment to come forward" could relieve employers of liability in certain situations.

An essential element of a sexual harassment claim is a showing that the alleged sexual advances were "unwelcome." In determining whether the alleged sexual harassment is unwelcome, objective evidence rather than subjective, uncommunicated feelings is most persuasive. For example, a federal court in Illinois found a plaintiff's allegations of sexual harassment unbelievable because she visited her alleged harasser at the hospital and at his brother's home, and allowed him to come into her home alone at night after the alleged harassment occurred. In another case, a New Jersey court rejected the plaintiff's claim that she was sexually harassed by her co-worker's language and gestures. The plaintiff had indicated in her personal diary that she did not welcome the sexual banter. But, she made no objection to her co-workers' behavior and indeed appeared to join in "as one of the boys."

In determining whether a work environment is hostile, the EEOC, in its Compliance Manual, states that relevant facts include: 1) whether the conduct was verbal or physical, or both; 2) how frequently it was repeated; 3) whether the conduct was hostile and patently offensive; 4) whether the alleged harasser was a co-worker, supervisor, or nonemployee third party; 5) whether others joined in perpetrating the harassment; and 6) whether the harassment was directed at more than one individual. Unless the conduct is quite severe, an isolated incident of offensive sexual conduct generally does not create a hostile environment.

When the alleged harassment is physical, the EEOC will presume that the unwelcome, intentional touching of an individual's intimate body areas is sufficiently offensive to alter the conditions of the individual's working environment and constitutes a violation of Title VII. When the alleged harassment is verbal, the EEOC will look to factors such as the nature, frequency, context, and intended target of the remarks in order to determine whether the environment is hostile.

Employer liability

Employers can be liable for sexual harassment under a variety of scenarios. Not only can employers be liable for sexual harassment by supervisors or co-workers, but also for harassment by nonemployee vendors, clients, and customers. In addition, an employer is liable if it had actual knowledge of the harassment, or if it should have known about the harassment. Although the most common sexual harassment claims still involve a female victim alleging harassment by a male supervisor, an increasing number of claims have been raised by male employees against their female supervisors. In addition, as will be explained later in this chapter, many courts are beginning to recognize a cause of action for same gender sexual harassment. The EEOC has issued guidelines on sexual harassment that codify the most liberal pro-employee court decisions. The guidelines are not law, but they provide the basis for how the EEOC will conduct its investigations and whether it will issue a finding of probable cause to believe discrimination actually occurred in any particular case. The guidelines enable employers to understand their potential liability in this volatile and highly emotional area of employee relations.

The EEOC would hold an employer responsible for harassment by its supervisors regardless of whether the specific acts complained of were authorized or even forbidden by the employer, and regardless of whether the employer knew or should have known of the occurrence. A lesser degree of liability is imposed on employers with respect to conduct between fellow employees. Only where the employer knows or should have known of the conduct complained of, will the employer be responsible for acts of sexual harassment between fellow employees. Liability for the acts of fellow employees can also be avoided by taking "immediate and appropriate corrective action."

But employer liability for sexual harassment under the EEOC guidelines does not stop with the actions of persons it actually employs. The guidelines provide that an employer may also be responsible for the acts of nonemployees who sexually harass employees in the workplace, where the employer (or its agents or supervisory employees) knows or should have known of the conduct and fails to take "immediate and appropriate corrective action." In determining employer liability for acts of nonemployees, the EEOC considers the extent of the employer's control over such persons and "any other legal responsibility that the employer may have" with respect to their conduct.

One of the more controversial guidelines provides a cause of action to employees other than the victim of sexual harassment. The employer may be held liable under the EEOC guidelines for unlawful sex discrimination against other persons who were qualified for, but denied, an employment opportunity or benefit where the opportunity or benefit was granted to an individual because that individual submitted to the supervisor's sexual advances or requests for sexual favors.

Prompt remedial action

If the employer has no actual or constructive knowledge of ongoing sexual harassment, and, upon learning about the harassment, takes immediate and appropriate action to correct the harassment and prevent its recurrence, the EEOC will not find a violation of Title VII. As mentioned above, the EEOC will presume "knowledge" by the employer, however, where the supervisor is the one doing the harassment.

The corrective action should reflect the severity of the conduct by the alleged harasser. The employer is expected to make follow-up inquiries to ensure that the harassment has not resumed and there has been no retaliation against the complaining employee. The EEOC and the courts look more favorably on the employer if the penalty is effective in eliminating the sexual harassment and the severity of the disciplinary action is appropriate for the gravity of the harassing conduct.

Obviously, an employer must take some action to avoid the hostile environment that has been created by its supervisors. A federal court in Virginia found a company liable for sexual harassment under Title VII where the company was aware that its supervisor behaved in an "overly familiar manner" to employees under his supervision and where management referred to the supervisor's staff as his "harem" or "the animals" but did nothing to remedy the hostile work environment that existed for females. The plaintiff established her claim of a hostile work environment by demonstrating that the workplace was pervaded by sexual innuendo, sexually oriented games, and intimate touching between the supervisor and his female subordinates. The plaintiff presented testimony that she was a victim of at least one unwelcome advance while working for the supervisor. She also testified that on several occasions, the supervisor made derogatory and degrading comments about women in general.

The court found that the supervisor intimidated those employees who did not approve of his behavior and specifically caused the plaintiff significant emotional distress. The court concluded that the supervisor's behavior created a work atmosphere that was inconsistent with the Title VII's goal of promoting sexual equality in the workplace. The court also said that the sexual horseplay was made possible by the "hands off" attitude of management toward the supervisor and his department. The employer was found liable because it waited too long to remedy the situation that existed in the workplace.

Even though employers are required to take "prompt and corrective" remedial action to ensure that the sexual harassment ceases and that the workplace is free from such harassment, they have received little guidance as to what form of remedial action is appropriate to ensure that the sexual harassment is eradicated. In fact, there is no "formula" for determining what the appropriate penalty should be for sexual harassment. A decision of the Ninth Circuit Court of Appeals illustrates, however, that merely threatening harsher discipline, but never imposing the additional punishment, will not relieve an employer from liability.

In this federal court case, the plaintiff had been involved in a personal relationship with a co-worker, but she ended the relationship.

Following the break-up of the relationship, the co-worker began to harass the plaintiff. During an 18-month period, the plaintiff filed 16 complaints of sexual harassment with management. When the first complaint was filed, management met with the harasser and directed him to cease all such conduct. He was also advised that if his conduct continued, further disciplinary action would be taken. The employer, however, never took any more disciplinary action despite the fact that the complaints of sexual harassment continued for the next 17 months.

When the plaintiff filed suit in federal court, the employer defended the action by claiming that it had acted promptly and reasonably in responding to the plaintiff's complaints. Although the employer was successful with this defense at the trial level, the appellate court ruled otherwise. Specifically, the court of appeals ruled that any remedial action that the employer takes must be "reasonably calculated to end the harassment." While declining to establish a specific list of disciplinary actions that an employer must take, the court stated that the precise nature of the disciplinary action is up to the employer, provided that it is "assessed proportionately to the seriousness of the offense." The appellate court found that the employer's remedial actions were ineffective because the harasser's behavior persisted and the employer was aware of that fact through the filing of the subsequent complaints.

The Ninth Circuit's decision is instructive in that it advises employers that some form of disciplinary action must be taken in response to a valid complaint of sexual harassment. Further, the degree of discipline that is imposed must correspond with the nature of sexual harassment. Simply issuing a disciplinary warning when the complained-of conduct is severe will not be found to be sufficient to redress the sexual harassment. Finally, if an employer's initial efforts to stop the sexual harassment are not successful then it is incumbent upon the employer to impose more severe discipline to ensure that the sexual harassment ends.

How pervasive is sexual harassment?

If newspaper articles and employment journal reports are any indication of the amount of sexual harassment that is occurring in workplaces across this country, the problem appears to be increasing in scope. Harassment as a workplace phenomenon has received considerable publicity in recent years, and employers have responded by enacting sexual harassment policies and educating supervisors as to the dangers of creating a hostile environment for women in the workplace.

....

The much-publicized Mitsubishi class action litigation is the most prominent of recent cases involving sexual harassment in the workplace. This is partially because the EEOC is the agency suing Mitsubishi and the agency's vice chairman, Paul Igasaki, has held press conferences publicizing the allegations against Mitsubishi. Describing the litigation as "strategic law enforcement" designed to focus the agency's resources on large-scale, egregious cases of employment discrimination, Igasaki said that as many as 400 women may have suffered sexual harassment at Mitsubishi in recent years. The EEOC alleges that male auto workers at the company engaged in numerous acts of harassment including grabbing female co-workers in their breasts, buttocks, and genitals; making drawings of female body parts and sexual acts on auto fenders and cardboard signs used on the assembly line; and calling female employees "sluts," "whores," and other insulting names. Mitsubishi has denied those allegations and is devoting substantial resources to a defense of the charges.

The EEOC, however, is currently overburdened with discrimination charges and its resources are limited. As a consequence, only a very small number of the complaints received by the agency are ever litigated by the EEOC's legal staff. In fact, more than 98 percent of the cases brought against employers for employment discrimination are handled by private law firms. It is these firms that are largely responsible for the large jury awards that get the most publicity.

For example, after a federal court jury in Pennsylvania awarded a female lab technician $4.2 million, the plaintiff's attorney told a national publication that the hostile environment for the woman included incidents where the lab manager and other male co-workers would read aloud Bible passages asserting women's inferiority to men while, at other times, co-workers gathered near her to discuss their sexual fantasies, including one man who said he wanted to rape and shoot her. The plaintiff's attorney also alleged that management ignored the plaintiff's complaints about the harassment. The article merely credited company management with denying that the plaintiff ever complained about harassment but did not give further details about the company's defenses at trial.

In California, a jury awarded $1.5 million in damages to a former department store employee who had alleged that she was sexually harassed by her male supervisor at the store. After the trial, the plaintiff's attorney said that the woman's supervisor harassed her with "sexual innuendoes and physical touching." The attorney said that the supervisor would touch the plaintiff's breasts and find ways to lean against her when they

....

were unloading boxes or moving merchandise. In response, the company's attorney said the company was investigating possible jury tampering by the plaintiff but refused to otherwise comment on the verdict.

Finally, two other cases merit attention, if only for the sheer size of the damages awarded to the victims of sexual harassment. A secretary in California was awarded $7.1 million in punitive damages in her sexual harassment lawsuit against the law firm that had employed her. The damage award amounted to more than $400,000 a day for each of the 15 days the secretary was forced to work for the offending law partner. The secretary said she was "terrorized" by the partner's harassment, which included conduct such as grabbing her breasts while he put M&M candies into her blouse pocket.

In another case, a female personnel recruiter for a national restaurant chain was awarded $8.1 million in damages after a federal court judge in Texas found that she had been subjected to severe and pervasive sexual harassment and the company had done nothing to remedy the situation. The court also found that the plaintiff was fired for complaining about the harassment.

The recruiter alleged that an assistant vice-president introduced her to other managers as "our Dolly Parton" (referring to the size of her breasts) and often told new recruits for trainer positions that a bonus for joining the restaurant chain would be a weekend with the plaintiff, who would be wearing a bikini. On another occasion, the assistant vice-president grabbed her blouse so he could take a look at her breasts. Other managers also harassed the plaintiff. A regional manager constantly interjected filthy comments into business conversations with her and made references to oral sex. Another district manager stuck a Polaroid camera under her skirt and took a photo of her crotch.

The troubling question about these cases is whether each is an aberration in today's workplace or an indication that sexual harassment of women continues to occur with alarming frequency. These cases may not be indicative of a lack of training by management in harassment avoidance but rather a failure to properly investigate complaints of harassment when they do arise. For example, in the case of the personnel recruiter and the restaurant chain, management was aware of her complaint, yet it accepted the denials of the assistant vice-president who was accused of harassment. Also, the company failed to discipline the district manager for the Polaroid incident even though another executive had witnessed the district manager's behavior.

....

Investigations into sexual harassment allegations can be embarrassing for both the person complaining and the alleged harasser and often result in emotional confrontations between employees. Often, it is one person's word against another and the investigator may be reluctant to make a credibility determination that might resolve the problem. However, the person investigating a complaint of sexual harassment must decide who is telling the truth, because the consequence of ignoring or rejecting a valid sexual harassment claim can be substantial monetary liability for the company.

One case that would strain credibility for any investigator of sexual harassment involved male employees charging their supervisor with an unusually explicit form of sexual coercion. The plaintiffs claimed that they were forced to observe and participate in various sexual activities with their boss's secretary. For example, they alleged that they were forced to witness their supervisor and his secretary engaging in sexual acts in the boss' office. The plaintiffs also were compelled to watch an after-hours strip-tease orchestrated by the supervisor and performed by his secretary. In addition, the plaintiffs said that they were required to participate in a strip poker game on company premises following a company Christmas party, and that the plaintiffs themselves engaged in sexual activity with their supervisor's secretary on orders from their supervisor, while he viewed the activities from an adjoining room. In all instances, the plaintiffs contended that they participated in the sexual activities because they feared they would lose their jobs if they did not comply with the sexual demands and orders of their supervisor. Following their separation from the company, the plaintiffs sued the company for sexual harassment under Title VII.

The U.S. District Court for the District of Rhode Island permitted recovery under both a *quid pro quo* and hostile work environment theory. As for the claim of *quid pro quo* sexual harassment, the district court found: "This is the quintessential *quid pro quo* case—the plaintiffs understood that they would lose their jobs if they did not submit to the sexual demands of [their supervisor]. In short, the harassment imposed a new condition on the plaintiffs' employment: If they wanted to keep their jobs, they needed to comply with the condition of sexual harassment." The court ruled that neither plaintiff welcomed sexual relations with their boss's secretary and eventually participated only because they feared that noncompliance would cost them their jobs.

As to the claim of hostile work environment sexual harassment, the court held that the sexual harassment inflicted upon the plaintiffs drastically altered the conditions of their employment and created a hostile and abusive work environment. The court noted, in this regard, that the frequency and nature of the unwelcome sexual activity certainly was severe and pervasive. Furthermore, "sexual advances to the plaintiffs were made for months, and the harassment completely infested their work environment."

Employer defenses

Not all cases result in liability for the employer. In some instances, the employer can show that the harassment was not pervasive enough to create a hostile environment for the plaintiff. In other cases, the employer may be able to show that the sexual behavior was not "unwelcome" to the plaintiff. Also, there have been court decisions that appear to be more willing to credit an employer's lack of knowledge of the harassment.

For example, the U.S. Court of Appeals for the First Circuit ruled that suggestive conduct on the part of a co-worker was insufficient to give rise to a claim for sexual harassment. In this case, the plaintiff alleged that a co-worker harassed him by asking him to dance at a Christmas party. The plaintiff also claimed that the co-worker stood behind him while he mopped the floor, causing him to bump into the co-worker, and that the co-worker stood next to him in the restroom and "peeped" at his "privates." The plaintiff was fired for hitting the co-worker during an altercation that took place outside the hospital. He sued the hospital under Title VII claiming that he was actually discharged because of his complaints of sexual harassment.

The First Circuit affirmed the district court's judgment that the plaintiff's allegations of sexual harassment failed to form a basis for a Title VII claim. The court of appeals agreed with the district court that "the conduct complained of in this case was neither sufficiently severe nor adequately pervasive to amount to the type of conduct deemed to be actionable under Title VII." The court concurred that "the conduct was not the type that would interfere with a reasonable person's work performance, nor would it seriously affect a reasonable person's psychological well-being, at least to the extent required by Title VII."

The "mixed signal" defense

In another decision dealing with the issue of whether certain conduct was indeed unwelcome, the United States District Court for the Eastern District of Virginia held that an employee has an affirmative obligation to clearly resist unwelcome sexual behavior. The plaintiff was hired as a secretary in November 1987, for the director of personnel of a company that performed work in the area of maritime administration. The plaintiff resigned in June 1988, alleging that she was a victim of sexual harassment. Her boss was alleged to have been affectionate and extremely attentive toward her by peppering her with little notes of appreciation, escorting her to the bathroom or to her car, and visiting her both at home and during her stay in the hospital. In addition, the plaintiff claimed that while the supervisor was reviewing a salary recommendation for her, he accused her of having an affair with a fellow employee. She believed that the supervisor was suggesting that she succumb to his desires as a condition for a salary increase. The plaintiff sued under Title VII of the Civil Rights Act of 1964, claiming that the conduct created a hostile or abusive working environment.

The U.S. District Court for the Eastern District of Virginia ruled that the conduct in question was not clearly unwelcomed. In so doing, the court observed that the plaintiff never made any realistic effort to end the alleged sexual harassment. The court noted: "[The plaintiff] did not once make a serious demand on [her boss] to stop paying such close attention to her. She indicated that she continually asked him [to stop]...yet it seems certain that her requests were not delivered with any sense of urgency, sincerity, or force. In essence, she was sending out mixed signals.... There was no evidence that she ever sat [her boss] down and explained the problem (if, in fact, it was a problem) or made any reasonably serious plea for him to [discontinue or curtail his behavior]."

In addition to finding that the plaintiff made no earnest attempt to avoid her supervisor's friendly overtures, the court held that the conduct complained of was not sufficiently severe or pervasive to create an abusive working environment. The court said that the alleged sexual harassment "did not have the effect of unreasonably interfering with the plaintiff's work performance" or seriously affecting her psychological well-being. The court determined that the plaintiff failed to prove that the supervisor's conduct in showering her with affection caused the severe distress and depression from which she was suffering at the time of her resignation.

The court also said that the plaintiff failed to show that the company was aware of the alleged sexual harassment so as to incur liability for the personnel director's conduct. The court determined that the company was never put on notice of the plaintiff's allegations. The court concluded that other company employees were wholly unaware of the supervisor's conduct. Furthermore, the plaintiff never took advantage of the company president's "open door" policy or sought to complain to any other people in the company. The Virginia federal court's ruling is novel because it requires employees to clearly indicate that attention in the form of cards, notes, and other indications of affection is unwelcomed in order to recover for sexual harassment.

Lack of knowledge as a defense

Several other cases demonstrate that not every court follows the EEOC's guidelines in calling for virtually automatic employer liability for harassment by a supervisor. In another decision out of Virginia, a federal court held that the appropriate standard for imposing liability on an employer for sexual harassment is whether the employer had actual or constructive knowledge of the existence of a sexually hostile working environment.

The plaintiff in this case had worked for the company for nearly 21 years. She claimed that, beginning in 1981, her immediate supervisor began to make unwelcome sexual advances to her, and that in 1981 and 1983 there were allegedly two incidents of explicit sexual contact. After each occasion, however, the plaintiff contended that her supervisor told her not to tell anyone about the incident and intimidated and harassed her. The plaintiff initially contacted the EEOC in 1987 to file a charge of harassment but did not follow through with it because of concerns about her supervisor. The plaintiff again considered filing a charge with the EEOC in 1989, but again did not follow through with it.

Six months after the resignation of her supervisor, the plaintiff finally reported the incidents of sexual harassment to her new supervisor. The company's policy on sexual harassment provided four separate avenues for reporting sexual harassment. When the employee finally filed suit against the company, alleging sexual harassment in violation of Title VII, the company claimed that it could not be liable for the unauthorized actions of its employee because it was not aware of the alleged sexual discrimination until long after its occurrence.

The district court granted summary judgment to the company, holding that the company had neither actual nor constructive knowledge of the sexually hostile working environment. Although it admitted that the perpetrator of the hostile acts was the plaintiff's supervisor with the authority to hire, fire, and discipline her, the court also noted that the company "had an adequate, if not exemplary, sexual harassment policy and procedure that the plaintiff failed to utilize." Of significance to the court was the fact that the company had "taken significant steps to create a strenuous anti-discrimination policy, as well as a positive environment for reporting the acts of sexual harassment."

This decision is noteworthy because the existence of a grievance procedure and a policy against discrimination, coupled with the employee's failure to invoke these procedures, were effective in insulating the employer from liability for sexual harassment. The decision underscores the importance of developing a sexual harassment policy that encourages employees to come forward and report harassment to management.

Prompt remedial action

As mentioned previously, an employer that takes prompt remedial action in response to a harassment complaint may be able to avoid substantial liability, even where a supervisor was the one doing the harassment. For example, in one case, the Eleventh Circuit Court of Appeals reduced a jury verdict for $300,000 to a nominal $200 because the court could find no evidence that management had condoned sexual harassment or acted with malice or reckless indifference. The plaintiff was a temporary staff employee who alleged that the company's supervisor had made lewd or suggestive remarks to her and other female employees. The supervisor allegedly suggested that the women he supervised should take jobs at a nude cafe so he could go and watch them. The plaintiff also claimed that the supervisor had massaged her shoulders.

The court of appeals, in setting aside the original verdict, found that the company had taken prompt remedial action. The company took the plaintiff's complaint seriously, immediately reprimanded the supervisor and reduced his pay, gave the plaintiff her job back after she had been replaced, paid her for the days she missed, and transferred the supervisor to another job on a different floor.

In another decision by the Eleventh Circuit, the court of appeals found that a well-enforced, widely distributed sexual harassment policy could rebut an employee's claim that the company should have known she was being harassed. The plaintiff claimed that a company dentist at an on-site medical facility had discussed his erotic dreams with her, kissed her over her objections, made remarks about her body, and told jokes of a sexual nature in her presence.

After the plaintiff complained, the company conducted a full investigation, concluding that neither the plaintiff nor the dentist were entirely telling the truth about their employment relationship. The company gave the dentist a written reprimand, removed him as a supervisor, and cut his salary and benefits. The plaintiff, a dental assistant with the company, refused to return to her position and refused all alternative jobs offered by the company. Ultimately, she was terminated.

The court rejected the plaintiff's argument that the dentist's behavior was so severe and pervasive that the company should have known about the hostile work environment even before plaintiff complained. The court said that an employer is insulated from liability on a claim premised on the employer's "constructive" knowledge of the harassment where "the employer has adopted an antidiscrimination policy that is comprehensive, well-known to employees, vigorously enforced, and provides alternative avenues of redress." The court was careful to note, however, that if the employer had actual knowledge of the harassment, and took no action, no policy could insulate the employer from liability.

Same gender sexual harassment

Traditionally, cases dealing with sexual harassment have involved unwelcome conduct of a sexual nature between a man and a woman. A developing frontier of employment harassment law involves an employer's liability for same sex or same gender harassment claims under Title VII. A number of courts have recognized claims of *quid pro quo* same gender harassment where the employee is promised or denied a benefit based on acceptance or rejection of the advances of a homosexual supervisor. Claims by homosexual employees of a hostile or offensive work environment have been accepted where the employee alleges that an "anti-male" or "anti-female" atmosphere pervades the workplace and that, "but for" the employee's sex, he or she would not be subject to this conduct. Finally, an increasing number of courts have found that same gender harassment claims, in situations involving heterosexual employees of the same sex, are viable under Title VII.

There appears to be general agreement among the courts that a claim by a homosexual employee of harassment by heterosexual supervisors and employees based on sexual orientation cannot be maintained under Title VII. The distinction appears to be that a homosexual may allege that he or she is being discriminated against because he is a male, but not because he is a homosexual. In other words, discrimination because of sex is prohibited by Title VII, but the Act does not apply to sexual orientation bias.

Same gender homosexual harassment

Some courts have been willing to recognize same gender harassment claims where the individual doing the harassing is a homosexual. The lower federal courts have taken various positions on the viability of same gender sexual harassment claims. For example, the U.S. District Court for the District of Maryland has ruled that Title VII did not provide a cause of action for an employee who claimed to have been the victim of sexual harassment by a supervisor of the same gender. In this case, the plaintiff alleged that throughout his eight years of employment, he was sexually harassed by his male supervisor. The plaintiff claimed he was subjected to a series of sexual jokes, pranks, comments, and gestures by his supervisor. The District Court left open, however, the question of whether it would reach the same conclusion if the harassment was *quid pro quo* involving a homosexual supervisor.

The Fourth Circuit Court of Appeals, in affirming the District Court's opinion, recognized the viability of same gender harassment but suggested that the homosexuality of the plaintiff and his harassers would be an essential element of such a claim. In another recent decision by the Fourth Circuit, the court affirmed the dismissal of an auto mechanic's same gender sexual harassment claim because no claim was made by the plaintiff that either the plaintiff or his harassers were homosexual. The plaintiff had been frequently and repeatedly teased about his sex life, and touched in sexually suggestive ways by his co-workers, who also exposed themselves to him.

Despite the continued harassment during the plaintiff's employment, the court approved the dismissal of his complaint because it did not believe the harassment was "because of the [plaintiff's] sex." The court said the harassment may have occurred because of the "vulgarity," "meanness of spirit," or "sexual perversion" of the harassers. The court was simply unwilling to allow plaintiff's claim without a showing that one or both of the individuals involved was homosexual.

In fact, there have been many cases that have recognized the viability of same gender harassment claims under Title VII where the harassment was of the *quid pro quo* variety and the supervisor was a homosexual. In a federal court case out of Tennessee, a male plaintiff alleged that he was harassed by his homosexual supervisor. The defendant moved for judgment on the pleadings, seeking a determination as to whether same gender sexual harassment was actionable under Title VII. The court found that the plaintiff's claim was actionable, holding that: "Sexual harassment of a subordinate by a homosexual supervisor of the same sex is an adverse employment action that the subordinate would not have faced but for his or her sex."

The Northern District of Alabama reached a similar result in a case where the male plaintiff alleged *quid pro quo* sexual harassment. The plaintiff alleged that after he rebuffed the advances of his supervisor, his supervisor then contrived a plan to terminate the plaintiff's employment. In response to the plaintiff's complaint, the defendant moved for summary judgment. The court stated that homosexual *quid pro quo* sexual harassment has long been recognized as a violation of Title VII. The court concluded that when a gay supervisor propositions or harasses a male subordinate, but not a female subordinate, the conduct is a violation of Title VII.

Same gender heterosexual harassment

Despite the judicial acceptance of same gender sexual harassment claims when the allegations involve *quid pro quo* harassment by a homosexual supervisor, a number of jurisdictions continue to reject same gender harassment claims that involve allegations of hostile environment harassment by heterosexual supervisors or co-employees toward a heterosexual plaintiff.

For example, in a federal court case out of Illinois, the plaintiff filed a Title VII action alleging that he had been sexually harassed by his co-employees. Specifically, the plaintiff claimed that during an eight-year period he was subjected to verbal taunts from his co-workers because he was not married and did not have a girlfriend, to comments about dating a particular female employee because of her sexual proclivity, to pictures of nude women, to statements that he was gay or bisexual and other sex-related comments, and to pokes in his buttocks with a stick. The co-employees who engaged in these activities were heterosexual males, as was the plaintiff.

The district court found that the type of conduct complained of by the plaintiff was not the type of behavior Title VII was intended to prohibit. Under the court's analysis, a plaintiff asserting a same gender sexual harassment claim must show that he was treated less favorably because of "anti-male" sentiment in the workplace. Because the plaintiff worked in a male-dominated environment, the court concluded that, while the plaintiff may have been harassed by his co-employees, the harassment did not create an "anti-male" environment in the workplace. Therefore, his claim did not come within the scope of impermissible sexual harassment under Title VII. This "exploitation/domination" requirement adopted by the Illinois federal court has been relied upon by several subsequent courts in ruling that a plaintiff alleging same gender sexual harassment has failed to establish a claim.

In 1994, for example, the U.S. Court of Appeals for the Fifth Circuit ruled in favor of a defendant in a same gender sexual harassment claim. The heterosexual plaintiff in this case alleged that on several occasions his male heterosexual supervisor approached him from behind and "reached around and grabbed his crotch area and made sexual motions from behind him." The employee complained about the conduct and the supervisor was disciplined. Nevertheless, the employee filed a lawsuit, alleging sexual harassment. In rejecting the plaintiff's claim, the court of appeals stated that "harassment by a male supervisor against a male subordinate does not state a claim under Title VII even though the harassment has sexual overtones."

Among those cases that have recognized the viability of same gender hostile environment harassment claims involving heterosexual employees is a decision by the Seventh Circuit Court of Appeals in July, 1997, that gave extensive treatment to the same gender harassment issue. The plaintiffs were two brothers who worked on a municipal cemetery work crew. During two months of employment, the brothers were subjected to continuous harassment. One of the brothers, who wore an earring, was called "fag" and "queer" by the older employees on the work crew. He was told to "go back to San Francisco with the rest of the queers." He was asked whether he was a boy or girl. One employee started calling the plaintiff his "bitch" and told him he was going to take him into the woods and have his way with him. One day, after the employee had been drinking at lunch, he grabbed one of the brothers by the testicles, and announced to the other workers, "Well, I guess he's a guy." The brothers finally quit their jobs and sued under Title VII.

The district court granted summary judgment in favor of the employer but, on appeal, the Seventh Circuit reinstated the brothers' claims, holding that "sexual harassment of a man by other men is actionable under Title VII." The court said there was sufficient evidence to infer that the brothers were harassed because of their sex. The court rejected the requirement of homosexuality as an element of a same gender harassment case, stating: "The fact that the [plaintiffs'] harassers are not gay— a fact that some courts view as dispositive—is, in our view, immaterial."

In a lengthy opinion, the court of appeals gave a broad reading to the phrase "because of such individual's...sex" in Title VII. Rejecting the notion that the harasser must be motivated to harass one gender and not the other in order to establish a viable harassment claim, the court said, "We must question whether it is appropriate to view sexual harassment as actionable sex discrimination only when the plaintiff is able to show that she was harassed because she was a women rather than a man, or vice versa. Proof that the harasser was motivated to target...one gender and not the other may be necessary where the harassment is not on its face sexual...but such proof would seem unnecessary when the harassment itself is implied with sexual overtones."

The dissenting judge in this decision pointed out some possible flaws in the majority opinion's reasoning. He said that the court had shifted the focus of the statutory language from "sex" to "sexuality." The judge said that "just because the harassment is overtly sexual, does not mean that it was motivated by the victim's sex." The dissenting opinion said that the plaintiff was harassed "because [he] wore an earring not because [he] was a male. Title VII does not prohibit discrimination on the basis of 'sexuality,' 'sexual orientation,' 'something linked to sex,' or anything else— only discrimination (or more specifically here, harassment) because the victim is a man."

This dispute over same gender sexual harassment as a viable claim under Title VII rages on in the federal courts. Hundreds of same gender harassment claims have now reached the federal courts. On June 9, 1997, the Supreme Court accepted a case for review that may decide the issue of whether Title VII is applicable to same gender harassment claims. The case involves a male employee who worked on an offshore rig and quit after alleged harassment and physical abuse by his supervisor and co-workers. In particular, the plaintiff claims that two of the employees threatened him with homosexual rape.

Although the Fifth Circuit Court of Appeals rejected the plaintiff's claim, the Supreme Court granted review after urging from the Department of Justice and the EEOC. However, the case may not be the best vehicle for resolving all issues relating to same gender harassment, because there was no factual record developed by the lower courts. It may be difficult to determine whether the case deals with homosexual harassment or harassment among heterosexuals of the same sex. Also, because the case arose in a work environment that was all-male, it may be difficult for the plaintiff to demonstrate that he would be successful in showing that he was discriminated against because of his sex. In other words, the plaintiff cannot show the workplace was dominated by females or that "but for his gender" he would not have been harassed.

Regardless of how the Supreme Court resolves this issue, employers should make sure that their harassment policies prohibit sexual "horseplay" or "hijinks" between individuals of the same sex. As was mentioned in Chapter 3, there is a legislative effort to bring sexual orientation under the protection of Title VII. If the Supreme Court rejects same gender sexual harassment as a viable claim under the Civil Rights Act, there will probably be an increased effort in Congress to pass a bill prohibiting harassment between individuals of the same gender. Harassment of individuals on any basis, if sufficiently egregious, can lead to tort liability. It just makes no sense for an employer to allow such conduct to continue in the workplace.

Tort causes of action for sexual harassment

Although a Title VII sex discrimination action is the most common legal recourse for sexual harassment, courts have also recognized causes of action grounded in tort law as a remedy for sexual harassment. Tort law is that part of the common law under which courts provide a civil remedy for the behavior of individuals that offend public policy. Among the tort actions that have been recognized as being implicated by sexual harassment are intentional infliction of emotional distress, assault, and battery.

As explained in Chapter 1, the basic test for liability for intentional infliction of emotional distress requires the plaintiff to demonstrate outrageous conduct by the defendant that causes the plaintiff to suffer severe or extreme emotional distress. The more outrageous the defendant's conduct, the less severe need be the injuries and distress required by the court for establishing a cause of action of intentional infliction of emotional distress. There are a number of decisions finding harassment in the workplace to be sufficiently "outrageous" to meet the conduct requirement of the tort of intentional infliction of emotional distress.

The related torts of assault and battery require a showing that either the victim was subjected to unpermitted physical contact or that he or she was put in apprehension that there would be harmful or offensive physical contact. A cause of action for battery may arise from such actions as grabbing another worker, attempting to kiss or embrace another employee, or touching parts of the individual's body in a sexually suggestive manner. Physical injury is not required; if the contact results in injury to a victim's feelings, a cause of action for battery is established. To establish an assault, no contact at all is necessary; rather, the cause of action is established if the victim was put in imminent apprehension of offensive contact. Apprehension does not mean fear or intimidation, but only a reasonable expectation of harm. Words alone do not generally constitute assault; however, words accompanied by gestures or movements directed at the victim can constitute assault.

The availability of tort causes of action as a remedy for sexual harassment means that victims of harassment will not just bring one cause of action against their employer, but many different theories of liabilities. Also, despite the fact that most courts have concluded that supervisors and co-employees cannot be personally liable for harassment in a Title VII action, there is no such limitation in a tort action. Plaintiffs can receive compensatory and punitive damages from individuals who have abused them, either physically or emotionally.

Are employers at risk if they don't discharge sexual harassers?

Recently, some employees alleging sexual harassment have expanded their lawsuits against employers to include a common law cause of action for the negligent hiring or the negligent retention of the alleged harasser. In a case out of Illinois, for example, a plaintiff sued her former employer, alleging that she had been sexually harassed. She claimed that her manager attempted to kiss and touch her body and place objects down the front of her blouse. She complained several times to upper management before they investigated her complaint. She also alleged that even after the company verified that sexual harassment had occurred, management took no corrective action. The harassment eventually ended, but the plaintiff claimed that she was terminated four months later because of her sexual harassment complaint.

In her civil suit, the plaintiff alleged, among other things, that the company was negligent in both hiring the manager and retaining him in its employ after they had knowledge of the harassment. Despite the urging of the employer, the Illinois appellate court refused to allow the dismissal of the plaintiff's complaint holding that the complaint stated a viable claim for negligence against the employer. The court found that all employers have "a duty to exercise ordinary and reasonable care in the employment and selection of careful and skillful co-employees and to discharge that duty with care commensurate with the perils and hazards likely to be encountered in the employee's performance of the job." According to the court, there is a foreseeable likelihood of sexual harassment occurring where a company hires a new manager whose staff will be primarily composed of persons not of the manager's gender. The court concluded that the duty of care that should be exercised by employers in such situations includes the obligation to make an inquiry of the potential manager's former employers in order to find out whether the manager had a work history of sexually harassing female co-workers.

What is unusual about this "negligent retention" decision is the fact that even though the employer conducted an investigation into the alleged harassment and the harassment stopped, the Illinois court nevertheless allowed the plaintiff to pursue a claim for negligent retention based on the employer's knowledge of the prior sexual harassment. Although the court disclaimed any intention to prohibit the continued employment of an employee with a history of sexual harassment, the decision clearly places an employer at risk when deciding not to discharge a manager who has engaged in sexual harassing behavior. Indeed, because the employer will have knowledge of prior sexual harassment, a court could find the employer liable even if the employer did monitor the supervisor's performance but the harassment occurred under situations that could not be monitored (as is true in most cases of sexual harassment).

The developing legal theories of negligent hiring and negligent retention place employers in a vulnerable position when they hire or retain a supervisor knowing that he or she has a history of sexual harassing behavior. Although the foregoing decision has application only in Illinois, courts in other states could adopt similar reasoning at the urging of an inventive plaintiff's attorney. If that occurs, employers may be tempted to discharge an employee who engages in any kind of sexual harassment, regardless of the severity of the harassment.

The danger in overreacting

Employers must not overreact to incidents of alleged sexual harassment. As explained below, a deliberate and thorough investigation should allow employers to determine who is telling the truth when a supervisor is accused of harassment. If harassment has occurred, the penalty should match the gravity of the offense. The employer need not discharge every employee who is implicated in an incident of improper sexual behavior in the workplace.

A recent decision illustrates the danger in overreacting to accusations of improper sexual behavior by supervisors. In the much-publicized *Seinfeld* case, a jury awarded $26 million to an executive who was fired after discussing an episode from the television show *Seinfeld* with a female employee. The episode involved a situation in which one of the show's characters, Jerry, could not remember his girlfriend's name, but recalled only that it rhymed with a female sexual organ.

The episode ended with Jerry recalling the girlfriend's name: "Delores." The next day at work, the executive recounted the episode to the female employee and showed her a dictionary page with the word "clitoris" on it. After she complained to management, the executive was fired. The executive sued his employer for misrepresentation. He also sued a vice president of the company for interference with his employment. His attorney said that the jury's verdict had little to do with sexual harassment; instead, it was a reaction to the defendant's interference with the plaintiff's employment. Nevertheless, it was reported that the jury viewed the *Seinfeld* episode during the trial and, therefore, considered it as significant evidence to support the plaintiff's claim. The company said it would appeal the $26 million jury award.

How to avoid harassment claims

Many employers have already adopted strong policies prohibiting sexual harassment. In light of the extension of sexual harassment principles to other forms of prohibited discrimination, it appears appropriate to expand these policies into general "harassment" policies that prohibit all forms of illegal harassment. Further, the policy should specifically state the prohibition's application to situations involving individuals of the same gender. Harassment should be forbidden regardless of the fact that the harasser and the victim are both male, or both female. A sample harassment policy is included in the Appendix on page 274.

It is imperative that the policy reference a procedure by which complaints of harassment can be brought to management's attention, and that ensure a quick and thorough investigation of these complaints. Once a complaint of harassment has been made, the employer must completely investigate the claim. Frequently, the complaining employee will tell the employer, either at the time of the complaint or shortly thereafter, that he or she does not want the complaint investigated or that he or she does not want the harasser to be terminated or disciplined. After the passage of many months or even years, the complaining employee will then allege that the employer was made aware of the harassment and did nothing. Therefore, once a complaint of harassment is made, the employer controls the investigation of that complaint and has a legal obligation to ensure that the investigation is thorough and complete.

Just as the complaining employee does not control the investigation of a sexual harassment claim, the complaining employee does not control the appropriate remedy for proven instances of harassment. Certainly, the employer should consult with the complaining party to determine what steps would make that employee comfortable. Not every instance of harassment merits immediate termination, however. The employer's obligation is only to take reasonable steps to remedy the harassment and not to give in to every demand of the complaining employee.

Although an employer may not be able to completely avoid claims of sexual harassment, an employer can limit its liability by making certain that its antiharassment policy: 1) expressly states the company's commitment to maintaining a workplace free from all forms of harassment; 2) specifically defines sexual harassment; 3) includes an effective complaint and investigation procedure that allows the victim of harassment to bypass his or her immediate supervisor or any other manager that may be involved in the harassment; and 4) sets forth adequate remedies for violations of the policy, including disciplinary measures. The scope of the policy should extend to all company-sponsored activities, including social functions. As mentioned, it should list as prohibited conduct horseplay that is in any way related to sex, comments of a sexual nature, and jokes that contain sexual connotations even when carried on between individuals of the same sex.

The employer should also issue a statement that explains what behavior constitutes prohibited sexual harassment. Penalties and sanctions for violating the policy, ranging from reprimand to termination, should be included in the statement. This information should be posted on bulletin boards and included in employee handbooks and supervisors' training manuals. By clearly communicating that harassment will not be tolerated, the employer helps insulate itself from a charge that it condones such unlawful behavior.

All supervisors must be held responsible for administering, enforcing, and adhering to the policy. Supervisors should be trained to respond quickly and effectively to complaints of inappropriate sexual conduct. They must be alert for comments and innuendo that indicate a potentially hostile environment. Moreover, they should be proactive during employee evaluations to allow individual employees to air any possible complaints regarding unwelcome sexual or racial conduct.

Employers should also specifically designate and thoroughly train all individuals who will be investigating harassment complaints. The company must make sure each investigator understands the methods for properly interviewing each witness, how to make credibility determinations, the need for confidentiality, and the value of obtaining written statements from the complaining party and/or witnesses. When an employer receives a complaint of harassment, it must engage in a thoughtful and careful process of addressing the concerns raised by the employee.

Ground rules for a harassment investigation

When an employer first becomes aware of a harassment complaint, the following steps should be taken: 1) The employee making the complaint should be given assurance that the complaint will be thoroughly investigated; 2) management should resist the temptation to comment on the credibility of the employee's story (for example, "Herb's such a nice guy. I can't see him doing that kind of thing!"); 3) the human resources manager should review the investigation process with the complaining employee and explain that although every attempt will be made to maintain confidentiality, the employee cannot be guaranteed anonymity; 4) if the complainant's supervisor is involved, the employer should consider making a temporary change in the reporting relationship so that the complainant can report to a different supervisor. If the allegations are particularly egregious (alleged physical touching, for example), the employer should consider suspending the supervisor while the investigation is ongoing. In either event, the supervisor should be informed that a complaint has been lodged and that he will have an opportunity to respond to the allegations. He should also be told not to communicate with the complainant unless absolutely necessary.

Conducting the harassment investigation

The manner in which the investigation is conducted is critical, and it must be started soon after the harassment complaint is received. The steps to keep in mind are as follows: 1) The employer should choose an appropriate impartial investigator; 2) the investigator should interview the complainant again to get the "full story," and ask the complainant to identify potential witnesses to the alleged conduct. The complainant can be asked to put the complaint in writing but it should not be a requirement for initiating an investigation. The investigator can summarize the complaint and ask the complaining employee to sign the summary attesting to its accuracy; 3) the investigator should interview the potential witnesses, letting them know that they will not be subject to retaliation for speaking honestly and stressing the confidentiality of the matter. If possible, witness statements should also be in writing; 4) the investigator should interview the accused harasser, allowing the person to tell his or her side of the story and inquiring whether the complainant might have had other motivations for coming forward (for example, a recent disciplinary action by the supervisor for performance problems, break-up of a consensual relationship, denial of promotion, etc.); 5) any additional witnesses should also be interviewed.

Making credibility determinations

Perhaps the most difficult part of the process is weighing the conflicting testimony and deciding what response, if any, should be taken. In weighing the evidence, the employer should consider the tenure and performance history of the complainant and the accused harasser, each individual's respective reputation for integrity and truthfulness, the demeanor and body language of the complainant and the alleged harasser, the testimony of other witnesses, and other potential motivations of the complainant.

Taking prompt and appropriate remedial action

Once the evidence has been weighed, the employer may be able to avoid liability if "prompt remedial action" is taken. Depending upon the seriousness of the allegations and the outcome of the investigation, the appropriate response with respect to the alleged harasser could be discharge, suspension without pay, demotion or transfer, counseling or sensitivity training, a written reprimand in the personnel file, or any combination of these. Not all investigations of harassment must result in the termination of the alleged harasser, but a simple admonition to "go and sin no more" is hardly remedial in nature. Of course, if the investigation does not support the allegations, the employer may take no action, although formally reminding the supervisor of the harassment policy may be appropriate in any case.

....

With respect to the complaining employee, there are also several options available, including an offer of transfer to another department. An employer should take whatever action is necessary to end the harassment and restore lost benefits or opportunities to the victim. Finally, if the investigation turns up evidence of broad-based, inappropriate conduct in a department that might be creating a hostile environment for other members of the complainant's sex or race, the employer should consider republishing and disseminating the company's harassment policy, as well as providing training or sensitivity sessions for managers and employees in the department.

Chapter 5

Give Abusive or Combative Employees the Maximum Penalty

Sam Goodwin's new job as a computer programmer was going well. He had been with the company for more than three years and had received good evaluations. He had been written up on one occasion for insubordination; otherwise, his performance had been good. Sam didn't socialize with the other employees in his department. Mostly, he just kept to himself. He even ate lunch alone, content to read sports magazines or maybe an occasional gun catalogue.

Lately, however, Sam seemed to be arguing with his supervisor Frank Chaplin over every little thing. He seemed to be much angrier than usual. He didn't understand it himself. On one particular occasion, Sam got so upset that he told Frank, "Get out of my face or I'll kill you." Frank gave Sam a one-day suspension, which was approved by Human Resources. Frank really didn't think Sam would attack him. In fact, he told Susan Childs, the HR director, that he believed Sam was merely "venting."

Upon his return to work, Sam was sullen toward Frank, often glaring at him when he passed him in the hallway. Sam also often followed Frank to his car after work. Still, because Sam also parked his car in the same lot, Frank was reluctant to confront him. Besides, since he returned from his suspension, Sam did everything Frank asked of him in the department.

One morning, not long after Sam's return to work, Frank overheard him tell a co-worker that he had a new gun, a .44 magnum. Frank asked security to keep an eye on Sam. After work that day, security personnel followed Sam to his car and watched as he pulled a brown paper bag out of the car. He held the bag as Frank passed, glaring at him. The security personnel stopped Sam as he was about to get in his car and seized the bag. Inside the bag, they found Sam's gun.

Sam was taken to Susan Childs' office where security personnel filled her in on the details of what happened. Sam was clearly in a lot of trouble—the company has a very strict policy against bringing firearms onto company property. Sam would have been fired, but he produced a permit to carry the gun and told the HR Director that he was receiving psychological counseling for his emotional outbursts.

"That may be, Sam, but having that gun on company property is a termination offense," said Susan. "What the hell were you going to do with it?"

"Now, wait a minute, Susan. The only thing I was doing was waiting for Stan Politski. I told him about my gun and he said he wanted to see it. I took it out of my car and I was waiting for Stan in the parking lot when these security guys jumped me."

Susan said, "Look, Sam, the bottom line here is that Frank Chaplin says you've been glaring at him, you've been following him to his car, and then today you're caught standing near his car with a .44 magnum in a brown paper bag. It doesn't look good, Sam."

"Oh, for Pete's sake, Susan," exclaimed Sam, "that gun wasn't even loaded. Just ask your security people." Susan didn't answer but glanced over at Joe Black, the chief of security, who nodded his head, confirming what Sam was saying.

Sam continued, "Susan, please, I've got to keep this job. I have a legal permit to carry that gun in my car. I know it looks bad, but all I was doing was waiting for Stan—you can ask him."

Susan said, "I'm going to suspend you pending an investigation for possible discharge. I'll want a written report from your psychologist and I also want to talk to him. We'll hold your gun here until we decide what to do. By all rights, I should probably turn you over to the police, but since the gun wasn't loaded, I guess I'll let that go for now."

Susan had her hands full during the next few days. She received the report from Sam's psychologist, which indicated that Sam was suffering from a bipolar condition, sometimes called a "manic-depressive" condition. The psychologist was very positive about Sam's chances for complete recovery and he was extremely distressed to hear that Sam might be discharged. He did not condone Sam's possession of a gun, but stated that, in his estimation, Sam's job was the "most positive, constructive part of his life right now." The psychologist minimized the risks toward other employees, saying, "Individuals with a bipolar condition are hardly ever physically aggressive. They may be verbally combative but, in Sam's case, the medicine I prescribed for him should control any of those outbursts."

Susan also talked to Stan Politski, the employee Sam was allegedly waiting for in the parking lot. Stan confirmed that he had asked to see Sam's gun and had arranged to meet him after work. "I didn't know he was going to pull it out in the parking lot, though," said Stan. "I thought we were going to go to the gun club to fire off a few rounds."

Susan decided to give Sam another chance. There was still the problem of Frank, however. She knew he would not be comfortable with her decision. Luckily, there was an opening in the electronic parts cage and Sam had the technical "know-how" to do that job. She decided to allow Sam to come back on the condition he take the transfer to the parts distribution job.

Upon his return to work, Sam was polite to Frank when he saw him, but he really didn't associate with any other employee except Stan Politski. One day, Sam and Stan were standing in the hallway adjacent to the company lunch room when Frank Chaplin went by. Frank nodded and kept on walking. Sam didn't say anything to Frank but smiled and turned to Stan Politski. "Did you read about the guy in North Carolina who blew away his supervisor with a sawed-off shotgun?" asked Sam. "Knock it off," said Stan, "Frank might hear you." Sam just continued to smile and told Stan he had to get back to work.

Several days later, Sam was again standing outside the lunchroom when Frank came to eat lunch. Frank saw Sam come toward him as he approached the lunchroom, but he thought Sam was just going back to the parts cage. Frank saw the flash of steel as Sam closed the distance between them very quickly. He didn't have time to react as Sam plunged a seven-inch knife into his abdomen and then again into his chest.

The police found Sam in the parts cage, blood on his hands and running down the front of his shirt. He was crying, but otherwise seemed to be routinely attending to some paperwork that needed to go out with a parts shipment. He calmly followed the orders of the police as they handcuffed him and took him out of the plant. No one heard Sam say anything to the police except, "They shouldn't have taken my gun."

Violence in the workplace

There is an increasing tendency of employees to react with violence after discharge or layoff from employment. Homicide is now the leading cause of death for women in the workplace and it is the third largest threat to workers overall. The violence that has so permeated our society in recent years does not end at the factory door. Workplaces are no longer islands of safety in an otherwise troubled society.

Recent studies would seem to indicate that these violent events are not simply isolated incidents but part of a larger trend of increased violence in the workplace. In a report issued by the National Institute for Occupational Safety and Health (NIOSH), statistics showed that homicides accounted for more than 12 percent of all work-related fatalities during the years 1980 to 1989. About 41 percent of all women killed in the workplace during this same time period were victims of homicide. And although these statistics do not distinguish between convenience store clerks killed in the line of duty and supervisors who are murdered by vengeance-seeking ex-employees, this latter phenomenon is undoubtedly increasing.

A Northwestern National Life Insurance Company study found that 25 percent of all workers had been either attacked, harassed, or threatened during the year-long period ending in July 1993. The report estimates that nearly 2.2 million workers were victims of physical attacks over the one-year period, while 6.3 million were threatened with harm. Moreover, 43 percent of the threats were never reported, yet nearly one in six attacks involved a lethal weapon.

Employers cannot be expected to accurately predict which of their employees may have the potential for workplace violence. Many times the acts of murder and vengeance have appeared to be totally out of context with the normal behavior of the employee. Experts say that there is a "profile" for the type of individual who may turn into a so-called "avenger" after a discharge from employment. Still, these "avengers" may have been model employees before they "snapped." Are there procedures that might have identified these employees' tendency toward violence? Is the employer responsible for hiring or retaining these violent employees?

In this chapter, we will explore a methodology for differentiating between simple antisocial or unfriendly behavior and truly violent or threatening conduct. We will review the steps that employers can take to protect their supervisors against potential attacks by "avenging" employees. Finally, we will take a practical look at the relative risks that exist in retaining hostile or threatening employees as compared with the risk of potential liability for the discharge of such employees. It may be that, in situations that mandate decisive action, discharge may be preferable to continued attempts at rehabilitating the hostile or aggressive employee.

Identifying the violent employee

In August 1989, when a postal worker went to his workplace in Escondido, Calif., and killed two of his co-workers, he had been a model employee for 27 years and had recently been nominated for "letter carrier of the quarter." What his employer did not know was that the employee's sister had killed his father years before. Psychologists have noted that past encounters with violence are common among workplace assailants.

Additionally, the employee may have been trying to warn co-workers when, in the weeks prior to the killings he made vague references to an Edmond, Okla., shooting where another letter carrier killed 14 people after he found out he was about to be fired. The California postal worker became angry when his employer instituted a new rule prohibiting employees from smoking in their Jeeps. Top management was not aware of his fascination with the Oklahoma shooting or the depth of his anger over the smoking prohibition.

Using a strange but similar signal of potentially violent behavior, an employee discussed the post office shootings before he went on a murderous rampage in San Diego, Calif., in June 1991. The employee returned to his former place of employment, an electronics plant, wearing a bandoleer of ammunition and carrying a rifle and a shotgun. He shot out the company's telephone network, detonated two bombs and killed two executives. The employee, a 41-year-old father of two, had a fascination with guns but no history of violent behavior. He was simply angry because he had been dismissed three months earlier.

In October 1991, a disgruntled female employee in Bennington, Vt., returned to her place of employment and shot and killed the plant manager and wounded two others. In January 1992, a 43-year-old man shot and wounded his supervisor and then killed another manager at a plant in San Diego. The shootings occurred immediately following a termination hearing at the plant where the employee was being afforded the opportunity to protest a layoff notice he had received a week earlier.

Although it is true that employees are more likely to be attacked by customers than by other employees, the incidence of violent attacks on supervisors by disgruntled employees is increasing. The latest studies now indicate that about two supervisors a month are murdered by an employee they supervised. Are there any clues for supervisors that might have alerted them to the potential dangers from so-called "avenger" employees?

Slam the Door on Employee Lawsuits

The "avenger" is usually a white male in the 30-55 age group who may be going through a midlife transition and is dissatisfied with his life. He is often a loner with a history of depression, paranoia, or violence. Often, the avenger will have no police record. The avenger is likely to resist authority, however, and thus may have a personnel history that demonstrates difficulty in getting along with supervisors. The avenger's anger may spill over and manifest itself in frequent disputes with co-employees. Finally, the avenger will often display a fascination with guns and other weaponry.

The general increase in violence in the workplace may be a result of factors other than the psychological failings of particular employees. Economic and social factors may be contributing to a more violent workplace. For example, corporate downsizing has caused layoffs in some industries. The sudden loss of employment can leave people without jobs for the first time in their lives and very angry. Those individuals who remain employed after a major layoff are apprehensive about their future. This insecurity breeds distrust of management and creates a more stressful work environment. Increased competition for available positions also adds to the tension in the workplace. Studies have found that highly stressed employees experience twice the rate of violence and harassment than employees in less stressful environments.

Substance abuse may also be a major contributor to a more violent work force. Many employees surveyed about violence in the workplace blame alcohol and drug abuse as the top reasons for violence. The need to finance a drug addiction is obviously a contributor to customer attacks against businesses, but experts say drug abuse has also caused an increase in employee thefts with related incidents of violence. Also, the availability of guns and the sensationalism of violence in movies and television may, to a lesser extent, be contributing to the tendency of employees to act out their frustrations in a more extreme and violent manner.

Employers may be escalating the potential for violence by not controlling environmental factors that can contribute to stress. For example, workers in a hot and noisy plant may be more prone to aggressive behavior. Similarly, noxious fumes in the workplace coupled with poor ventilation can be a substantial source of irritation for employees already pushed to the breaking point by time pressures, tedious assembly line work, and frequent overtime. Obviously, an employer who allows horseplay or aggressive interaction between employees to go on unabated is asking for trouble.

There are actions that employers can take to protect themselves against potential attacks by violent employees. First, managers should be alert for warning signs, such as sudden behavioral changes by employees. Alcohol or substance abuse by the employee is an obvious signal of potentially erratic or violent behavior. If the employer is aware that an employee is undergoing a period of private stress such as a divorce or a death in the family, the employee should be offered counseling through an employee assistance program (EAP) if one exists at the company. If the company has no EAP, supervisors can nevertheless offer to speak privately with the troubled employee.

Companies may also wish to implement a "hotline" that employees can use to provide confidential information about a potentially violent situation. As discussed above, many workplace assailants have given clues to their impending blowup in conversations with other employees. Sometimes, an actual threat will have been communicated to another employee. All such threats should be treated seriously even if the facts ultimately show that the employee was not serious in his comments.

In situations where no overt threat has been identified, but the employee is clearly challenging a supervisor's authority with disdainful remarks, security can be alerted to begin more intensive monitoring of the troubled employee. Obviously, if an aggressive, combative employee has already been discharged, security can increase perimeter protection for the plant and even alert local police authorities if necessary.

Finally, managers and human resources personnel who will be implementing discharge decisions should become acquainted with the profile characteristics of the avenger employee. The termination process must be handled in the most humane manner possible. Managers should never allow their own anger to complicate and intensify a discharge interview. If a manager feels he cannot control his emotions in dealing with an employee who must be discharged, another manager or a human resources officer should handle the discharge interview. If appropriate, severance benefits, outplacement services, and retraining can be offered to the discharged employee to ameliorate the impact of the termination.

Employers who are reluctant to invest time and effort to reduce workplace violence should be aware that the National Institute for Occupational Safety and Health (NIOSH) has issued an alert that recommends that employers take certain steps to protect employees from violence. In its 1993 alert, NIOSH reminds employers that they have a general responsibility to provide a safe workplace for their employees.

....

NIOSH recommends that employers install good external lighting, use drop safes to minimize cash on hand, and post signs indicating that only a limited amount of cash is on hand. It also recommends that employers close their establishments during high-risk hours, increase security staffing, and install silent alarms and protective barriers. Finally, NIOSH suggests that employers should provide training in conflict resolution and nonviolent response to workplace frustrations.

At a minimum, employers may want to implement a policy to deal with workplace violence in the manner that they have addressed sexual harassment in the workplace. The policy should include a strong statement against aggressive or antisocial behavior, a promise of discipline for violent behavior, a confidential procedure for reporting threats by another employee, and a crisis plan for responding quickly to violence by employees or customers.

Negligent hiring and retention

Employers who fail to take action to control abusive, belligerent, or combative employees often find themselves embroiled in litigation. For example, some injured employees have sued their employer for the negligent hiring or the negligent retention of the alleged employee who caused their injuries. Typically, these suits have alleged that the employer failed to accurately check references, criminal records, or general background information that could have shown the employee's likelihood for criminal or tortious behavior. In other cases, employers have been sued because they failed to dismiss or reassign employees after they found out that the employee was a potentially violent or abusive person. These negligence theories are premised on the unreasonable conduct of an employer in placing a person with certain known propensities for criminal or tortious behavior in an employment position where the individual poses a threat to others.

The negligent hiring and negligent retention theories of liability have been recognized in a number of states. For example, in a decision by an appellate court in Illinois, a supermarket chain was found liable for negligent retention of an employee who attacked a 4-year-old boy outside one of its stores. The employee, a manager for the supermarket chain, stopped by his store while off-duty, allegedly after he had been drinking. He saw an older boy urinating on the side of the building. He chased the boy to a car where he shouted racial insults at the driver, the boy's mother. He then pulled a younger 4-year-old boy out of the car and threw him through the air. The boy was injured, spent four days in the hospital, and required medical attention for a month. The jury awarded the child $150,000.

In affirming the jury award, the appellate court took note of prior incidents of violence by the manager. Seven years before, the manager had thrown a milk crate at a co-worker. He was not disciplined for the incident. The manager had also been convicted of aggravated battery for an attack on his own son at his home. The court said that even if super-market officials did not know about these prior incidents, the manager's friends and co-workers knew. Thus, the court said the defendant had "corporate knowledge" of the attacks and could be found liable for negligent retention of the manager.

The Court of Appeals of Maryland has, in several cases, explored the duty of employers to inquire into the criminal record of prospective employees. In an early decision, the court concluded that a tavern owner was not liable on a theory of negligent hiring for injuries sustained by a patron who had been assaulted by a bartender. The court found that the owner had conducted a reasonable investigation into the bartender's fitness for employment and could not have foreseen that the bartender would shoot one of the patrons in the tavern. Unknown to his employer, the bartender had a significant criminal record, including several convictions for assault. The tavern owner had made no inquiry concerning a possible criminal record. The plaintiff contended that because the bartender necessarily had frequent contact with the public, the proprietor had a duty to investigate the employee's criminal record.

The court of appeals noted that an employer has a duty to use reasonable care in the selection and retention of his employees and that this duty would be owed not only to other employees, but to members of the general public. The court found that this duty was satisfied because the tavern owner had a good recommendation from the bartender's former employer and the tavern owner also had prior personal knowledge of the bartender. The court said that there was no evidence that the tavern owner should have known that the bartender was potentially dangerous, and therefore, the owner was not liable under the doctrine of negligent hiring.

In another decision by the Maryland Court of Appeals, the court was again faced with a negligent hiring claim when a woman sued her land-lord, the Housing Opportunity Commission, after she was raped by an inspector who was an employee of the Commission. The inspector had been convicted of robbery, assault, and burglary, and at the time of his hire was under indictment for rape. Although the jury found that the plaintiff did not prove that the Housing Commission was negligent in hiring the inspector, the court of appeals overturned the verdict because the lower court had excluded evidence concerning the inspector's criminal convictions and the accessibility of that information to the Housing Commission. The court of appeals stated that the question of whether the plaintiff had established a relationship between the hiring of the housing inspector, his criminal record, and the rape was one for the jury to decide.

A decision out of Minnesota demonstrates that the mere fact of a criminal record will not necessarily give rise to negligent hiring liability, but retention of that same individual after several threatening incidents will be negligent if the employee subsequently murders another employee. In this case, the employer rehired a former employee who had spent time in jail for the strangulation death of a co-worker. They assigned him to a maintenance crew where he became enamored with another female member of the crew. After the female employee rejected the advances of the ex-convict, he began to harass her and threaten her both at work and at home.

Finally, the female employee found a death threat scratched on her locker door. She reported the threat but the male employee never returned to work and 10 days later resigned his employment with the company. Eight days after his resignation, the male employee went to the female employee's home and killed her with a close-range shotgun blast. The female employee's heirs sued the company for negligent hiring and negligent retention.

The court found that the company was not liable for negligent hiring because they had hired him as a maintenance worker whose duties entailed no exposure to the general public and required only limited contact with co-workers. As to the negligent retention count, however, the court found evidence of a number of incidents during the ex-felon's employment that demonstrated a "propensity for abuse and violence towards employees." He had sexually harassed female employees and challenged other employees to fights. With regard to the female employee who was murdered, the ex-convict was involved in several workplace outbursts directed at her and he eventually scratched the words "one more day and you're dead" on her locker door. Citing the employer's duty to maintain a safe workplace, the court found that violence toward a co-worker was foreseeable.

Where members of the public will be unusually dependent upon the competence of an employee, the employer may be required to conduct a more exhaustive investigation before hiring the employee. For example, a court of appeals in Georgia held that where the hospital employed an orderly who had been convicted as a "peeping tom," the hospital was required to exercise ordinary care in determining the competency of its employees after the orderly molested a minor child who was a patient in the hospital. The court said that the jury was entitled to consider whether the hospital acted reasonably in not inquiring into the criminal record of the orderly when he applied for employment.

In another decision dealing with access to especially vulnerable members of the public, the Virginia Supreme Court held that the mother of a 10-year-old girl who was raped by a handyman could state a claim for negligent hiring against the church that had employed him. The supreme court stated the test of negligent hiring to be whether the employer has negligently placed an unfit person in an employment situation involving an unreasonable risk of harm to others. The plaintiff alleged that the church knew, or should have known, that its employee had recently been convicted of aggravated sexual assault on a young girl, and that he was on probation for this offense and that a specific condition of his probation was that he not be involved with children. The complaint alleged that the church gave the employee free run of its building in a job that brought him frequently into contact with children, and that as a result, plaintiff's daughter had been raped "numerous times." The court concluded that these allegations were sufficient to support a claim of negligent hiring.

These decisions make it clear that employers do have an obligation to take precautions when hiring their employees. At the very least, employers should ask about the applicant's previous criminal convictions. If the applicant will be working with vulnerable individuals like children or hospital patients or where the employee must deal with the public as part of his or her regular duties, the employer should take further precautions before hiring the employee such as doing a further background check on the applicant. The phenomenon of negligent hiring suits is not going to go away and all employers must take steps to guard against the substantial liability that these suits can engender.

Intentional torts

Employers can also be vicariously liable for the intentional torts of violent or abusive employees. The possible causes of action include assault, battery, false imprisonment, and intentional infliction of emotional distress. Although an intentional tort like battery may seem like it is beyond the scope of employment, the current trend is to extend responsibility to the employer. This is especially true where there is some expectation that the employee may have to use force in the performance of his duties. For example, security duties or any assignment where an employee may be required to restrain a customer or co-employee may give rise to an increased obligation on the part of the employer to check the background of any potential security personnel before hiring them for employment.

For example, the Nevada Supreme Court held that an employer could be held liable for the conduct of its security guard during an eviction of an employee from a rental unit owned by the employer. Two resident managers accompanied by a security guard went to the plaintiff/employee's apartment to evict her. When the plaintiff would not let them in, the security guard tried to force his way into the apartment. The plaintiff put her hand on the security guard's chest to prevent him from coming in. In response, the security guard pulled a gun, pushed it into plaintiff's stomach and said, "You push me again, bitch, and I'll bash your face in." The resident managers immediately grabbed the security guard and left plaintiff's apartment.

The plaintiff sued the resident managers, the security guard, and the employer for assault and battery. She was awarded $2,500 in punitive damages against the individual defendants and $25,000 in punitive damages against the employer. The court said that the jury's conclusion that the security guard was acting within the scope of his employment when he tried to enter plaintiff's apartment was not clearly erroneous. Vicarious liability was appropriate because the resident managers and the security guard were agents of the employer. Further, the court said there was evidence that would allow the jury to find that the security guard was acting at the direction of the resident managers and not as an "independent actor."

Violence and mental disabilities

How far must an employer go in accommodating the antisocial or even violent behavior of an individual with a mental disability? If the ability to work amicably with co-workers is an essential function of an employee's duties, an employee who is surly or antisocial can be disciplined for failing to cooperate with other employees or his supervisor even if the behavior is the product of a mental disability. If the behavior continues and the employee's behavior is not just antisocial but combative or abusive, discharge is appropriate.

Persons with mental disabilities are protected by the ADA as long as they can perform the essential functions of their position, with or without accommodation. As explained in Chapter 6, the courts and the Equal Employment Opportunity Commission (EEOC) have broadly defined the term "mental disability" to include many different kinds of psychiatric infirmities. The issue for discussion here is whether the employer's accommodation burden under the ADA requires the employer to "put up" with eccentric or bizarre behavior by mentally disabled employees.

The ADA allows an employer to discipline an employee with a mental disability for misconduct as long as other nondisabled employees would also be disciplined for such misconduct. The EEOC would require the conduct rule to be job-related, however. The agency, in a recent enforcement guidance on psychiatric disabilities, gives the following example concerning the requirement for the "job-relatedness" of a conduct rule:

> *An employee with a psychiatric disability works in a warehouse loading boxes onto pallets for shipment. He has no customer contact and does not come into regular contact with other employees. Over the course of several weeks, he has come to work appearing increasingly disheveled. He also has become increasingly antisocial. Co-workers have complained that when they try to engage him in casual conversation, he walks away or gives a curt reply. When he has to talk to a co-worker, he is abrupt and rude. His work, however, has not suffered. The employer's company handbook states that employees should have a neat appearance at all times. The handbook also states that employees should be courteous to each other. When told that he is being disciplined for his appearance and treatment of co-workers, the employee explains that his appearance and demeanor have deteriorated because of his disability that was exacerbated during this time period.*

The EEOC concluded that discipline of the warehouse employee in this situation would violate the ADA because the employer's dress code and co-worker courtesy rules are not "job related for the position in question and consistent with business necessity." In other words, a general rule of courtesy toward others does not support discipline of antisocial employees as long as their particular job requirement did not necessitate cooperation with others. This problem might have been addressed by inserting a clause in the warehouse employee's job description stating that cooperation and courteous interaction with other employees was an essential function of the position. Certainly, the situation might be different if the employee does not cooperate with his supervisor or engages in abusive or threatening behavior instead of just behaving in a "curt" or "antisocial" manner.

Again, the EEOC's enforcement guidance addresses this issue. It gives the example of an employee who has a "hostile altercation with his supervisor and threatens the supervisor with physical harm." The employer immediately terminates the individual's employment, consistent with its policy of immediately terminating the employment of anyone who threatens a supervisor." If the employee reveals a mental disability and asks for leave in lieu of termination, the EEOC says the employer is not required to rescind the termination and offer the leave as an accommodation because "reasonable accommodation is always prospective...an employee is not required to excuse past misconduct." Where the employee violated a rule that is consistent with business necessity—in this case, prohibiting threats against supervisors—and the rule has been uniformly enforced, the discharge can stand.

The ADA allows employers to discharge individuals who pose a "direct threat" to the safety of others. The EEOC's regulations, however, interpret "direct threat" to mean "a significant risk of substantial harm to the health and safety of...others that cannot be eliminated or reduced by reasonable accommodation." In its enforcement guidance, the EEOC describes a significant risk as "high, and not just a slightly increased risk." The EEOC expects the employer to identify the specific behavior that would pose a direct threat. The EEOC says this includes "an [individual] assessment of the likelihood and imminence of future violence."

In its enforcement guidance, the EEOC gives a rather easy example of a direct threat as guidance for employees. The agency poses the hypothetical situation of an employer considering the application of an individual who is mentally disabled and who was discharged two weeks earlier by another employer for: 1) telling a co-worker "that he would get a gun and get his supervisor if he tries anything again"; 2) engaging in several altercations during his past employment, including one where he had to be restrained from fighting with a co-worker; and 3) punching the wall outside his supervisor's office. Not surprisingly, the EEOC said the employer would be justified in not hiring the applicant.

Unfortunately, the decisions faced by employers in this troubling area of the law are never that easy. What if the mentally disabled employee does not say anything but engages in glaring and stalking behavior? What if the threat by the mentally disabled person is ambiguous as to the time and manner in which he will "get [the other employee] back"? What if the person claims he was only joking? How much credibility is an employer expected to afford an employee with a history of bizarre behavior? What if the disabled employee's threat is only to destroy property, and is not directed at an individual supervisor? Destruction of property can still result in injuries to other employees. The EEOC would undoubtedly say that the foregoing issues can only be addressed on a case-by-case basis and an employer's enforcement of a general prohibition against violent behavior will be scrutinized very closely by the agency.

Several courts have given a flexible interpretation to the direct threat defense and allowed employers to discharge mentally disturbed employees. For example, in a case decided by a federal court in Pennsylvania, an employer's decision to discharge an employee was upheld where an employee had repeatedly used abusive language in response to his supervisor's criticism; directed demeaning and insulting language at a nurse while trying to retrieve his urine sample; and, on one occasion, hit his supervisor over the head with a plastic tub. The court said that the employee's disruptive and abusive behavior demonstrated that he could not meet the reasonable demands of his job. Further, the court said continued employment with his employer would unduly burden the defendant because "defendant's employees would be exposed to a hostile and potentially threatening work environment."

In another case, an employee who repeatedly used abusive language in the workplace was discharged. When she sued under the ADA, the court said she was not a "qualified individual with a disability." Noting that the plaintiff had, on one occasion, told another employee, "If you don't leave me alone, I'm going to throw you out a window," the court said that plaintiff's "continued use of threatening statements to express herself" and the fact that she did not seem to be able to control such behavior, "even if [she] had no intention to do harm to anyone, made plaintiff a direct threat to the health and safety of the other workers." The court concluded: "The ADA does not require unreasonable accommodation. Thus, [the employer] was not required to employ plaintiff with the risk that others would be hurt by plaintiff's continued employment."

························

These cases appear to support discharge where the "direct threat" to other employees is not "imminent" but merely a potential risk. Arguably, the cases require the threatening behavior to be substantial or, at least repetitive, and not merely a one-time "off-hand" remark made in the heat of anger. Employers must balance the risk of harm to other employees by allowing a potentially violent employee with a mental disability to remain employed against the risk of liability if the employee is discharged and then sues the employer in an ADA action. When all employees are put on notice that threatening or abusive behavior of any kind will not be tolerated and where cooperation with other employees and non-threatening behavior is inserted as an essential function in all job descriptions, the discharge of a potentially violent mentally disabled employee—assuming the potential for violence is supported by objective medical evidence—may be a risk worth taking.

Preemployment inquiries can curtail workplace violence

The law allows employers to ask prospective employees whether they have ever been convicted of a crime. As explained above, the employer may have a legal duty to make such an inquiry because of the negligent hiring theory of liability. An employee or member of the public who is injured by a violent employee will claim the employer knew or should have known by the exercise of reasonable care that an individual had violent tendencies. For this reason, employers should try to investigate the applicant's past behavior during the interview process.

During the interview process, employers are prohibited from inquiring into the existence of a mental disease that might produce violent or abusive behavior. The interviewer can ask about violent behavior, however. Thus, it would be permissible to ask the applicant whether he or she had ever been disciplined or discharged for fighting. Also, questions such as "Have you ever been disciplined or discharged for insubordination?" or "Have you ever been disciplined or discharged for harassment?" are also permissible. Although you are not likely to get an affirmative response to any of these questions if the applicant is willing to lie to get a job, additional open-ended questions might give clues to behavioral problems. Thus, the interviewer could say, "Please describe the most difficult employee you've ever had to work with and tell me how you were able to interact with that employee." Or, more simply, the interviewer could ask, "How did you get along with your supervisor at that company?"

An employer conditioning a job offer on a medical examination can ask about mental disease in a questionnaire or make a psychiatric examination part of the post-offer medical inquiry. The only requirement under the ADA is that all potential employees must receive the same medical examination. If the employer does uncover a history of mental disease, rescission of the job offer must be job-related and "consistent with business necessity." The EEOC also very clearly states that "an individual does not pose a direct threat simply by virtue of having a history of psychiatric disability or being treated for a psychiatric disability."

Employers should also look for suspicious gaps in the applicant's employment history or contradictions on the application form. Employers should also check references provided by the applicant. Although these follow-ups don't usually provide much information, if an employer fails to make a simple phone call and the individual turns out to be a convicted rapist who attacked a female employee, the employer will face significant liability.

Criminal background checks—do you really need to know?

Many employers have now begun to use criminal background checks to assess the applicant's predisposition toward violent or abusive behavior. Even though the doctrine of negligent hiring may establish a duty to investigate an applicant's criminal background in certain circumstances, an employer's access to criminal records may be restricted by statute.

The laws vary from state to state with respect to the privileged nature of criminal records. Although there are a number of states that have no restrictions on employer access to criminal conviction records (e.g., Texas, Maine, West Virginia, and Wyoming), many states require employers to petition for such information from state repositories for criminal record information, the state police, or local law enforcement agencies. The right of access is not absolute; there may be a standard that the employer must meet to get criminal record information about an applicant.

For example, in Maryland, criminal records are maintained in a Criminal Justice Information System Central Repository. Criminal background checks are by petition to the Secretary of Public Safety. To get access to the records, the employer must "convincingly demonstrate" that the prospective employee will "have the capability to: a) jeopardize the life or safety of individuals; b) cause significant loss or damage by illegally accessing or misusing the fiscal or nonfiscal assets of the employer;

or c) otherwise engage or participate in criminal conduct in violation of state, local, and federal law." Similarly, in Alabama, an employer must petition the Alabama Criminal Justice Information Center Commission to access criminal records and the employer must demonstrate a "need to know" or a "right to know" such information. In Virginia, criminal background history information is maintained by the Virginia State Police Central Criminal Record Exchange. Under Virginia law, however, an employer may only secure criminal record history information by requesting the prospective employee to authorize release of the information. Under such circumstances, the state agency will allow release of the information to the employer as long as the employee has signed the release form and authorized disclosure to that particular employer.

Some states will only allow access to criminal conviction information when the employer is hiring employees for particular positions. For example, certain employers in California (such as financial institutions and certain health care facilities) are permitted to access criminal records. In addition, employers who plan to hire employees who will have supervisory or disciplinary authority over minors may ask the California Department of Justice for conviction records of such employees relating to sex or drug crimes or crimes of violence. Other states will allow access to criminal conviction information but require some kind of notice to the applicant or employee (e.g., Oregon, Pennsylvania, Georgia). Still other states will limit the time period for consideration of criminal conviction records, in other words, the employer cannot access convictions older than seven years (Washington) or 10 years (District of Columbia) or 15 years (Massachusetts). Because of the wide variance in statutory regulation of criminal records from state to state, employers must check their local laws before attempting criminal background checks.

One general trend is apparent, however. Increasingly, many states are relaxing restrictions on the release of criminal records in specific situations where it is not only advisable but mandatory to have employers checking the criminal history of applicants for specific positions, especially those positions where the individual will have unsupervised access to children, the elderly, or the infirm. For example, many states require criminal background checks for childcare licensees and their staff. Schools and teachers are closely regulated also. Finally, nursing homes or long-term care residential facilities for the elderly are increasingly being required to do criminal background checks on their employees. Again, the specific requirements vary from state to state.

Title VII and the use of criminal records

The practice of using a criminal conviction as one of the selection criteria for employment, even though neutral on its face, may violate Title VII because studies indicate that minorities are convicted more frequently than nonminorities. The EEOC and the courts have held that an employer may not lawfully deny employment to an applicant (or discharge an employee) merely because of a criminal conviction unless the conviction can be shown to be related to the job for which the applicant is applying.

The EEOC and the courts require the examination of several factors in determining whether a specific individual who has been convicted may be disqualified for employment in a particular position. Consideration should be given to factors such as the age of the individual when the conviction occurred, the length of time since the conviction, and whether the individual is rehabilitated. "The most important factor and the most often cited by the courts is the relationship of the conviction to the specific position the applicant is seeking." Consequently, employers should make a separate evaluation for each person who has been convicted of a crime against the requirements of the specific job.

For example, the relationship between the conviction and the job were found to be too remote to justify disqualification if an employer: 1) refused to hire an applicant as a mechanic because of a gambling conviction; 2) discharged a utility operator who was convicted of unlawful delivery of marijuana; and 3) failed to hire a crane operator because of a conviction for armed robbery. In other cases, job-relatedness was established where an employer: 1) did not hire an individual with a history of convictions for property-related crimes for a "security sensitive" position; 2) refused to hire an applicant for a custodial job because of a felony conviction involving robbery, especially where the job required possession of a master set of keys for the facility; and 3) discharged an apartment manager who had unsupervised access to apartments and rent receipts because of three convictions for theft-related offenses.

Even though the EEOC permits an employer to give fair consideration to the relationship between a conviction and the applicant's fitness for a particular job, the EEOC recommends that employers who inquire into criminal convictions on employment application forms include a statement that a "yes" answer will not disqualify an applicant from consideration for employment. The following statement should also be part of the employer's application form: "A conviction record will not necessarily bar you from employment. Each application will be individually considered on its merits, taking into account such factors as the nature and seriousness of the violation, how long ago it occurred, and rehabilitation."

Dealing with violent employees during employment

Reducing the incidence of violence during employment starts with a strongly worded "nonaggression" policy. This policy should state the employer's determination to keep the workplace free of aggressive, abusive, or violent behavior. It should identify the conduct by which employees will violate the policy. Most important, the policy statement should put employees on notice that they are subject to termination if they violate the policy.

The nonaggression policy should make reference to the company's employee complaint procedure so that employees who are subjected to aggressive or abusive behavior know how to report such conduct. A confidential employee hotline should be developed as an adjunct to the reporting system so that employees who are not victims of intimidation and abuse but see it going on in the workplace can report such conduct without fear of reprisal from the abusive employee.

The company's EAP should also be referenced in the nonaggression policy and referral to EAP should be mandatory for all persons who violate the non-aggression policy. It should be made clear, however, that referral to EAP will not be a substitute or alternative for discipline under the nonaggression policy. A sample "Non-Aggression Policy" is included in the Appendix on page 274.

An employer should also have a policy that strictly prohibits weapons of any kind on the employer's property, including the parking lot. Thus, even in those states that now allow individuals to carry concealed weapons in their cars or on their person, employers can legally put employees on notice that guns cannot be brought to work. In some states, especially at certain times of the year (for example, during hunting season), employees may want to carry rifles or shotguns in their cars or trucks. This is an employee relations issue, not a legal issue. In other words, it is legal for an employer to ban activity on its private property that may be legal off the premises. Nevertheless, an employer may have to address a morale problem among employees caused by a "zero-tolerance" weapon policy.

Employers should revise job descriptions to emphasize that cooperation with other employees is an essential function of the job. Almost any position description can be written in a manner that highlights those job duties that require courteous interaction with other employees.

Supervisors must be trained to spot obsessive, panicky, or troubled employees. Obviously, a supervisor must keep her eyes and ears open for threatening behavior or verbal threats directed at another employee. Specific members of management must be trained in conflict resolution and nonviolent response to aggressive challenges to authority.

Security personnel should also monitor employees who fit the profile of an "avenger" employee or who have previously engaged in threatening behavior. Obviously, this will only work if the company has a sophisticated security team. Otherwise, supervisors must be aware of the characteristics most common to the avenger. Admittedly, many avengers were model employees until they "snapped"; still, in most cases, there were at least some clues that might have forecast the violent events.

Finally, the NIOSH recommendations should be followed as applicable. They include:

- Posting signs noting that there is only a limited amount of cash on hand.
- Installing silent alarms and surveillance cameras.
- Increasing staff during times when robberies may occur.
- Installing drop safes.
- Increasing security presence.
- Improving external lighting.
- Providing bullet-proof barriers or enclosures.
- Increasing the number of random police drive-bys.
- Closing establishments during high-risk hours late at night.

Avoiding violent situations during layoff or discharge

The primary rule in avoiding violence during or after employee terminations is not to be afraid to discharge employees who engage in aggressive or abusive behavior. The discharge decision should only be mitigated where the employee was provoked, such as by racial or sexual harassment. Even then, aggressive behavior after provocation is only necessary as a reasonable act of self-defense. Termination of more than one employee may be appropriate where an employee has been provoked but overreacts with abusive and aggressive behavior.

Angry feelings can obviously be precipitated by a discharge from employment. Employers should increase security presence if there is a potential for violence during a discharge conference. Normally, however, security personnel need not be present in the interview room where the discharge will be discussed unless actual threats or violent behavior pre-existed the discharge decision. In most cases, it is sufficient to have security personnel standing by to escort the employee from the premises if necessary.

For layoffs or discharges of employees for reasons that have nothing to do with aggressive or abusive behavior, supervisors should avoid being cold, impersonal or angry when handling a discharge or layoff conference. If a supervisor can't control his emotions, he should get another supervisor to assist in the discharge meeting. Layoffs are obviously very disconcerting to long-term employees. Employers should attempt to give as much notice as possible to avoid the shock of a layoff. If it is economically feasible to provide severance or outplacement services to departing employees, this will obviously reduce the hardship for those employees chosen for layoff.

Finally, employers should develop crisis response teams to deal with incidents of violence in the workplace. Employers should work with EAP professionals and counselors or therapists who specialize in violence or abuse situations. A crisis response team should be headed up by a member of management with sufficient authority to make quick decisions. Security managers, human resources officers, and in-house medical personnel are also appropriate candidates for this team.

Chapter 6

Assume That Every Workplace Injury Will Be an ADA Disability

Joe Lyons has worked as a truck driver for Ace Mattress Company for about two years. The company manufactures mattresses and box springs and sells them to retail outlets. Joe delivers the product to Ace's customers but he is not normally required to either load or unload the product from his truck. Occasionally, however, he has to straighten a load that shifts in the truck so that the merchandise can be unloaded with a forklift.

Although Joe believes he is a loyal company employee and a terrific driver, his supervisor, Charley Rhodes, keeps "harassing" him about his absenteeism. Joe has been warned several times about the number of absences he was accumulating. Charley also mentioned that he noticed that Joe was most often absent either on Mondays or Fridays.

Finally, Joe reached the point in the company's progressive discipline procedures where one more absence in the following 30-day period would result in termination. Charley Rhodes was careful to let Joe know that if he was absent again, he would be fired. That night, at the local tavern, Joe complained to his friend Bob about his boss, "He's picking on me for no good reason. Other drivers are late for work and he doesn't do a thing about it. He's scared of them."

Bob proceeded to tell Joe about his back problems and how he told his company that he hurt his back lifting boxes at the plant. Bob said, "Not only did I get to take time off with pay and get all my doctor's bills

*paid—anytime I feel like staying home, I just tell them my back is
acting up again." Joe replied, "Hell, I get back pains all time from
riding in that truck. I just take a couple of aspirin, though, and the
pain goes away. I don't think I could get away with faking a more severe injury." Bob laughed, "Joe, my man, you're just too honest. You've
got to use the system—that's what those workman's comp dollars are
there for!"*

*Several days later, on Monday, Joe was absent again. He slept
right through his alarm and didn't call in to work until 10 a.m., at
which time Charley Rhodes fired him. Still half asleep, Joe mumbles
something about going to the doctor and said he would stop by to pick
up his check. Charley hung up, relieved to finally be rid of a problem
employee. He reported the disciplinary action to Human Resources.
Meanwhile, Joe immediately called his friend Bob and asked, "I need
to see your back doctor right away—can you get me in?" Bob promised
to do what he could. Joe then called work again and asked to talk to
the Human Resources director. When the director answered the phone,
Joe told him about his back "injury."*

*A few hours later, Charley Rhodes received a call from the HR direc-
tor, who told him that Joe injured his back on Friday and that that
was why he could not come to work. The HR director reminded Charley
of the exception that was placed in the absenteeism policy for time lost
due to workplace injuries. It seemed that some employment lawyer had
suggested that the company adopt such an exception to avoid any
possible claim for retaliation under the worker's compensation law.
Charley protested that Joe did not mention the back injury when he
brought his truck in on Friday. The HR Director replied, "Joe claims
he did not begin to experience the back spasms until Sunday evening."*

*Instead of termination, Joe was placed on leave. Charley Rhodes
was told to find temporary help to perform Joe's truck driving duties.
Meanwhile, Joe went to see Bob's doctor and contacted Bob's attorney.
The attorney filed a worker's compensation claim for Joe that attributed his back injury to his efforts at fixing a shifted load in the truck.
Joe's doctor filed a report that is somewhat vague as to both the cause
of Joe's back problems and the permanency of his injury. As a result,
the company's worker's compensation insurance company vowed to
continue to fight Joe's claim for permanent partial disability compensation and to investigate Joe's leisure time activities.*

*After two months of doctors' visits and physical therapy sessions,
Joe was still not ready to come back to work full-time. Joe's physical
therapist believed he was ready to go back to work without restrictions.
Joe wanted to work part-time and his doctor eventually agreed to write*

Joe a prescription restricting his total driving time to no more than five hours per day.

Joe called Charley Rhodes and proposed a schedule that would allow him to drive two and a half hours in the morning and two and a half hours in the afternoon, with an hour break for lunch. In addition, Joe requested that a helper be assigned to assist him in case there was a load shift requiring that mattresses and box springs be realigned on their pallets. Charley felt that he could not possibly accommodate Joe without adversely affecting the delivery schedule.

As a compromise, the company offered Joe the opportunity to work only mornings and agreed to allow the temporary driver to act as Joe's assistant on the morning runs, then drive the truck without Joe during the afternoon. Joe was warned that he was still subject to discipline under the company's absenteeism policy and that he must meet the requirements of the morning schedule. Joe's lawyer obtained an agreement from the company that any absences in the morning that are caused by recurring back spasms will not be counted against Joe.

All went well for about two weeks, then Joe approached the HR Director and told him that he needed a special seat to relieve the discomfort he feels in his back while driving. The seat he requested cost about $600. Company officials had had enough, however, and refused to grant Joe's request. Instead, Joe was given a new back support pillow.

Four days later, Joe did not report for work at his scheduled time. He called in and said he had a cold and that the coughing was aggravating his back. The HR director told Joe that he would need a certification of illness from his doctor. The next day Joe called and said that he was quitting because he couldn't stand the constant harassment he was receiving from the company. That same day, the HR director learned that the worker's compensation insurance company had paid Joe a substantial settlement for his back injury.

Six weeks later, the company was served with a civil complaint wherein Joe was suing the company for discrimination under the ADA, retaliation under the FMLA, wrongful discharge, breach of contract, intentional infliction of emotional distress, and loss of consortium. The HR director reviewed the papers and let out a huge sigh.

Dealing with the ADA

The Americans with Disabilities Act (ADA) became effective on July 26, 1992. It now applies to any employer with 15 or more employees. As with other federal employment discrimination laws, aggrieved individuals can access the remedies provided in the ADA by filing a charge of discrimination with the Equal Employment Opportunity Commission (EEOC).

The new statute has overburdened the EEOC, however, by creating a tremendous increase in the number of claims filed with the agency each year as well as by presenting the agency with a different type of claim that takes much longer to investigate. Most states also have laws that protect disabled individuals from discrimination. Often, these state laws are patterned after the ADA and may govern the actions of businesses with less than 15 employees.

The ADA was intended to enhance the opportunities of disabled persons in the workplace. Employers initially feared that the Act would act as a massive affirmative action plan for the disabled requiring preferential hiring for unqualified applicants and hampering their business operations. However, the hiring aspects of the ADA have not proven to be an extraordinary burden for employers. Generally, disabled applicants have proven to be productive employees and the specter of numerous failure-to-hire discrimination lawsuits has not become a reality. Employers have been able to preserve their hiring discretion by specifically defining the essential functions of the positions in their work force and then requiring disabled individuals to meet those job specifications.

This is not to say, however, that the ADA has not had its troublesome elements. As illustrated by Joe, the truck driver in the opening sketch, there are always employees who will abuse the protections of the statute. Employers have struggled with the employee who appears to be using an alleged disability as an excuse for poor performance. In particular, the issue of regular attendance has been a dilemma for employers looking for reliability and productivity from each of its employees. Reasonable accommodation as a litigation issue deals not so much with demands for assistive devices from disabled employees but unreasonable expectations from disabled employees that an employer can always change a schedule without undue hardship, can grant extended leaves of absence without difficulty, and can always convert a full-time job with overtime requirements into a part-time position with extended break periods.

This chapter is intended as a guide for those employers who are willing to hire and promote qualified disabled persons but who do not want to face legal challenges and financial liability when they must discharge an employee with a disability. The answer is not, as one client suggested to me, to stop doing any hiring. After all, an employee without a disability today can be asking for accommodation tomorrow because he or she has suffered a workplace injury with chronic long-term consequences. Instead, the answer is to use policies and procedures that ensure that employment decisions are performance-based and exercised with due deliberation.

ADA—the definition of disability

The definition of disability in the ADA is very broad and many physical and mental conditions have come within the scope of the protections set forth in the Act. The ADA defines an "individual with a disability" as a person who: 1) has a physical or mental impairment that substantially limits one or more of that person's major life activities; 2) has a record of such impairment; or 3) is regarded as having such an impairment.

A decision out of Vermont serves as a vivid example of the potential breadth of the term "disability" under the ADA. Although the decision was construing the Rehabilitation Act of 1973, the definition of a "handicapped person" in the Rehabilitation Act is identical to the definition of a "disabled person" in the ADA. In this case, a chambermaid at a ski resort lost her job because her dentures were too painful to wear. The employer sent the plaintiff a letter telling her that she would not be able to return to work without dentures. The letter warned: "Employees will be expected to have teeth and to wear them daily to work." Seeking to upgrade the resort's image to secure a "four star" rating, the employer decided the plaintiff was unfit to be seen by customers.

The court allowed the plaintiff to go to trial on her handicap bias claim stating that "lack of upper teeth is a physical impairment within the meaning of the Act because it is a cosmetic disfigurement and an anatomical loss affecting the musculoskeletal and digestive systems." Further, the court found that the employer had regarded plaintiff as a handicapped individual even though the cosmetic disfigurement did not limit any major life activity other than the ability to work. In the court's view, the employer treated the plaintiff as though she had a visible physical impairment that prevented her from fulfilling the duties of her position.

In a more recent decision construing the definition of disability under the ADA, a federal court of appeals ruled that a telemarketer with 18 missing teeth, who was discharged after three days of work by a Chicago publisher because he allegedly mumbled on the telephone, should be able to take his ADA claim to trial on a theory that the employer regarded him as having a disability. The court said that the "toothless telemarketer" did not need to have an actual impairment to establish his claim under the ADA. If the employer regarded him as being impaired, the employee was "disabled" under the Act. The court did say, however, that the employer should have a chance to show that the employee's alleged "mumbling" would prevent him from being an effective telemarketer.

In another case, a federal court in the District of Columbia accepted a plaintiff's claim that she was disabled because she had a stuttering problem. The employee alleged that the employer had denied her a promotion because of her stuttering, had denied her a partition around her desk to shield her from visual contact with co-workers, refused to assist her disability by reducing audio-induced stress, and denied her request for leave without pay to obtain speech therapy. The court concluded, however, that plaintiff's stuttering was not the cause for the denial of a promotion, but rather was caused by her inadequate application and interview for the supervisory position.

Many back injuries have been determined to be covered disabilities under state and federal acts. A back condition can be a covered disability even though the individual with the back problem is not currently suffering any distress from the condition. For example, in one reported case, two drivers were discharged from employment after a physical examination revealed that one employee had a small spur on his spine and another had a condition known as spondylolysis, a fusion of the vertebral joints. Neither employee had experienced previous back problems and each had been performing their truck driving duties for almost 60 days during their probationary period. The court determined that the latent back conditions were disabilities under the Maine Human Rights Act because the asymptomatic condition of each of the men constituted a "malformation" of the spine.

The foregoing cases demonstrate the potential coverage of the ADA. Employers must assume that any impairment, no matter how minor, may be construed as a covered disability. Because the courts have said that the determination of a disability is best suited to a case-by-case determination, the scope of the term "disabled person" is often dependent on the particular philosophy of the judge who may be handling a particular case. It is incumbent on employers, therefore, to consider their potential liabilities under the Act where the poor performance of an employee may have some relationship to a physical or mental impairment.

ADA—the two-stage hiring process

The ADA mandates a two-stage procedure for inquiring about disabilities. During interviews prior to actually offering a job to an applicant, an employer may ask questions about the individual's ability to perform specific job functions, but is prohibited from making inquiries that are likely to uncover information about a disability. For example, an employer may describe or demonstrate job functions and inquire whether or not the applicant can perform the functions, with or without accommodation. Preemployment physical agility tests are also permissible. The physical agility test must be job-related, however. You can't give a laborer a dexterity test that requires fine motor skills.

Once a conditional job offer has been made, an employer may conduct a medical examination or ask health-related questions. All candidates who receive a conditional job offer in the same job category must be required to take the same examination or respond to the same inquiries. Any exam criteria that cause a disabled applicant to lose a job offer must be job-related and consistent with business necessity.

An employer may also state attendance requirements and inquire as to whether the applicant can meet them. It is also permissible to ask an applicant questions that might reveal whether he or she abused their sick leave privilege with a previous employer. For example, you could ask an applicant how many days he was absent on a Friday or a Monday during the past year. However, employers may not inquire about an individual's worker's compensation history during the pre-offer stage.

Prohibited inquiries during the hiring process

The basic prohibitions with respect to *pre-offer* inquiries are as follows: 1) An employer may not make any pre-employment inquiries about a disability on application forms, in job interviews, or in background or reference checks; 2) an employer may not make any medical inquiries or conduct any medical examination prior to making a conditional offer of employment.

EEOC regulations construing the ADA list numerous questions that may *not* be asked on application forms or in job interviews. Some of these are:

♦ Have you ever been treated for any of the following conditions or diseases? (Followed by a checklist of various conditions and diseases.)

♦ Have you ever been hospitalized? Please describe the reasons for such hospitalization.

♦ Have you ever been treated by a psychiatrist or psychologist? If so, for what condition?

- Is there any health-related reason why you may not be able to perform the job for which you are applying?
- Have you had a major illness in the last three years?
- How many work days did you miss because of illness last year?
- Do you have any physical defects that prevent you from performing certain kinds of work? If yes, please describe your specific work limitations.
- Are you taking any prescribed drugs?
- Have you ever been treated for drug addiction or alcoholism?
- How often did you use illegal drugs in the past?
- Have you ever filed for worker's compensation insurance?

Permissible inquiries

Information that may be requested on application forms or in interviews includes the following:

- An employer may ask questions to determine whether an applicant can perform specific job functions. The questions should focus on the applicant's *ability* to perform the job, not on a disability.
- If an individual has a *known* disability and the employer reasonably believes that it will interfere with the performance of job functions, he or she may be asked to describe or demonstrate how he or she will perform these functions even if other applicants are not asked to do so.
- If a known disability would *not* interfere with performance of job functions, an individual may only be required to describe or demonstrate how he or she will perform a job if this is required of all applicants for the position.
- An employer may condition a job offer on the results of a medical examination or on the responses to medical inquiries if such an examination or inquiry is required of all entering employees in the same job category.
- An employer may ask about work attendance records with previous employers as long as the inquiry does not refer to illness or disability.

Interviewing tips

Employers should make sure that their recruiters or any employee doing substantial interviewing of candidates for employment adhere to the following guidelines.

♦ Do not make assumptions about an individual's disability or how that disability may or may not affect the person's performance on the job.

♦ Focus the interview on ability, not on disability.

♦ Do not make gratuitous statements about the person's disability. For example, do not express sympathy for the individual's condition or express concern for any discomfort that the individual may be experiencing because of the disability.

♦ Watch facial expressions and body language. The interviewer should not convey any discomfort about interviewing the disabled person, or that he or she is doing the applicant a favor by conducting the interview.

♦ Do not make notes on either the application, resume, or the interview sheet that are not job-related statements. Do not make any notes that relate to the person's physical or mental condition unless it relates to the applicant's request for accommodation.

♦ Treat all applicants for a position the same way—do not selectively ask some applicants some questions, while avoiding those questions with other applicants.

♦ Be responsive to the applicant if an accommodation is requested with respect to a testing device or the performance of an essential function.

♦ Do not use language that is offensive to the applicant or that shows bias.

Use of job descriptions

The importance of drafting or revising job descriptions to list the essential functions of each job cannot be overemphasized. The ADA requires disabled individuals to possess an ability to perform the essential functions of available positions. Obviously, employers cannot expect to defend a charge of failing to hire a disabled applicant if they have not identified the essential functions of each position within their organization.

Essential functions are fundamental job duties, not marginal functions. You must focus on the truly job-related requirements of the position when drafting the job description. A function may be essential because the reason the position exists is to perform that function. For example, drawing blood from patients is an essential function for a phlebotomist. Typing 70 words per minute may be an essential function for a secretary.

A function may also be essential because it is the employer's judgment that a function is essential. That judgment is reinforced if the essential function is listed on the job description before the interviewing process for hiring or a promotion decision. It is much easier to convince the EEOC that a function is essential if it has been made part of the job description prior to the personnel decision that provoked the charge of discrimination. The agency will be very reluctant to credit an employer's belief that a job function is essential if it was omitted from an existing job description that lists position guidelines. Also, employers can better validate a list of essential functions by having position incumbents "sign off" on job descriptions or participate in the process of creating them.

Finally, job descriptions can be effective in defining the minimum productivity standards and setting the quality and quantity of work that must be accomplished by a person performing the job. The importance of having well-defined productivity standards is illustrated by two contrasting decisions interpreting the reasonable accommodation requirements of the Rehabilitation Act.

In the first case, a state court ordered an employer to allow a "team cleaning approach" as an accommodation for a nursing home housekeeper who had suffered a cerebral hemorrhage, even though the cost of a second full-time housekeeper was $18,928. According to the court, the accommodation was reasonable because the co-worker would not actually be doing the disabled employee's work. The court characterized this accommodation as merely "restructuring the schedule so that the two housekeepers worked together on the [same] floor."

The court noted that the job description used by the employer required only "minimal job qualifications." The nursing home had not incorporated productivity standards into the housekeeper's job description. The court concluded that the mentally impaired employee could still perform the essential functions of her job. The case may have been decided differently if productivity standards had been established and incorporated into the job description for this position.

Under a slightly different set of facts, a federal court decided that an accommodation requested by a disabled employee was not reasonable. In this case, a head nurse suffered from severe depression and other emotional disorders. As a result of her mental condition, it was difficult for her to start work at the scheduled hours of 7:30 or 8 a.m. Based on the nature of a head nurse's responsibilities and job duties as set forth in her job description, the hospital refused to alter her tour of duty to start work at 10 a.m.

The court found the hospital had the right to prescribe the regular tour of duty for its nursing personnel. In light of the documented job requirements for the head nurse position, the court agreed that rescheduling was not a reasonable accommodation. Discussion in the decision indicates, however, that staff nurses did not have similar job duties. Thus, if the situation involved a staff nurse with a similar mental disability, the hospital may have been required to reschedule the employee as a reasonable accommodation.

Reasonable accommodation

The ADA requires employers to provide reasonable accommodation to enable workers with disabilities to perform the essential functions of their jobs, unless doing so would impose an undue hardship on the business. Thus, a disabled person cannot be discharged for performance problems related to the disability until the employer determines whether some type of reasonable accommodation will allow the employee to perform the essential functions of her position or a vacant position that the employee might also be qualified to perform.

An employer is obligated to make accommodation only to the known limitations of an otherwise qualified individual with a disability. In other words, an employer is not required to provide accommodation if it is unaware of the need for such accommodation. Normally, it is the responsibility of the employee to inform the employer that an accommodation is needed to perform the essential functions of the position. Thus, although adequate prevention suggests that employers be prepared for the possibility that almost every injury or illness will later be construed as an ADA disability, it is not necessary to concede this issue in conversations with injured employees. In other words, consider the possibility of accommodation for an injured employee, discuss the injured employee's "prognosis" with him or her (for example, ask when he or she will be able to return to work as a full-time productive employee), but do not suggest

....

possible accommodation for the employee unless it is obvious that the employee has an ADA disability and is requesting assistance to do the job.

The EEOC's *Technical Assistance Manual for the ADA* states that "if an employee with a *known disability* is not performing well or is having difficulty in performing a job, the employer should assess whether this is due to a disability." Also, an applicant does not have to specifically request a reasonable accommodation, but must only let the employer know that some adjustment is needed to do a job because of limitations caused by a disability. Finally, remember that plaintiffs who are seeking large damage awards often testify about conversations with supervisors in a manner that supports their cause of action. Supervisors should not be surprised, therefore, when an ex-employee "remembers" telling her supervisor about her need for accomodation when, in fact, no conversation ever took place.

The Act sets forth various examples of reasonable accommodation, such as: making existing facilities used by employees readily available to and usable by individuals with disabilities; job restructuring; part-time or modified work schedules; reassignment to a vacant position; acquisition or modification of equipment or devices; adjustment or modification of examinations, training materials or policies; the provision of qualified readers or interpreters; and other similar accommodation. The list of examples in the Act was not intended to be exhaustive nor is any item mandatory.

A reasonable accommodation is any modification or adjustment in the work environment or in the way things are customarily done that allows an individual with a disability to enjoy equal employment opportunities. The process for determining whether an employer can provide a reasonable accommodation is a case-by-case approach. The employer must analyze the particular job in question and determine its purpose and essential functions. Then, the employer should consult with the disabled individual to determine his precise job limitations and how they may be overcome. After that, the employer should identify potential accommodations.

Finally, the employer must select and implement the most appropriate accommodation. The employer may consider the preference of the individual to be accommodated but it is not necessary to be governed by the disabled employee's demands. Remember also that reasonable accommodation may include removing physical barriers that inhibit or prevent access of an individual with a disability to job sites. Thus, on an individual basis, an employer may be required to modify facilities and equipment so that a disabled individual can perform the essential functions of a job.

Undue hardship

A failure to provide reasonable accommodation may be justified if an employer can demonstrate that the proposed accommodation would impose an "undue hardship" on the operation of its business. Undue hardship means "significant difficulty or expense incurred." The factors to be considered include: 1) the net cost of accommodation considering availability of tax credits or deductions; 2) the overall financial resources of the employer (the employer may have to show that the net cost of accommodation is an undue hardship when compared to its overall budget); 3) the type of operations of the employer; 4) the impact of accommodation on operations of a facility, including the impact on the ability of other employees to perform duties and the impact on the employer's ability to conduct business.

For large employers, it is often very difficult to establish an undue hardship on financial grounds. Courts generally seem willing to require an expenditure of money to accommodate requests for assistive devices for disabled persons. The most difficult cases are those where the disabled person demands a change in the employer's operations as an accommodation. Courts are more reluctant to sanction requests for radical changes in an employee's schedule or in the required duties of the position.

For example, in one case, a police officer who suffered from chronic fatigue, a sleep disorder, and susceptibility to blackouts in high-stress situations sued her employer because she claimed her employer had not reasonably accommodated her disability. The plaintiff claimed she was able to perform a light-duty assignment at the station house. The court agreed with the employer and found that the plaintiff had not shown that she was capable of performing the essential functions required of a police officer even with reasonable accommodation such as light duty. The court noted that one of the essential duties of a police officer is to protect the public at large. The court stated that the plaintiff's injuries prevented her from fulfilling this fundamental duty. Even a police officer who works at a desk must be capable of responding in a professional manner to various crises that could occur in the station house. In addition, a police dispatcher must remain clear-headed and calm in emergency situations. As explained by the court, the risk of blackouts prevented the plaintiff from protecting the public at large, remaining calm in emergency situations, and responding in a professional manner to various crises that could occur in the station house.

The safety defense

An employer may refuse to hire an applicant for employment or discharge a disabled individual when the employee poses a "direct threat" to their own health or safety or the health and safety of others. A risk can only be considered a direct threat when it poses a significant risk—a high probability of substantial harm. A speculative or remote risk is insufficient to support the defense.

As with other issues arising under the ADA, the determination of whether an individual poses a significant risk of substantial harm must be made on a case-by-case basis. Regulations construing the ADA list four factors that must be considered: 1) the duration of the risk; 2) the nature and severity of the potential harm; 3) the likelihood that the potential harm will occur; and 4) the imminence of the potential harm.

Relevant evidence may include input from the individual with the disability, the experience of the individual with the disability in similar positions, and the opinion of medical doctors, rehabilitation counselors, or physical therapists who have expertise in the disability and/or direct knowledge of the individual with the disability. The determination must be based on individualized data and not on stereotypical or patronizing assumptions about the nature of the disability in general.

The employer must also consider whether any potential accommodation will eliminate or reduce the risk (the risk need not be eliminated entirely). In cases where the employee will put his or her own safety at risk, the employer must be careful that its desire to protect the employee is not clouding its judgment as to the nature of the risk. There are cases, however, that demonstrate that a disabled employee cannot always assume the risk at his peril. For example, an employer would not be required to hire an individual as a carpenter where the individual is disabled by narcolepsy, random and uncontrollable bouts of sleep. Because the carpenter would be required to operate a power saw as a regular part of his duties, no accommodation exists that will reduce or eliminate the risk of injury to the carpenter. Similarly, firing a construction inspector who had Parkinson's disease would not violate the law because he could not perform the essential functions of the job safely. The inspector position required a lot of climbing and physical exertion that would be dangerous to the disabled individual.

When an employee has a psychological problem that has the potential to cause the employee to react in a violent or aggressive manner, a discharge for safety reasons may not be justified when the condition is controlled by medicine and the employee has demonstrated reliability in taking his prescribed dosage of medicine. As explained in Chapter 5, however, where there is actual evidence of violent or aggressive behavior, or threats directed at other employees, the safety defense probably can be established even though the harm to others is only a potential risk. It is not necessary to wait until the mentally disabled employee pulls out a gun. If the employee is acting in a threatening manner, the employer should protect other employees and remove the mentally disabled employee from the workplace.

There are several issues that are particularly troublesome for employers in applying the requirements of the ADA. The following examples are frequently confronted by employers and the legal issues arising out of such controversies are recurring in nature. The next sections suggest ways of dealing with these problems.

Workplace injuries and the ADA—the light duty dilemma

Since the effective date of the ADA, employers have questioned its application to work-related injuries covered by state worker's compensation laws. In September 1996, the EEOC issued a directive entitled *Enforcement Guidance: Worker's Compensation and the ADA* ("the *Guidance*") that addresses certain ADA issues relating to workplace injuries, including the creation of light-duty jobs and the obligation of employers to keep a position open for an employee on leave with a disability-related occupational injury.

Although the *Guidance* concedes that not every person with a work-related injury is disabled within the meaning of the ADA, it is clear from the language of the *Guidance* and previous EEOC regulations that all work-related injuries have the potential for being construed as a protected disability under the ADA. The *Guidance* offers the following example to illustrate how a temporary impairment can find protection under the ADA: "An employee is fully recovered from an occupational injury that resulted in a temporary back impairment. The employer fires the employee because it believes that, if he returns to his heavy-labor job, he will severely injury his back and be totally incapacitated. The employer regards the employee as having an impairment that disqualified him for a class of jobs (heavy labor) and therefore is substantially limited in the major life activity of working. The employee has a disability as defined by the ADA."

The *Guidance* states unequivocally that an employer may not fire an employee who is temporarily unable to work because of a disability-related occupational injury unless the employer can show that providing leave to the injured employee would be an undue hardship. Further, the injured employee is entitled to return to his or her same position unless the employer can demonstrate that holding open the position would impose an undue hardship. This latter requirement calls into question an employer's ability to cap the amount of time an employee on worker's compensation leave is allowed to remain on leave and still retain his position.

Generally, employers hold open an injured employee's position only for a limited amount of time. For example, some employers have adopted the 12 week limitation in the Family and Medical Leave Act as the termination point for reinstatement rights. According to the *Guidance*, however, the reinstatement rights of an employee with a disability-related occupational injury are not subject to arbitrary time limitations and may be curtailed only if holding open the position would impose an undue hardship on the employer. For example, if an employer had a clerical employee out on worker's compensation leave and the employee could show that she had an ADA disability that required her to be on leave for an extended period of time, the employer would have to hold her position open for the duration of her leave unless it could demonstrate that covering the position with temporary help or assigning other employees to perform the employee's duties would result in an undue hardship.

In order to expedite an employee's return from worker's compensation leave, many employers have created so-called "light-duty" jobs, so that injured workers can provide some measure of productivity to the employer. The creation of light-duty positions to get employees off worker's compensation leave can complicate things if the employee has a protected disability under the ADA.

An employer that creates light duty positions for employees with occupational injuries does not have to create such positions as a reasonable accommodation for employees with disabilities who have not been injured on the job. As explained by the *Guidance*, an employer may feel a "special obligation" to create a light duty position for an employee who is injured while performing work for the employer. Such a practice would not be construed to be discrimination under the ADA simply because the employer does not extend the same privilege to disabled employees who were injured off the job.

Those employers who have reserved light-duty positions, however, may have to explain why they did not offer such positions to disabled persons as a reasonable accommodation. Reassignment to a vacant position is specifically listed as a form of reasonable accommodation under regulations construing the ADA, absent any undue hardship. The *Guidance* states that an employer would not be able to establish that "reassignment to a vacant reserved light-duty position imposes an undue hardship simply by showing "that it would have no other vacant light duty positions available if an employee became injured on the job and needed light duty."

The key to maintaining light-duty jobs for work-related injuries is not to reserve specific jobs as light duty, but to assign light-duty tasks on a case-by-case basis and make them temporary assignments. As explained in the *Guidance*, "an employer is free to determine that a light duty position will be temporary rather than permanent." Thus, if an employer provides light-duty positions only on a temporary basis, it need only provide a temporary light-duty position for an employee with a disability-related occupational injury.

The ADA and alcoholism

Although alcoholism is a protected disability under the Americans with Disabilities Act, an employer may nevertheless discipline or discharge an individual whose use of alcohol adversely affects job performance. Courts have ruled that an employer does not violate the ADA by firing an employee for misconduct stemming from his alcoholism. This is especially true where the employer can establish that it had no knowledge of the employee's alcoholism and thus was never asked to assist the employee in controlling his destructive behavior.

For example, a federal court in Minnesota ruled that accommodation was not required under the ADA where the plaintiff was fired after he was arrested for drunk driving and assault after work hours. Prior to his arrest, the plaintiff had a pattern of unexcused absences including one when he called his supervisor at 2 a.m. to ask for two days off to attend the funeral of an individual who, in fact, had not died. The company maintained that the plaintiff's discharge was justified by his pattern of absenteeism and his arrest.

The plaintiff argued that his discharge violated the ADA because it was based on his alcoholism. He claimed that his employer failed to provide him with counseling and other accommodations for his alcoholism. The court agreed that the ADA requires reasonable accommodation but only where the employer knows the employee is disabled. In this case, the plaintiff had not told the company about his disability and in fact openly denied having an alcohol problem. The court said that because of the employee's denial, the employer could not be said to have had knowledge of the employee's alcoholism.

Even if an individual denies being an alcoholic and thus does not come within the express definition of "individuals with a disability" under the ADA, there may be a quantity of evidence that is sufficient to show that the employer should nevertheless still be liable because it perceived the individual to be an alcoholic. In one reported case, an operating room nurse told her supervisor that she smelled alcohol on the breath of an operating room technician during surgery. The supervisor required the technician to go directly to the hospital's employee assistance program, but would not allow him to drive to the appointment. Instead, the technician was escorted by two hospital security officials from the operating room control center to the security chief's office to wait until a friend arrived to drive him to the Employment Assistance Program appointment.

The technician alleged that the hospital discriminated against him because it perceived him to be an alcoholic. At the trial, the court ruled that the plaintiff was covered by the ADA. The hospital presented testimony, however, showing the potential dangers of alcohol impairment in the operating room and argued, therefore, that its actions were appropriate and a business necessity. The jury agreed, finding against the plaintiff on the cause of action for disability discrimination, apparently concluding that the hospital's responsibility to ensure the health and safety of its patients justified the discharge of the technician.

Misconduct connected with work, regardless of its connection with alcoholism, should allow an employer to discharge an alcoholic employee without liability under the ADA. Where the signs of alcoholism are obvious, however, employers should provide assistance to the employee. If the individual refuses assistance or accommodation, disclaiming any problems with his or her drinking, the employer is in an even better position to defend against an ADA claim.

Drug addiction as a disability

Disability is defined broadly enough to include persons addicted to drugs; however, there is a specific exclusion in the Act for employees or applicants who are "currently engaging in the illegal use of drugs." This exclusion indicates a congressional intent to relieve employers from liability for testing, disciplining and discharging employees for drug use. The ADA allows employers to:

♦ Test applicants and employees. Drug tests are not medical exams under the Act.

♦ Discharge employees using drugs in the workplace.

♦ Discharge employees under the influence of drugs in the workplace.

Nevertheless, the exclusion for current drug use leaves some questions unanswered. For example, what is a "current user"? What if the applicant says he stopped using drugs yesterday? Is he no longer a current user? What if he stopped two weeks ago? Or perhaps 30 days ago? Unfortunately, there is no bright line for delineating past users from current users. The EEOC says the exclusion is intended to apply to an individual whose use of drugs occurred recently enough to justify a reasonable belief that the person's use is "current." In other words, at some point, a "current" user becomes a "former user."

It is important to remember that individuals addicted to drugs who have completed a drug rehabilitation program or have otherwise been rehabilitated are protected by the ADA. Thus, self-help programs such as Narcotics Anonymous could serve as rehabilitation programs. Also, a former addict who is currently participating in a supervised rehabilitation program is covered under the Act. Even an individual who is erroneously regarded as engaging in drug use, but who is not so engaging, may be covered by the Act's protections.

For example, if an employer discharges a employee who is rumored to be using drugs, it does not matter that the employee has only occasionally used marijuana in the past. The employee will be covered under the Act even though he is not addicted to drugs because his employer regarded him as an addict. The employee would not be protected if the employer could convince a judge or jury that it regarded the employee as only a "social" user of marijuana and not an addict.

It is important to note that an employer does not violate the Act by adopting or administering reasonable policies or procedures, including drug testing, that are designed to ensure that a recovered drug addict is, in fact, no longer engaging in the use of illegal drugs. Thus, requiring an employee to participate in a rehabilitation program and making continued employment contingent upon the employee submitting to random drug tests after completion of the rehabilitation program would not be considered a violation of the ADA.

An individual addicted to drugs must still meet the minimum qualifications for the job and be able to perform the essential functions of that position, with or without a reasonable accommodation. For example, an essential function for the position of a visiting home health nurse who works with terminally ill patients may be the administration of narcotic drugs. If a nurse, because of past drug addiction, is prohibited from administering such medication, she would not be able to perform an essential function of the job.

In summary, employers may not arbitrarily disqualify a recovered drug addict from employment solely because of the disability. An employer must consider the recovered addict's ability to handle the position actually sought. On the other hand, even under the regulations, the employer may impose an absolute ban against the possession and use of drugs in the workplace and can use drug testing as a method of detecting current drug users as well as to determine whether recovered addicts continue to be drug-free.

Mental disability and the ADA

The ADA's provision for protection of employees with mental disorders can be extremely troublesome for employers. Many psychological disorders have already been identified as "disabilities." For example, employers have faced claims dealing with manic-depressive conditions, stress reactions, anxiety-depression syndrome, claustrophobia, acrophobia, carbon monoxide phobia, paranoid schizophrenia, personality disorders, mental retardation, and learning disabilities. Although certain mental diseases and deficiencies are easily recognized as truly disabling, to what extent must an employer accept employee claims of more esoteric mental illness to explain aberrational behavior in the performance of their duties?

On March 25, 1997, the EEOC issued an enforcement guidance on the application of the ADA to individuals with psychiatric disabilities. In the guidance, the EEOC addressed the definition of psychiatric disability, what major life activities can be substantially impaired by this type of disability and the issue of reasonable accommodation. As is often true with EEOC guidances, the position taken by the EEOC in its latest enforcement guidance runs contrary to court decisions, and therefore leaves employers with more questions than answers.

As to what constitutes a psychiatric disability, the EEOC states in the guidance that the term "mental or psychological disorder" includes many of the traditional emotional or mental illnesses such as: major depression; bipolar disorder; anxiety disorders, including panic disorders, obsessive compulsive disorders, and post-traumatic stress disorders; schizophrenia; and personality disorders. The EEOC also said that, while "stress, in itself, is not automatically a mental impairment," it may be shown to be related to a mental or physical impairment.

Courts, however, have ruled that an employee's inability to accept criticism from a supervisor or to handle workplace stress, even if linked to a mental or physical impairment, does not establish grounds for a violation of the ADA. For example, a federal court in Maryland held that an employee who displayed several incidents of bizarre and insubordinate behavior, such as insulting her supervisor and using obscenities, was not able to perform the essential functions of the job and therefore did not state a viable claim under the ADA. Likewise, the U.S. Court of Appeals for the Sixth Circuit has found that an employee who could not accept any criticism, who exhibited signs of extreme anxiety when his doctor suggested that he return to work, and who threatened to kill himself was not qualified to return to work.

As with physical disabilities, a mental impairment must "substantially limit one or more major life activities" to come within the protection of the ADA. The EEOC states that the question of what constitutes a major life activity differs from person to person and that a major life activity can include "concentrating and interacting with others." If an employee has "some" difficulty getting along with a supervisor or a coworker, the EEOC would not regard this trait as a substantial limitation on a major life activity. If, on the other hand, an employee's relations with others are characterized "on a regular basis by severe problems," the individual would be substantially limited in a major life activity.

The EEOC's opinion in this respect appears to be at odds with a decision of the First Circuit Court of Appeals where the court said that the ability to get along with others "does not generally constitute a major life activity." The court stated that the "concept of 'ability to get along with others' is remarkably elastic...and to impose legally enforceable duties on an employer based on such an amorphous concept would be problematic."

························

One other area of the enforcement guidance that is particularly troublesome is the question of reasonable accommodation. The EEOC states that an employee requesting a reasonable accommodation because of a mental disability need not mention the ADA or use the phrase "reasonable accommodation." According to the EEOC, if an employee asks for time off because he or she is "depressed and stressed," or if the employee has communicated a request for change at work or time off, the employer is on notice that the employee is requesting a reasonable accommodation.

Several court decisions dealing with mental disability and coverage under the ADA have provided hope to employers struggling with this aspect of the Act. For example, a federal court in Texas has ruled that a grocery store manager who claimed he was suffering from depression could not sue for disability discrimination following his discharge because he had not adequately notified his employer that he was being treated for a mental disability. Even though the employee had been given extensive disciplinary counseling for poor work performance, he never once told his supervisor that he was being treated for depression.

The employee did give his employer a note from a physician recommending that he be allowed to take a six-week medical leave for a "health disorder." The note, however, did not specify the nature of the illness. After he returned from his leave of absence, the employee gave his employer two other notes from doctors recommending that he be allowed to transfer from grocery manager to clerk. Although one of the notes was typed on paper bearing the letterhead of a psychiatric hospital, neither of the notes explained why he needed a transfer.

The court dismissed the employee's claim holding that the correspondence provided by the employee to his employer did not constitute proper notice to the employer of a mental disability. The letters simply did not inform the employer that the employee was suffering from depression. Although the court acknowledged that an employer does not need to be aware of the exact diagnosis and full nature of the employer's disability in order to be charged with discrimination, the law requires the employer to have "some knowledge" that the employee has a disability covered by the Act.

This decision appears to be a very close case. The ruling could easily have gone the other way. If the court had ruled that the employer had notice of a psychiatric illness, the employer might have had an obligation to offer reasonable accommodation or at least talk to the employee to determine whether anything could be done to assist the employee's performance of essential functions. Determining the extent of accommodation that must be provided an employee suffering from a mental disability can be quite problematic. For example, the EEOC in its regulations instructs employers that they must provide accommodation unless to do so would be an "undue hardship." That "guidance" is of little assistance to employers where the term "undue hardship" remains undefined.

It appears clear that an employer need not provide an entirely stress-free work environment in order to accommodate an employee's mental disability. In a case decided by the U.S. Court of Appeals for the Sixth Circuit, the court ruled that a tool room attendant who suffered from extreme depression was not a "qualified handicapped person" and thus could be legally discharged from his position. The plaintiff would become extremely anxious and depressed at even the slightest hint of rejection or criticism. In fact, when his doctor suggested he try returning to work, he burst into tears.

The court found that the tool room attendant position was already the least stressful position in the employer's plant. It concluded that the plaintiff was not able to perform the essential functions of his job where he would be incapable of getting along with his supervisors and co-workers. The court said, "It would be unreasonable to require that [the employer] place plaintiff in a virtually stress-free environment and immunize him from criticism in order to accommodate his disability."

Finally, when an employer provides an accommodation to an employee's mental disability and the disabled employee fails to take advantage of the accommodation, the employee will have difficulty in proving disability discrimination after he is discharged for other misconduct. In one case, a federal court of appeals ruled that a postal worker who punched his boss was properly discharged even though he claimed to be suffering from a psychiatric illness that was aggravated easily by stress. The Postal Service was aware of his illness but permitted the plaintiff to leave his work station and go scream in the men's room until his stress was relieved. However, the employee never availed himself of this accommodation and on one occasion, after receiving a direct order from his supervisor, "phased out" and then proceeded to assault the supervisor until restrained by other employees. The attack was so severe that the supervisor was sent to the hospital.

The court ruled that the plaintiff was not a "qualified handicap person" because no amount of accommodation would allow the employee to perform the essential functions of his job without endangering the health and safety of other employees. The court rejected the employee's argument that the company should have provided him with a work environment that was free of stress-producing situations.

Judicial decisions have upheld the rights of employers to discharge employees with mental disabilities where their disability renders them unable to perform their job duties or results in erratic behavior that poses a serious threat to other employees. However, employers should not automatically assume that erratic behavior will lead to workplace violence. Discharging a mentally infirm individual without a reasonable pattern of hostile, bizarre, or threatening behavior can lead to potential liability under the ADA.

ADA and obesity

In recent years, the issue of weight restrictions, specifically denial of employment because of obesity, has been challenged as discrimination on the basis of a disability. Is obesity a disability, an immutable condition that cannot be controlled, and thus protected under the ADA, or is it a condition resulting from voluntary action? The ADA does not specifically address the issue of obesity as a covered disability. The EEOC's *Technical Assistance Manual* states, however, that weight that is within a "normal" range and not the result of a physiological disorder is not a disability, thus implying that obesity that *is* a result of a physiological disorder may be a covered disability. If obesity is found to be a disability, employers would not only be prohibited from discriminating on the basis of an individual's weight, but would also be required to provide reasonable accommodations to assist the individual in performing the essential functions of the position. Courts interpreting state and federal antidiscrimination laws are split as to whether obesity is a protected disability.

A California jury awarded $1 million to a morbidly obese man who had brought suit alleging that he had been fired because of his weight. The man brought suit under California's disability discrimination law. The verdict was based on a theory that obesity is covered under California's disability discrimination law if the individual can demonstrate that there is a "physiological, systemic basis for the condition." In this case, the plaintiff was required to prove that his obesity was the result of a physiological condition that interfered with a major life function such as walking, standing, or sitting. The limitations on his ability to function were evident in the courtroom as he rose and sat down with great difficulty.

The plaintiff weighed about 250 pounds when he was hired, but by the time he was fired, he weighed more than 400 pounds. The plaintiff used an expert witness to establish a physiological basis for his condition. The expert witness testified that 80 percent of obesity is physiological and 20 percent is environmental. Although the company claimed the employee's discharge was for cause, the plaintiff was able to present evidence of disparaging comments about his weight. He also alleged that the company had denied his requests for assistance with a weight loss program despite the fact that the company had programs for employees with drug and alcohol addictions.

In another decision, the federal District Court for the District of Rhode Island concluded that obesity may be a disorder qualifying as a disability to the extent that it is caused by systemic or metabolic factors and constitutes an immutable condition that cannot be controlled, but it would not be a handicap to the extent that it was a condition resulting from voluntary action or inaction. This decision is illustrative of how the EEOC will apply the ADA to obesity because when the case was appealed to the U.S. Court of Appeals for the First Circuit, the EEOC filed an amicus brief with the court arguing that morbid obesity of sufficient duration and with a significant impact on major life activities can constitute a disability and should not be rejected as a covered disability simply because it was a product of the voluntary actions of the individual or because it was not an immutable condition. The EEOC further argued that morbid obesity is similar to other disabilities, such as alcoholism, diabetes, emphysema resulting from smoking, and heart disease resulting from diet and smoking, all of which result from or are exacerbated by voluntary conduct.

Although the EEOC's standard is very liberal in allowing coverage for all types of obesity, no matter what the cause, such a standard would, in fact, be easier for employers to apply. Under the standard that finds that obesity is a disability only if it is caused by a physiological disorder, employers are left with the dilemma of trying to determine the cause of a weight problem. Employers who conclude that an employee's weight problem is not attributed to a physiological disorder without adequate medical authority to support their decision would certainly be challenged by plaintiffs with medical diagnoses supporting their contention that they did not voluntarily eat themselves into an obese condition. Ultimately, the determination as to discrimination might depend on which party retained the most convincing expert medical witness.

....

AIDS and the ADA

There is no question that AIDS is a covered disability under the ADA. And, although the decisions are not entirely in agreement, many courts have also said that an individual who is infected with the virus that causes AIDS—is HIV-positive—but who is also asymptomatic for AIDS, is also protected from discrimination under the Act. Despite the considerable precedent that exists for concluding that HIV-positive status is a covered disability, employers continue to violate the ADA by discriminating against employees on this basis.

For example, in December 1996, a federal jury in New York found that an HIV-positive bartender was fired in violation of his rights under the ADA and the New York Human Rights Law. The jury awarded the bartender more than $1.4 million. In this case, the plaintiff had alleged that supervisors at the hotel where he worked took unwarranted disciplinary action against him after they learned he was HIV-positive. The hotel claims the plaintiff was discharged for refusing to open the bar's back gate for entry by employees of the hotel restaurant, for leaving his replacement alone, and for displaying a negative and uncooperative attitude to hotel staff.

The bottom line for employers when dealing with an HIV-positive employee is to treat the individual like any other disabled employee. If the employee can do the essential functions of the position without creating a direct threat to himself or others, he or she must be retained. If the employee is not a qualified disabled employee, he or she can be discharged. Employers should not make unwarranted assumptions about the infectious status of HIV-positive employees. In most cases, the risk of transmission to other individuals is very remote. Even in cases where HIV-positive health care employees are engaged in direct patient care duties, the courts have said that "universal precautions," such as the use of gloves and other protective protocol, would be sufficient to safeguard against the risk of transmission.

ADA preparation steps

The financial risks of not doing anything to insulate an organization from potential liability under the ADA are substantial. The remedies provided by the ADA include backpay, reinstatement, or injunctive relief along with compensatory and punitive damages. Thus, it makes little sense to ignore the ADA and think it will never affect your work force.

....

At a minimum, the following steps should be taken to avoid difficulties with the ADA:

+ **Review your company's application form.** Remove any questions regarding an applicant's physical or mental condition that cannot be shown to be directly related to the job that the applicant seeks.

+ **Draft or review job descriptions.** List *all* job functions that are essential to the position. Add "cooperation or courteous interaction with other employees" as an essential function in all job descriptions.

+ **Review hiring procedures to determine accessibility for the disabled.** Is the location where applicants apply, interview, and/or are tested wheelchair accessible? Are forms, tests, etc., available in a format that is accessible to the blind, the hearing impaired, and other disabled individuals?

+ **Review tests.** Do results accurately reflect job-related skills or aptitude rather than the disabilities of the applicant or employee?

+ **Review procedures for medical examinations.** Are preemployment examinations given only after a conditional offer of employment?

+ **Review confidentiality of medical information.** Access to medical information on employees or applicants must be restricted.

+ **Develop centralized procedures for employment decision-making.** Develop a set procedure for determining when an accommodation is necessary, what accommodations are possible, and whether any of the possible accommodations are reasonable. Ensure that each factor in the process is documented.

+ **Review physical and mental standards for jobs.** Are these standards really necessary for job performance?

+ **Ensure that disabled applicants or employees seeking promotion are not denied a job because of possible risk of future injury.** There must be "significant risk" of "substantial harm" that cannot be eliminated by reasonable accommodation.

- **Secure a source of medical evaluation and expertise.** Medical evidence will be required to support employment decisions. Make sure your medical expert is informed as to the requirements of the job and is prepared to stand by his or her opinion.

- **Review social and recreational activities.** Are they accessible to all disabled employees?

- **Secure the ADA poster.** The federal equal employment poster should be in an accessible location.

- **Train interviewers.** Make sure job interviewers know what questions they can and cannot ask job applicants.

- **Train supervisors.** Make sure supervisors understand the duty to accommodate employees with disabilities and what that duty entails.

Chapter 7

Never Assume an Employee Is Exempt

Anne is a secretary for a large Baltimore law firm. She is paid on an hourly basis and she receives her paycheck weekly. Because the firm is extremely busy with various kinds of litigation, Anne regularly works 50 to 55 hours a week. The firm understands its obligation to compensate Anne for working more than 40 hours in a week, but in lieu of cash payment, she is asked to take hours off. There is no restriction with respect to when Anne can take the paid time off or "comp" time as long as the work of the firm gets done. The firm is very accurate in its calculation of Anne's accrued "comp" time and she is awarded one hour of "comp" time for each hour she works over 40.

Anne complained to the managing partner of the law firm regarding its "comp" time pay practice. She pointed out that federal law requires hours worked over 40 to be compensated at a time-and-a-half rate, and thus she claimed that she should be awarded one and a half hours of "comp" time for every hour she worked over 40. The managing partner agreed and immediately adjusted Anne's accrual rate for overtime purposes. Under the new policy, Anne may use her "comp" time whenever she desired.

Barry, Anne's husband, is a limousine driver for a large government contractor. He and several other individuals are employed by the company to drive busy executives and clients to meetings, government hearings, or the airport. Barry gets paid on a biweekly basis. Because Barry's hours fluctuate from week to week, the company has made each of the limousine drivers sign a written agreement by which they promise to work no more than 75 hours in a payroll period. Barry has some flexibility to schedule when he works, but if he works 50 hours in week one of the payroll period, he is allowed to be scheduled for only 25 hours of work in week two of the payroll period. The company has used this contractual pay practice with great success, having never paid an hour of overtime to any driver.

The company's need for drivers fluctuates quite a bit—executives are asked to request a driver ahead of time, but sometimes they forget to make the necessary arrangement with the dispatcher. Also, when meetings downtown are postponed or canceled, the driver is not needed. As a result, the drivers often end up sitting around at the garage waiting for another assignment. The company responded to this problem by issuing pagers to the drivers and sending them home during slack periods to wait for a call from the dispatcher regarding their next assignment. In this way, the company also avoided the cost of unnecessary overtime hours. Barry received no pay when he was sent home.

Barry always had his doubts about the legality of the "contract" he was forced to sign with his employer. When his wife Anne came home and bragged about her success in convincing her boss that she should accrue "comp" time at a time-and-a-half rate, Barry decided he would also go in to work and demand that he be paid overtime whenever he worked more than 40 hours in a week. The next day, when Barry raised the issue with his boss, he was told to "stop making trouble and get back to work." Several days later, when Barry tried to convince several of the other limousine drivers that they were being cheated and that they should file a complaint with the Department of Labor, Barry's boss fired him, calling Barry a "loud mouthed S.O.B." The written termination form listed "poor driving record" as the reason for Barry's discharge.

Several weeks later, however, management at Barry's company announced a new pay practice for drivers. They would no longer be required to sign a contract. Instead, they would be paid $600 a week on a biweekly basis at the rate of $300 a week for a 40-hour work week. If any driver worked more than 40 hours in the first week of the payroll period, the company accountant was to figure out how much overtime was owed the driver and then notify the driver's supervisor as to the maximum amount of hours the driver would be allowed to work in the second week of the pay period to ensure that the driver would make no more than $600 in the payroll period.

Barry could not find another job right away. But he was paid some vacation time when he was discharged and he decided to relax for a couple of weeks at the beach. Anne couldn't go with him because the law firm was too busy. Despite the assurances from her boss that she could use her accrued comp time whenever she wants, she was told that taking some time off to be with her husband would be impossible.

After Barry got back, he decided to call the Department of Labor and report what happened. All he got was a recording and he was directed to leave his phone number and someone would get back to him. It took a few days but Barry was finally able to talk to Mr. Pickering, a wage/hour specialist for the DOL. He seemed interested in Barry's story and took a written statement. However, Barry didn't tell the investigator about his poor driving record.

After about 10 days, Mr. Pickering called the Human Resources department at Barry's company and made an appointment to see the Human Resources manager, Ms. Applewright, at the corporate offices. When Mr. Pickering arrived at the company's Bethesda location, he was ushered right in to see Ms. Applewright. She was very helpful and had Barry's personnel file available for his review. Mr. Pickering was surprised to see that Barry had a very poor driving record, and Ms. Applewright assured him that Barry's numerous accidents, albeit minor "fender-benders," were the reason for his discharge and not his complaint about the 75-hour contract. Ms. Applewright told Mr. Pickering that the company had recently revised its pay practice with regard to the drivers and explained in detail the differences between the old and new compensation plans. Mr. Pickering listened carefully, then told Ms. Applewright that he believed the prior plan for compensating drivers was in violation of the Fair Labor Standards Act. He asked to see all time records for drivers for the previous three years.

Ms. Applewright immediately complied with Mr. Pickering's request and placed him in an office near the time clock to review the records. She told him, "I really don't think you'll find much overtime—we send the drivers home when there isn't much to do. Then we call them at home if we get a driving assignment for them." "Do they have to wait by the phone?" asked Mr. Pickering. "Well, they used to," said Ms. Applewright, "but now they carry a pager." "When were the pagers issued?" asked Mr. Pickering. "Oh, about nine months ago," said Ms. Applewright. "I think I'm going to need to talk to each of the drivers, Ms. Applewright," said Mr. Pickering. "Can you arrange that for me?" Ms. Applewright said she would be happy to oblige.

At the end of the day, Mr. Pickering went to see Ms. Applewright. He told her that he was not able to complete his investigation but he believed that the company might owe overtime to a number of drivers. He explained, "I think your current pay plan for drivers is legal but, as I told you, your old plan did not properly compensate drivers for overtime on a workweek basis." Ms. Applewright interrupted, "But, Mr. Pickering, I can't believe they worked that many hours." "That may be true," said Mr. Pickering, "if you only count recorded hours of work. The problem is that I think the on-call time before the drivers were given pagers was compensable time. If you add that in, I think you will find that they worked considerable overtime hours. I won't know for sure, however, until I talk to all the drivers. I'll get back to you."

About two weeks later, Mr. Pickering called to tell Ms. Applewright that he had completed the computation of wage liability for the company's drivers. He said he would meet with her in person to discuss his findings but he said that the company owed various drivers a total of $39,307 for uncompensated hours of work and overtime pay. Ms. Applewright was flabbergasted and said, "I think I better talk to my boss, Mr. Pickering. I am going to have to call you back." As he put down the phone, Mr. Pickering realized he was not going to get the same level of cooperation from Ms. Applewright any more.

The DOL investigator is not your friend

There are many friendly, personable investigators working for the Department of Labor (DOL). They are always quite courteous, and often downright engaging, when they call on employers to do a wage/hour investigation. Time and time again, I am called by clients after they have allowed a wage/hour specialist to review their payroll records. I am frequently told, "He seemed like such a nice young man," or "She said she didn't think we had a lot of problems." Only later do they receive a back-pay computation that absolutely "floors" them.

The basic rule to remember when dealing with a DOL investigator is: *"These people are not your friends."* Ask them to wait if they show up uninvited at your office. Call your employment attorney. Do not automatically turn over all your payroll records or allow them to peruse time cards at their discretion. Do not sit there and answer question after question about compensation practices. Talk to your attorney first. The fictitious example above is not atypical of what can happen during a DOL investigation. What started out as a simple inquiry into Barry's retaliation claim resulted in considerably more wage/hour liability for the company. It also points out another principle of wage/hour liability: If you don't handle one complaint, the government may end up auditing your entire workforce for proper wage/hour compliance.

It is illegal under the Fair Labor Standards Act (FLSA) to fire an employee simply because he or she has asserted his or her rights under the Act. Barry's poor driving record, however, may have provided the company with a defense to his claims. The payroll practice implemented by the company in response to Barry's complaint appears to be a legal "time-off" plan because the employer was actually compensating the drivers at an overtime rate for hours worked over 40 in the first work-week. Of course, the issue may be complicated by the potential "on-call" time liability, but we'll deal with that issue later in this chapter.

The "time-off" plan differs from the illegal contractual agreement used by the company before Barry complained, because during that time period, the drivers were not compensated on an overtime basis for hours over 40 in a week. The company was operating under an erroneous as-sumption that as long as the employees worked less than 80 hours in the two-week payroll period, no overtime need be paid. Overtime must be calculated on the basis of a single workweek, and employers are forbid-den from averaging hours over two or more workweeks in order to avoid paying overtime.

The legality of "comp" time

In the introductory narrative, the law firm where Anne works is vio-lating the Fair Labor Standards Act (FLSA) by not paying Anne each payroll period for the overtime she has earned. There is no such thing as "comp" time for nonexempt employees working for private-sector employ-ers. An employer may not "credit" an employee with compensatory time off (even at a time-and-a-half rate) for overtime hours. It does not matter that Anne may have agreed to the "comp" time arrangement. Employees cannot waive their rights under the FLSA, and the practice is illegal.

Because many employees would like the option of taking time off in-stead of overtime pay, legislation has been introduced in Congress that would make "comp" time legal. The bill, titled the "Working Families Flexibility Act," cleared the House of Representatives in 1996 but got stalled in the Senate. In 1997, Republican leaders in the House and Sen-ate again said they would give "comp" time legislation high priority. In January 1997, a group of House Republican women endorsed the "comp" time bill as "family friendly" legislation. Despite this expressed support, "comp" time legislation continues to face stiff opposition from union lead-ers who view such legislation as an attack on the 40-hour workweek.

"Comp" time may soon be a permitted pay practice under federal law. But until such legislation is signed into law, employers should not ask employees to accept time off with pay as an alternative to the regular payment of overtime. There are still many issues to be resolved before "comp" time becomes a reality for private sector employees, not the least of which is who will determine when "comp" time can be used.

This chapter explores the most frequent headaches for employers in dealing with the maze that is federal and state wage/hour regulation. As many employers have found out, compliance with wage/hour law is not easy. Often, it is better to resolve an individual complaint by making a small payment to the employee, even though you may be totally correct in your legal position, rather than risk a full-scale audit by wage/hour investigators.

Keeping a lid on wage liability

At first glance, compensation issues seem fairly straightforward. It would seem reasonable to begin the payment of wages when an employee actually starts work and to cease any accumulated wage calculation when an employee stops work. Similarly, it seems fair to deny compensation when an employee is eating lunch. Employers must be cautious, however, when denying or limiting compensation to employees. The intricacies of federal wage and hour law may authorize compensation in unexpected situations.

For example, employers often assume that certain activities in preparation for work are not compensable. Similarly, an employee working at her desk during lunch doesn't have to be paid, does she? What about the employee who cleans up his work area after his allotted shift. There is no need to pay him for this time, right? Finally, if there is a short training meeting on Saturdays, should employees really expect to be paid for their attendance at such meetings? Employers are often surprised to learn that, depending on the facts of any particular situation, employees may be entitled to compensation for such activities pursuant to regulations construing the Fair Labor Standards Act.

What is compensable time?

The FLSA mandates that an employer pay employees for all time that it "suffer[s] or permit[s an employee] to work." Therefore, unrequested work that an employer allows to occur must be included in hours worked. Even if an employer has a policy that prohibits overtime work unless authorized, the employer may still be required to pay employees who work overtime without permission. Often, the only legal recourse the employer has for curbing such unauthorized overtime is to discipline the employee.

The FLSA also requires that the time spent by employees in activities before or after their regular work day be counted as time worked if the activities are "an integral and indispensable part of the employees' principal activities." Whether activities are "an integral and indispensable part of the employees' principal activities" is a fact-specific determination.

Under normal conditions, time spent by employees before or after their regular workday in changing clothes, washing, or showering is not compensable. Time spent on these activities is compensable, however, if the activity is required by law, by an employer's rules, or by the nature of the duties. Thus, if an employer requires employees to wear a specific uniform while working but does not allow employees to wear the uniform off-site, the time the employees spend changing from street clothes to the uniform would be compensable.

Training time

An employer need not compensate employees for the time they spend attending lectures, meetings, and training programs that are held outside working hours as long as the following conditions are met: 1) Attendance is voluntary; 2) the course, lecture, or meeting is not directly related to the employee's job; and 3) the employees do no productive work during the meetings or training.

This standard is applied narrowly, however. If the training sessions are not truly voluntary, that is, if nonattendance has an adverse effect upon employment status, compensation for attendance would be required. Similarly, if the training is designed to make employees more effective in their current jobs and not to teach different job skills, the time spent in training would be considered compensable.

Meal periods

Although the FLSA does not require rest or meal periods, the Act has been interpreted to require employers to treat rest periods of short duration (usually 20 minutes or shorter) as hours worked or compensable time. On the other hand, meal periods of greater duration during which an employee is totally relieved of duties are not considered work time under the FLSA.

To constitute a *bona fide* meal period, three conditions are examined: 1) It must be a period set aside for a regular meal and must be long enough to allow the employee to use it for that purpose; 2) it must occur at a scheduled hour or within a specified period at a time of day which, in the light of the employee's working hours, is suitable for a normal meal period; and 3) it must be an uninterrupted period during which the employee has no duties whatever to perform. If meal periods are frequently interrupted by calls to duty, the entire meal period must be counted as hours worked. Similarly, the employee who is allowed to eat lunch at her desk while she continues to perform work, even in a limited manner, must be compensated for the lunch period.

A startling case involving compensation for a lunch period was decided on July 31, 1997, when the Second Circuit Court of Appeals decided that certain craft workers who were restricted to their job site during their lunch period as a security presence for certain valuable company equipment at the site were entitled to compensation for the 30-minute lunch period. In this case, the court awarded the employees more than $14.5 million dollars in back pay and liquidated damages.

The employer in this case provides telephone services to consumers throughout the state of Connecticut. The company employed certain "outside craft workers" to perform such tasks as installing and replacing telephone poles and cables, splicing cable, working on lines between telephone poles, and other maintenance work. In performing their duties, these outside craft workers used valuable company equipment that included trucks, fresh air ventilation systems, water pumps, gas testing and fiber optic devices, cable and wire, and various handheld tools. It was their responsibility to maintain this equipment and protect it from theft.

The employees were allowed 30 minutes for lunch during which time they were expected to stay at the job site and secure the area and the equipment. Otherwise, the employees engaged in passive activity at the site, eating their lunches in the truck or near a manhole, trench, or telephone pole. The employer did not compensate the employees for this lunch period and it was not counted for the purpose of calculating overtime hours. The court concluded that the employer should have compensated the employees for this time, because by remaining at the job site, the employees were performing duties that were "predominantly for the benefit of the employer." In addition, the court said this time should be compensated at an overtime rate because it pushed the employees' total hours to more than 40 in a week.

The company argued that the time should not be compensable, because the outside craft employees were free to enjoy their lunch without interruption—that the services they were performing for the company were "entirely passive." The court rejected this argument, emphasizing the importance of the security function being provided to the employer. The court said that if the employees were not required to stay at the job site, the employer would have been required to pay others to perform the service for the employer. In effect, the court said, the employer "was receiving free labor."

On-call pay

Some employers require employees in certain positions to remain at their homes in order to be available to do work if called. These "on-call" hours, as they are called, may be noncompensable if the employees are free to engage in any personal activity they desire, while they remain available for work if called.

According to federal regulations, an employee who is required to remain on call on the employer's premises or close enough that he or she cannot use the time effectively for his or her own purposes, is working while "on call." An employee who is not required to remain on the employer's premises but is merely required to leave word at his or her home or with company officials where he or she may be reached is not working while on call. Time spent at home on call may or may not be compensable, depending on whether the restrictions placed on the employee preclude using the time for personal pursuits.

In applying this standard, the U.S. Supreme Court has said that the test is whether the time is spent predominately for the employer's benefit or for the employee's benefit. The issue is always a question of fact to be resolved by the trial court. For example, in a case out of Kansas, on-call time for fire fighters was deemed to be compensable working time. The fire fighters were required to report to a call-back within 20 minutes and answer the call-back or be subject to discipline. The number of call-backs ranged from zero to 13 and averaged three to five every 24-hour period. The court also considered significant the fact that the fire fighters had difficulty trading on-call shifts and experienced difficulty in obtaining or maintaining secondary employment.

Likewise, a federal district court granted summary judgment to the plaintiff in *O'Brian v. DeKalb-Clinton Ambulance*, because a five-minute response time requirement was considered too restrictive to allow the employee to use the on-call time for his or her own benefit. In this case, the calls averaged only one per 24-hour shift. Although there was evidence that the employee could run errands and do routine chores while on call, the court considered the time compensable because the five minute restriction interfered with the employee's ability to leave the city limits.

On the other hand, where the restrictions are not onerous and the calls are infrequent, courts have ruled that on-call time is noncompensable. For example, an ambulance service telephone dispatcher who was on duty at home from 5 p.m. to 8 a.m. five nights per week was not considered to be working all the hours during the period. According to the Fifth Circuit Court of Appeals, the employee answered a "small number" of calls per night and could use the on-call time effectively for herself—she visited friends, entertained guests, slept, watched TV, did laundry, and baby-sat. In addition, she could leave her house if she wanted and forward her calls to where she was visiting.

Generally, on-call issues can be handled in a manner that will avoid claims for compensable time. For example, if an employee is frequently called to work while on-call, there is very little you can do to avoid compensating the employee for the on-call period. Where the call-backs are infrequent, however, the compensation issue can be avoided by providing a pager to the employee or allowing the employee to call in with a forwarding number when he or she is away from home while on-call. In this way, the employer can argue that the employee is free to use the time predominantly for his or her own benefit. In such a case, the time should not be construed to be compensable time.

Exempt employees

Wage and hour protections for employees can be a very dry subject. There are many CEOs who could care less about the "salary basis" requirement for exempt status. They just want to group all their "white collar" employees into FLSA exempt categories and not have to worry about overtime pay for these employees. The exempt classifications under the Fair Labor Standards Act are never as inclusive as management thinks they are. You cannot simply label a secretary as an "administrative assistant" and expect to be relieved of any obligation to pay him or her overtime if all the employee does is type the supervisor's letters.

The "salary basis" test

The FLSA requires that employees be paid at least the minimum wage for all hours worked and time and a half for all hours worked over 40 in a workweek. Certain employees are "exempt" from the overtime requirements and there are also industry-specific exemptions. The most widely used exemptions are applied to employees who are classified as "executive," "administrative," or "professional." To be classified as exempt, the employee must perform certain types of job duties and be paid on a "salary basis." The Department of Labor's regulations state that an employee will be considered to be paid on a "salary basis" "so long as the employee receives on a regular basis a predetermined amount that is not subject to reduction because of variations in the quantity or quality of the work performed." Subject to the exceptions discussed below, the employee must receive his or her full salary for any week in which the employee performs any work without regard to the number of days or hours worked.

The first exception from this rule provides that an employee need not be paid for any workweek in which the employee performs no work. Second, deductions may be made from an employee's salary when the employee is absent from work for a day or more for personal reasons, other than sickness or accident. Thus, if an employee is absent for a day or more to handle personal affairs, deductions may be made from the employee's salary for the days of work that are missed.

Also, deductions may be made from an exempt employee's salary for a day or more for absences occasioned by sickness or disability if the deduction is made in accordance with a *bona fide* plan, policy, or practice of providing compensation for such absences. If an employer has a sick leave or disability policy, an employee need not be paid his or her salary for days for which the employee receives compensation for leave under the policy. Moreover, deductions may be made for absences of a day or more because of sickness or disability even before the employee is covered under the policy or after the employee has exhausted the employee's leave allowance under the policy.

As previously noted, the consequences of misapplying these rules can be severe. Not only will docking an exempt employee entitle that employee to overtime compensation, the fact that all exempt employees are subject to a docking policy may convert those employees into nonexempt employees and require the payment of overtime compensation. For example, in some cases, the DOL has asserted that such employees are entitled to overtime compensation for the entire period they have worked under the policy, going back as far as three years. Not surprisingly, an employer's monetary liability for violating this rule can be staggering.

Despite the "salary basis" requirement in federal regulations, it continues to be a common practice among many employers to withhold pay or "dock" exempt employees for time missed from work for less than a day. This practice, however, has come under close scrutiny by the Department of Labor and may subject employers to significant monetary liability. Employers should also remember that uncompensated time for salaried employees that is later ruled to be work time is also work time for purposes of calculating overtime. Thus, an employer may end up paying wages owed to employees at a time and a half rate. Employers must make sure their wage and hour practice with respect to the "salary basis" requirement is in compliance with the law. Otherwise, a denial of overtime wages under a mistaken assumption that an employee is exempt can give rise to extraordinary liability.

"White collar" exemptions—the"duties" test

As mentioned, the minimum wage and overtime pay provisions of the FLSA do not apply to "any employee in a *bona fide* executive, administrative, or professional capacity." In addition to paying these employees on a "salary basis," an individual will not be exempt unless she meets the "duties" requirement of the exemption that is claimed by the employer. Determining whether an employee is exempt from the overtime requirement of the FLSA depends solely on the particular duties of the individual in question, not the job title, job description, or the nature of the employer's business.

It is well settled that any exemption from the FLSA's protection is to be narrowly construed against the employer asserting it. Accordingly, the application of an exemption is limited to those circumstances that "plainly and unmistakably come within the statute's terms and spirit." Thus, it is the employer's burden to prove affirmatively that its employees come within the exemption.

Executive employees

In order to be exempt in the executive category, the employee must be paid on a salary basis of not less than $155 per week and must meet all the following requirements: 1) The employee's primary duty is management of the company or a department or subdivision of the company, 2) the employee must customarily and regularly direct the work of two or more other employees, 3) the employee must have authority to hire or fire other employees or to make recommendations as to hiring, firing, advancement, promotion, or change of status of employees, 4) the employee must customarily and regularly exercise discretionary powers, and 5) the employee must not devote more than 20 percent of the hours worked in any one workweek to activities that are not directly and closely related to the performance of exempt work.

If the employee is paid on a salary basis of at least $250 per week, the employee will qualify for the exemption if his or her work meets the following two conditions: 1) The employee's primary duty is management of the company, department, or subdivision; and 2) the employee customarily and regularly directs the work of two or more other employees. This is known as the "short test" for the executive exemption.

Examples of management duties include: interviewing, selecting, and training employees; setting and adjusting employees' rates of pay and hours of work; directing employees' work; maintaining employee production or sales records for use in supervision or control; evaluating employee performance for the purpose of recommending promotions or other changes in status; handling employee complaints and grievances; disciplining employees; planning the work and determining the techniques to be used and the types of material, supplies, machinery, tools, or merchandise to be bought, stocked, and sold for the operation; appropriating the work among the employees; controlling the flow and distribution of materials or merchandise and supplies; providing for the safety of the employees and property.

Furthermore, under either the short or the long test, the amount of time spent on managerial duties, the amount of independent discretion the employee has and the number of employees that are supervised are critical factors in determining whether the employee is, in fact, an exempt executive employee.

Administrative employees

To be considered as an exempt administrative employee, the individual must meet the same salary requirements as that imposed on the executive employee. In addition, the employee must: 1) perform work where the primary duty is office work or nonmanual work that is directly related to management policies or general business operations of the company or the company's customers; 2) customarily and regularly exercise discretion and independent judgment; 3) regularly and directly assist someone employed in an executive or administrative capacity, or perform work under only general supervision that requires special training, experience, or knowledge, or execute special assignments and tasks under only general supervision; 4) not spend more than 20 percent of his or her time each week in work that is not directly and closely related to the performance of the administrative job.

The administrative exemption focuses on the "general business operation of management policies" as distinguished from "production" type activities. This prong of the test limits the exemption to persons who perform work of substantial importance to the management or operation of the business. For example, an insurance claims investigator was not considered to be an administrative employee because the court found that he was involved in the "production" of information, not administration of management policies of the company. In a 1990 decision by the U.S. Court of Appeals for the Fifth Circuit, a television station's general assignment reporters, producers, directors, and assignment editors were held to be nonexempt from the FLSA because they were production workers. Similarly, the Tenth Circuit Court of Appeals has concluded that a microwave system engineer was not an exempt administrative employee. According to the court, the duties and responsibilities of the position, the amount of time involved and the overall importance of the work showed that the primary duty was maintenance and not administrative in nature.

Federal regulations group administrative employees into three basic types: 1) executive or administrative assistants to a proprietor, an executive, or another administrative employee that can include employees with such titles as executive secretary, administrative assistant or assistant manager; 2) staff or functional employees, such as advisory specialists to management and includes employees such as tax, insurance, or sales research experts and investment consultants; and 3) those who perform special assignments that may often be away from the employer's place of business and that might include employees such as lease buyers, field representatives, and location managers.

Regardless of the classification, the employee must "customarily and regularly exercise discretion and independent judgment" in performing these duties. The regulations distinguish work that includes the use of discretion and independent judgment from the mere application of skill or knowledge. Thus, an employee who merely applies her knowledge in following prescribed procedures or determines what procedure to follow, or who determines whether specified standards are met or whether an object falls into one or another of a number of definite grades, classes, or other categories, with or without the use of testing or measuring devices, is not exercising discretion and independent judgment. Consequently, many employees fail to meet the administrative exemption because they are found not to be regularly exercising discretion and independent judgment.

Employees who are involved with the planning, scheduling, and coordination of activities required to develop systems for processing data or to obtain solutions to complex business, scientific, or engineering problems of an employer or an employer's customers may qualify under this exemption. Key punch operators, computer operators, junior programmers, and program trainees generally do not exercise the required discretion and independent judgment to be exempt as administrative employees. The requirement of discretion and independent judgment is not satisfied by, for example, preparing a flow chart or diagram that shows the order in which the computer must perform each operation, preparing instructions to the console operator who runs the computer, running the computer, and debugging a program. For example, a federal district court in Tennessee found that programmer analysts, programmers and members of technical staff who were hired to implement previously designed computer systems for employer's customers were not exempt administrative employees because employees performed work at which they exercised job skills and not discretion and independent judgment.

Professional employees

The exemption for professional employees is one of the more complex of the white-collar exemptions. In order to be exempt as a *bona fide* professional, the employee must be paid on a salary basis of at least $170 per week and meet the following requirements: 1) The employee's primary duty must be to perform work requiring knowledge of an advanced type in a field of science or learning customarily acquired by a prolonged course of specialized intellectual instruction and study; 2) the work must require the consistent exercise of discretion and judgment in its performance; and 3) the work must be predominately intellectual and varied in character; and 4) the employee does not devote more than 20 percent of the hours worked in any one workweek to activities that are not an essential part of the work described above.

A short version of the test may be applied for professional employees who are paid $250 per week or more. To qualify for the exemption under the streamlined or short version of the test, the employee must meet either of the following two conditions: 1) The employee's primary duty must consist of the performance of work requiring knowledge of an advanced type in a field of science or learning, including work that requires the consistent exercise of discretion and judgment; or 2) the employee's primary duty must consist of the performance of work requiring invention, imagination, or talent in a recognized field of artistic endeavor.

The requirement that the "primary duty be to perform work requiring knowledge of an advanced type...customarily acquired by a prolonged course of specialized intellectual instruction and study" is an educational requirement that generally dictates that the knowledge be attained from a course of study undertaken at a four-year college or university. The regulations state that, "generally speaking, the professions that meet the requirements for a prolonged course of specialized intellectual instruction and study include law, medicine, nursing, accounting, actuarial computation, engineering, architecture, teaching, various types of physical, chemical, and biological sciences, including pharmacy and registered or certified medical technology."

In determining professional exemption status, the employee must exercise discretion and judgment in carrying out his or her job assignment. Work that is purely mechanical or routine is not considered professional work. It is the employee's actual work duties that control the exemption. For example, an individual who has an accounting degree but is employed in a job in which the duties are merely bookkeeping and do not require the exercise of independent judgment will not be found to be exempt as a professional.

Government wage specialists who audit personnel classifications almost always give a very narrow reading to the regulations and the available exemptions. For example, the Department of Labor has for years been fairly strict about the four-year college degree requirement for considering someone to be an exempt professional employee. Thus, regardless of the years of technical training or experience that an employee possesses, he must be classified as nonexempt. Employers working in the computer industry were perhaps hardest hit by the four-year degree requirement for an exemption.

The computer personnel exemption

In 1990, the FLSA was amended to permit computer systems analysts, computer programmers, software engineers, and other "similarly skilled" professional workers to qualify as exempt employees regardless of the fact that they did not possess a four year degree or that they were being paid on an hourly basis. To qualify for the exemption employees must receive an hourly rate that exceeds six and a half times the minimum wage. Thus, only employees making almost $28.00 an hour will be exempt under this exemption.

In addition to the wage requirement, there is also a duties test. To qualify for this computer-related exemption, federal regulations provide that an employee's primary duties must consist of one or more of the following: 1) The application of systems analysis techniques and procedures, including consulting with users to determine hardware, software, or system functional specifications; 2) the design, development, documentation, analysis, creation, testing, or modification of computer systems or programs, including prototypes, based on and related to user or system design specifications; 3) the design, documentation, testing, creation, or modification of computer programs related to machine operating systems; or 4) a combination of the aforementioned duties, the performance of which requires the same level of skills.

This exemption for highly skilled computer professionals does not include employees engaged in the operation of computers or in the manufacture, repair, or maintenance of computer hardware and related equipment. Also specifically excluded are employees whose work is highly dependent upon or facilitated by the use of computers and computer software programs, such as engineers, drafters, and others skilled in computer-aided design software like CAD/CAM, but are not actually in computer systems analysis and programming occupations.

In 1992, the Department of Labor published its final regulations implementing the 1990 amendment to the Fair Labor Standards Act permitting computer systems analysts, computer programmers, software engineers and other "similarly skilled" professional workers to qualify as employees exempt from the FLSA's overtime requirements. After numerous public comments, the DOL concluded that the exemption for highly skilled computer professionals is not limited to employees whose pay exceed six-and-a-half times the minimum wage. Instead, under the final rule, highly-skilled computer professionals who are paid on a salary basis are exempt from the FLSA even though they earn less than six-and-a-half times the minimum wage or do not qualify as administrative or executive employees. Only those highly skilled computer professionals who are paid on an hourly basis must earn six-and-a-half times the minimum wage to qualify for the exemption.

Deductions from accrued leave for exempt employees

Some employers have a policy by which accrued leave time is banked in an account for vacation, sick leave, and personal leave. Exempt employees are then asked to use their accrued leave time to cover absences in any amount including increments of less than a day. Some employers even allow employees to run negative leave balances to cover unexpected absences.

All courts and the Department of Labor hold that deductions from an exempt employee's salary for absences of less than a day destroy the exempt status of the employee. They do not agree, however, as to whether leave policies that require exempt employees to use leave time in increments of less than a day invalidate an employee's exempt status. The DOL has stated that such a leave policy would not destroy exempt status. In a July 1987 Letter Ruling, the DOL stated, "Generally, deductions for absences of less than a day are not permitted under the regulations for any reason. However, an employer may require an employee to substitute paid leave for such absences without losing the exemption."

Subsequently, the U.S. Court of Appeals for the Fourth Circuit ruled that a policy of docking leave or accrued compensatory time for absences of less than an entire day does not defeat the salary status of exempt employees. In *Firefighters Local 2131 v. Alexandria*, the Court of Appeals said, "While personal leave, sick leave, and/or compensatory time may be part of an employee's compensation package, it does not constitute salary." In 1993, in *McDonnell v. Omaha*, the Eighth Circuit Court of Appeals also adopted this standard.

Other courts have not adopted the reasoning of the Fourth and Eighth Circuits but have found that deductions in leave time for amounts of less than a day destroy the exempt status of an employee, as would a deduction in salary. For example, in *SEIU Local 102 v. County of San Diego*, the District Court for the Southern District of California stated, "Docking an employee's leave time for absences from work is as contrary to the notion of salary status as the docking of base pay. In both instances, the employee's compensation is reduced as a direct consequence of the quantity of hours worked. Such a reduction is entirely inconsistent with salaried status."

It is important to note, however, that even courts that allow the docking of leave time for absences of less than a day find that a violation occurs if the salary is reduced as a result of an employee exceeding accrued leave time. The U.S. District Court for the Eastern District of Virginia held that a policy by which the employer docked an employee's salary for absences of less than a day when the employee had exhausted all accumulated leave balances violate the FLSA. Because the employer's action resulted in a direct deduction in wages, the court held that the company had violated the FLSA. Whether the results of this case would have been different if the excess leave time was charged to a negative leave account and later deducted from the accumulated leave is uncertain.

In light of some courts' holdings that leave time does not constitute salary and the Wage-Hour Administrator's similar interpretation of its regulations, employers who have a policy requiring the use of leave time to cover absences of less than a day may be able to successfully argue that the policy does not violate the "salary basis" provision of the FLSA because it does not reduce salary, only leave time. As explained above, however, the decisions are in conflict on this issue. Thus, continuation of a leave procedure for exempt employees that is applied to absences of less than a day is not without risk.

On the other hand, based on current case law, any accrual of negative leave time as a permitted component of an employer's leave policy may be problematic. As long as the employer charges excessive leave time against future leave time and does not reduce earnings, an argument can be made that the employee's salary is not subject to any reduction in salary, and therefore, the policy does not violate the FLSA. Under this type of policy, however, if an employee is terminated and is in negative leave time status, the employer would not be able to recover money from the employee's final paycheck for this advanced leave time.

Overtime compensation for exempt employees

Sometimes employers want to provide additional compensation to exempt employees for working long hours even though they have no legal obligation to make such payments. Employers may have legitimate concerns regarding the legality under federal wage and hour law of paying exempt employees extra compensation for overtime work. In particular, employers are concerned that payments to otherwise exempt employees at a straight time hourly rate for hours after 40 in a week will destroy the exemption because such employees would no longer be paid on a "salary basis" as that term is defined in the regulations.

An aggressive legal approach to an employer's desire to provide extra compensation to hard-working exempt employees favors an interpretation of federal law that would conclude that extra compensation to exempt employees for hours worked over 40 in a week will not destroy the exempt status of these employees as long as the other requirements of the salary basis test are met. Although there are certain court decisions that have questioned whether overtime payments are consistent with the salary basis test, most courts and the Department of Labor reject this latter interpretation of the salary basis test.

The Department of Labor has rejected any argument that additions to an exempt employee's salary will destroy the exemption. Federal regulations specifically state that "additional compensation besides the [employee's regular] salary is not inconsistent with the salary basis of payment." The DOL is even more specific on this issue in its *Wage and Hour Division Field Operation Handbook*, which states: "Extra compensation may be paid for overtime to an exempt employee on any basis. The overtime payment need not be at time and one-half, but may be at straight time, or flat sum, or on any other basis."

A number of federal courts have held that overtime that is calculated on an hourly basis will not defeat the exemption. For example, in *District of Columbia Nurses' Assn. v. District of Columbia,* the federal district court for the District of Columbia ruled that additional pay for hours worked in excess of standard workweek did not mean nurses were paid on an hourly basis. In *Hartman v. Arlington County, Va.,* a federal district court in Virginia said that payment to the plaintiff of additional pay at an hourly rate for each hour worked beyond the regular schedule was held to be expressly permitted by the federal regulations and did not defeat the executive exemption.

Although there are decisions that are in conflict with the foregoing decisions, the argument that extra compensation for exempt employees should not destroy the exemption is the more persuasive interpretation of the FLSA. Admittedly, the "safest" and most conservative legal advice would be to advise employers not to pay such overtime compensation to exempt employees. Overtime compensation for exempt employees does enhance productivity, however, and provides a morale boost for these employees too. An employer who is apprehensive about the conflicting decisions in this area could give additional compensation to exempt employees for working more than 40 hours a week by paying a flat sum regardless of the actual hours worked. Although such a policy change is not legally mandated, it might reduce the risk of a challenge to the exempt status of employees receiving this money. Employers could also pay this additional compensation in a separate check so that the regular salary of employees would not reflect a variation from week to week. Again, although such changes are probably not necessary, it is understandable that employers knowledgeable about the "salary basis" requirement for exempt employees become concerned when exempt employees have a portion of their earnings calculated using an hourly rate.

Calculating overtime for nonexempt employees

The Fair Labor Standards Act requires employees to pay overtime to any employee who works more than 40 hours in a week, unless the employee comes within one of the exemptions discussed above. Although some states may require overtime after eight hours in a day, or even double-time pay in certain situations, most states follow the FLSA standard of requiring payment at one-and-one-half times the employee's "regular rate" for hours worked over 40 in a week.

The employee's "regular rate" for overtime purposes can be simply the hourly rate assigned to the employee by the employer. If employees are paid by piece rate, commission or any combination of hourly compensation, piece rate and commission, the regular rate is usually determined by dividing the total compensation for the week by the total hours ultimately worked by the employee. As explained above, overtime is calculated on a workweek basis and, except for a special 14-day overtime provision for hospitals and residential care facilities, employers may not average the number of hours worked over a two-week payroll period to avoid their obligation to pay overtime under the Act.

When calculating a regular rate for overtime purposes, it is important to remember that extra compensation in the form of bonuses, prizes, or other monetary awards, if they have some relation to the employee's "quality, quantity, or efficiency of work," must be included in the regular rate. Therefore, the regulations provide that money paid as bonuses for "cooperation, courtesy, efficiency, highest production, best attendance, best quality of work, greatest number of overtime hours worked, etc." must be allocated over the period it was earned and added to the regular rate for that period.

Gifts, discretionary bonuses, and wages

The federal Wage and Hour Division considers bonuses as remuneration for employment and, as such, must be included in an employee's regular rate. It is generally true that regularly paid bonuses will be considered wages and will be included in calculating the regular rate for overtime purposes. Any type of "incentive bonus," such as production bonus, shift premium, length-of-service bonus, or attendance bonus also falls within this category. Certain payments to employees, however, may be viewed as "gifts" and thus will be excluded from the calculation of the regular rate.

Christmas bonus—gift or guarantee?

Many employers have a long-standing tradition of giving their employees Christmas gifts or end-of-year bonuses. Christmas gifts or end-of-year bonuses may be eliminated or changed as long as they are discretionary and there is no express or implied promise, agreement, or contract that the bonus will be issued. With regard to the effect such bonuses have upon an hourly employee's wage rate, as long as the bonus paid at Christmas or on other special occasions is a gift or in the nature of a gift, it may be excluded from the regular rate, even though it is paid with regularity and the employees have an expectation that they will receive it. If, however, the gift is so substantial in amount that the employees consider it part of their regular wages, it must be included in the regular rate that is used to calculate overtime. If measured by hours worked, production, or efficiency, the payment is considered to be geared to wages and hours during the bonus period and is no longer deemed to be "in the nature of a gift."

An employer may also exclude discretionary bonuses, such as amounts paid in recognition of services during a given period, from regular rate computations. For this exclusion to apply, however, two conditions must be met: 1) the employer must retain discretion both as to the fact that payment will be made and as to the amount of the payment until a time quite close to the end of the period for which the bonus is paid; and 2) the payments must not be pursuant to a prior contract, agreement, or promise that causes the employees to have an expectation that the payments will be forthcoming on a regular basis.

If the employer has promised in advance to pay a bonus, the employer will be deemed to have abandoned its discretion with regard to the bonus. For example, if an employer announces in June that it intends to pay its employees a bonus in December, the employer has thereby abandoned its discretion regarding the fact of payment by promising a bonus to its employees. Such a bonus would not be excluded from the regular rate and must be included in calculating overtime rates. Similarly, if bonus payments are substantial in amount and have been paid over a period of years, the bonus no longer is discretionary because employees come to expect it and regard it as part of their regular pay.

Merit or incentive bonus

An incentive bonus that is paid to employees for doing good work would be construed as wages. When employees receive an incentive bonus, the bonus must be taken into account in figuring overtime compensation. If such a bonus is based on a percentage of the employees' total earnings, that is straight salary plus overtime payments, it can be paid without running into overtime complications. The reason is that such a bonus already includes a proper allowance for overtime pay because it is figured as a percentage of the employee's total earnings.

A bonus based on a percentage of an employee's base salary or straight-time earnings will not satisfy the requirements of the FLSA. In such a case, the regular hourly rate would have to be recalculated to include the bonus, and additional overtime would have to be paid on the basis of the new rate.

Calculation of merit bonus in regular rate

When the calculation of the bonus is deferred over a period of time longer than a workweek and the bonus is to be included in the regular rate, the employer need not consider the bonus in computing a regular hourly rate until the amount of the bonus can be determined. When the amount of the bonus can be ascertained, it must be allocated back over the period during which it may be said the bonus was earned. This is most easily done by dividing the amount of the bonus by the number of hours worked by the employee in the period covered by the bonus. Then, for each overtime hour worked by the employee in the period, the employee is given an additional amount equal to one-half the hourly bonus figure.

For example, suppose an employer has established that the annual merit bonus is 5 percent of straight time salary. Suppose also that an employee at the top of the wage progression is earning $20 an hour, or $41,600 per year. The bonus payment for this employee would be $2080. During the year, however, this employee worked a total of 2,500 hours— 2,080 straight time hours and 420 overtime hours.

The procedure used to determine the employee's regular rate of pay is as follows: Divide the amount of the annual bonus by the total number of hours worked by the employee during the year ($2,080 / 2,500) = $.832. The employer is required to pay the employee one-half the amount ($.416) for each overtime hour worked during the year ($.416 x 420) = $174.72.

Compensation plans in lieu of overtime

Employers are often interested in any kind of compensation plan that will avoid the cost of overtime. There are really only two types of payment plans or compensation arrangements permitted by the Act that may be used in lieu of payment of overtime. They are a "time-off" plan and a "Belo" agreement. Neither of these plans is easy to administer nor will they be appropriate when work requirements mandate a large number of hours in excess of 40 in a week in consecutive weeks.

Under a "time-off" plan, an employee is given time off at a rate of one and one-half times the amount of overtime worked within the same pay period. For example, if an employee works two hours of overtime in the first week of a pay period, he or she must be given three hours off during the second week of the pay period. It should be noted that in a two-week pay period, the overtime may be worked either in the first or the second week. However, if the time-off given in the first week for overtime worked in the second week is not sufficient to pay the employee time and one-half off for the overtime worked, the employer must pay the employee the difference in overtime compensation for that pay period.

The "time-off" plan requires that very specific records be maintained by the employer. This compensation arrangement is difficult to administer and an employer risks inadvertently violating the Act if detailed and accurate records are not maintained. Because the recordkeeping involved is an administrative burden for employers and they risk being in violation of the Act if proper records are not kept, most employers do not adopt this plan.

There is a another payment plan recognized by the regulations that permits an employer to pay the same compensation each week to an employee even though the employee works overtime and the hours of work vary from week to week. This arrangement, known as a "Belo" agreement, is set forth in Section 7(f) of the Act. A "Belo" agreement must be made pursuant to a *bona fide* individual contract or pursuant to an agreement as a result of collective bargaining. All employees paid under these agreements must agree to the method of compensation in advance of performing the work.

Under a "Belo" agreement, an employee is paid a constant weekly income even though the actual hours worked will vary from week to week. The hours worked must fluctuate both above and below the 40-hour per week statutory limit. Fluctuations only above 40 hours per week will not qualify for a "Belo" agreement.

The most significant requirement for a "Belo" agreement is that the duties of employees paid under such an agreement must necessitate irregular hours of work. The regulations specify that regularly scheduled workweeks or scheduling involving alternating fixed workweeks do not qualify for compensation under a "Belo" agreement. Further, these agreements are not permitted when the hours of work vary from week to week at the discretion of either the employee or the employer. They only apply when neither the employer nor the employee can control or anticipate with any degree of certainty the number of hours the employee must work from week to week. The Wage and Hour Division gives the following examples of employees whose duties would necessitate irregular hours of work thus permitting a "Belo" agreement: 1) outside buyers, 2) on-call servicemen, 3) insurance adjusters, 4) newspaper reporters, 5) those engaged in the motion picture industry, 6) firefighters, and 7) "other like employees."

Neither the "time-off" plan nor a Belo agreement is a practical solution for controlling overtime costs. Inventive employers have devised other "schemes" to try and circumvent the overtime requirements of the FLSA. The Wage and Hour investigators are very wary of such plans, however, and will strictly construe the overtime requirement in the Act. Employers must control inadvertent or unauthorized overtime by supervisory oversight of a written policy forbidding overtime without authorization. If employees continue to violate policy by working overtime, they should be disciplined.

Retaliation protections under the FLSA

The Fair Labor Standards Act (FLSA) provides an individual with several options for seeking relief under the Act. The individual may file a complaint with the Department of Labor, triggering an investigation by the Wage and Hour Division. The individual may also file a private action in state or federal court. Additionally, the Secretary of Labor may bring an action under the Act for unpaid overtime compensation. The Secretary of Labor may also seek injunctive relief to restrain employers from violating the law. Finally, the Department of Justice may bring criminal actions for willful violations of the Act. An individual who institutes, or causes to be instituted, any of these proceedings is protected from retaliation under the Act.

Some employees have argued that the intent of Congress in enacting the Fair Labor Standards Act was to protect individuals making informal complaints regarding overtime. As noted recently by a federal court in Virginia, if Congress had intended to provide this type of broad protection to employees claiming retaliation for voicing internal wage/hour complaints, Congress would have expressed that intent in broad language such as that found in the retaliation provisions of Title VII of the Civil Rights Act of 1964, the Age Discrimination in Employment Act of 1967, the Americans with Disabilities Act of 1990, and the Family and Medical Leave Act of 1993. Each of these statutes prohibits retaliation against an individual "because he has opposed any practice made an unlawful employment practice" by that statute. No such broad "opposition clause" is found in the Fair Labor Standards Act.

The plain language of the FLSA demonstrates that employees who do not file a formal complaint with the government should have no cause of action under the Act. Section 15 of the Fair Labor Standards Act protects an employee from retaliation "because such employee has filed any complaint or instituted or caused to be instituted any proceeding..." Where an employee fails to file a formal complaint, courts should not allow a recovery. As yet, however, the decisions are in conflict on this issue.

Steps to take to avoid wage/hour liability

Employers continue to tamper with an employee's predetermined salary thereby destroying the individual's exempt status and exposing the employer to overtime and minimum wage liability. The primary rule for avoiding wage/hour liability can thus be stated as follows: Do not use payroll practices that reduce the exempt employee's salary.

Here are some common practices that destroy an employee's exempt status:

- ◆ **Deductions in salary**. Docking exempt employees' wages for being late or for absences of less than a full day destroys exempt status. Exempt employees are compensated not for the amount of time spent on the job, but rather for the general value of services performed. Additionally, deductions are not permitted for absences caused by jury duty, attendance as a witness, or temporary military leave unless the employee does no work for an entire week.

- ◆ **Hourly deductions in leave balances**. Some exempt employees have supported claims for overtime wages by demonstrating that they were treated like hourly employees rather than salaried workers because hourly deductions were made from the employees' leave balances. Currently, the Department of Labor permits such deductions to be made from accrued leave balances. Some courts have ruled otherwise. To avoid any risk, do not make such deductions. If you do choose to deduct time off from leave balances, do not create a negative balance in the leave bank.

- ◆ **Overtime pay and compensatory time**. Many employers who otherwise pay exempt employees on a salary basis may also pay some form of overtime compensation. While the FLSA specifically allows employers to pay exempt employees additional compensation beyond salary, a few courts have questioned whether overtime payments are consistent with the salary basis requirement. The DOL's Field Operations Handbook states that overtime payments to exempt employees need not be at time and one-half, but may be a straight time, or a flat sum, or on any other basis. Payment to exempt employees for "overtime" work that is not calculated on a strict hourly basis reduces the risk of this pay practice.

♦ **Disciplinary action**. The DOL regulations permit a disciplinary deduction to be made in an exempt employee's salary only when the penalty is assessed in good faith for infractions of safety rules of major significance. Examples cited by the DOL include smoking in an explosive plant, oil refinery, or coal mine. Conversely, the DOL ruled that an employer could not make disciplinary deductions from the salary of a registered nurse for patient care violations. Avoid deductions for disciplinary reasons.

♦ **Recording of time and requiring set hours**. Requiring exempt employees to keep careful track of their time and to turn in time sheets or other forms may create a salary basis problem, although no case has been decided solely on this basis. As explained below, however, keeping a record of starting and stopping times for exempt employees may be invaluable in wage and hour litigation.

FLSA record-keeping requirements

A failure to keep proper payroll records can be an independent violation of the Fair Labor Standards Act. Also, an employer who has not kept proper records is at a distinct disadvantage in wage/hour litigation. The burden is on the employer to prove that an employee did not work as much overtime as he or she claims. Without proper records, the employer is lost. In general, employers are required to maintain and keep payroll or other records, for a period of three years, containing the following information:

♦ Employee's full name and employee identification number, if used.

♦ Employee's home address, including zip code.

♦ Date of birth, if under 19.

♦ Sex and occupation in which employee is employed.

- Time of day and day of week when workweek begins.
- Regular hourly rate of pay for any workweek in which overtime pay is due.
- Hours worked each workday and total hours worked each workweek.
- Total daily or weekly straight-time earnings or wages due for hours worked, exclusive of premium overtime compensation.
- Total premium pay for overtime hours.
- Total additions to or deductions from wages paid each pay period.
- Total wages paid each pay period.
- Date of payment and the pay period covered by payment.

For exempt employees, employers are expected to keep information regarding the basis on which wages are paid, for example, salary per month and total remuneration paid to each exempt employee. Employers are not required to record a regular rate, hours worked, straight time earnings and weekly overtime pay for exempt employees. Because exempt employees are usually the individuals who will later come back and sue the employer for unpaid overtime, employers should nevertheless document the total hours worked by exempt employees each week. Obviously, these records can come back to haunt an employer if an exempt employee is later ruled not to be exempt and the records show many hours worked over 40 in a week. Nevertheless, disgruntled ex-employees who are mad because they did not get overtime pay will usually grossly exaggerate the number of hours they actually worked. Without records to show that these employees are lying, the employer will be required to compensate these employees for every hour they claim they worked. Exempt employees can be made to fill out a daily time sheet showing their starting and stopping time each day without violating the FLSA. These time sheets should be reviewed for accuracy by the exempt employee's immediate supervisor and both the employee and the supervisor should sign the time sheet.

Audit job descriptions

Although it is true that wage/hour investigators will look at the actual work being performed by "white collar" employees to determine whether they should be exempt, language in job descriptions that underscores the educational requirement of a position or the expectation that an employee will use discretion and independent judgment in performing the duties of the position can be very helpful. It is also important to have incumbents in the position sign off on the job description as agreeing with the job duties set forth in the description.

Annual evaluation forms that require exempt employees to describe their duties and accomplishments for the year are also very helpful during wage and hour litigation. Employees will usually "puff up" their duties and accomplishments in such evaluations. It is easier to impeach the credibility of a plaintiff who says he did not perform as an exempt employee if an evaluation, signed by the plaintiff, contradicts that point of view.

It should be remembered that wage/hour enforcement is often a negotiable incident. The government will threaten an employer with litigation and "liquidated damages" but it must gauge the time and cost of litigation, too. Thus, if an employer has comprehensive job descriptions or evaluations signed by the putative plaintiff, it will certainly be in a better position to bargain for a reduction in backpay liability.

Don't stand on principle

Wage/hour litigation is as expensive as any other litigation. Often, however, the amount that must be paid to a complaining employee is only a minor fraction of the total backpay liability and litigation expenses that may result if the government audits payroll records and sues the employer in court. Certainly, there are times when payment to one employee will have a "ripple" effect on other employees. Nevertheless, it is often better to take care of small problems in this area of the law by settling wage disputes early rather than standing on principle and paying a huge price later.

Chapter 8

If They Don't Need to Know, Don't Tell

Alex Irving, owner of Alexir Metal Fabrication, was in a bad mood. His shop superintendent, Larry Simpson, had just given him the results of his August tool inventory. It was dismal again. The company was losing money hand over fist because of employee theft. Hand tools and power tools were disappearing. "Larry," said Alex to his superintendent, "this has got to stop! I thought you said the installation of security cameras would put an end to this thievery."

Larry said, "Look, Alex, I try to watch these guys but I can't be everywhere at once. They leave at lunch time, they stop work at different times because of the stupid "flex scheduling" you instituted; you even let them come in on weekends to do personal jobs. I can't control all these comings and goings!"

"All right, calm down," said Alex. "There must be something else we can do." "Well, there is one thing we should start doing," replied Larry. "We can institute a random tool box check—you know, search their tool boxes when they leave." "Is that legal?" asked Alex. "Yeah, I think so," said Larry. "They used to do that at Acme Tool and Die when I worked there."

Alex told Larry Simpson that he wanted him to be in charge of the tool box searches. In fact, he told Larry that he did not want anyone else involved in the searches; only Larry would be doing the random checks. As the meeting was ending, Alex said, "This better work, Larry. We need to get things under control." Larry replied, "Don't worry about a thing, Alex. It will work; I'll see to that."

Larry knew what he would do. There was one young, long-haired loudmouth, Rick Samsom, who Larry thought was a troublemaker. He had only been working for the company for about six months and already Larry had written him up for insubordination. The company tools were clearly marked; it would be simple enough to slip one into Rick's tool box when he wasn't looking. He just had to watch out for Billy Jasper, Rick's buddy and only real friend at the shop.

About 20 minutes before quitting time on Thursday, Larry called Rick on the intercom and said, "I need you and Billy to clean up that scrap metal out back before you leave. In fact, you may have to stay about a half hour overtime. Just bring your gloves, you won't need any tools."

About a half hour later, after checking on Rick and Billy, Larry made his way through the shop to the work bench where Rick always kept his tool box. He found it without a problem and it was unlocked. Although most of the guys in the shop had left, there were still a few people finishing up. Glancing around quickly to make sure everyone in the shop was otherwise occupied, Larry saw his opportunity. He lifted the top tray of Rick's tool box and slipped a power screwdriver belonging to the company into the bottom of the box.

About 20 minutes later, Larry stopped Rick and Billy as they headed out of the shop. "Hold on, boys," Larry said, "I need to check your tool boxes." "No problem, Boss," Rick said sarcastically, smiling at Billy. First, Larry checked Billy's tool box and lunch box. It was clean. Then, he had Rick open up his tool box. He lifted the top tray, reached in, and pulled out the power screwdriver belonging to the company.

"What's this, Mr. Samsom?" asked Larry accusingly. Rick looked shocked, "How the hell did that get in there? I didn't put that in there!" Billy chimed in, "Hey, man, I was just looking in Rick's tool box for a wrench right before you called us to go out back to clean up. That screwdriver wasn't in there." "Well, it's in there now," said Larry. "Let's go to the office, Rick." Rick protested, "Look, I'm telling you. I've been set up." Larry smiled and said, "Come with me, Rick. I'll put your statement on the discharge form."

The next day, Larry told Alex what happened. Apparently, Billy Jasper had been in to see Alex first thing that morning, but Alex was not there yet. Billy left a written statement for Alex recounting the fact that he had looked in Rick Samsom's tool box just before Larry had sent him and Rick to clean up and the screwdriver wasn't in there.

Alex asked Larry, "What did Rick have to say when you fired him?" Larry replied quickly, "Nothing much, just what he wrote on that form there. You know, that he was set up. Of course, all crooks claim they were framed, you know that." Alex thought a minute and said, "What *about this statement from Billy Jasper?" Larry said, "Billy is Rick's drinking buddy. He'll say anything to save Rick's job."*

Alex said, "Have you said anything to the other guys?" "No, not yet," said Larry. "I thought you might want to handle that."

"Do I have to say anything?" asked Alex. "They all probably know anyway." Larry answered Alex quickly, "Are you kidding? This is our chance to stop all this thievery once and for all. We need to make an example of this kid. You tell them what happened—that we found company property in his toolbox and that when that happens, the employee has to be fired. They'll get the message."

Alex decided to go along with Larry's idea. He was worried about the loss of inventory and felt that making an example of Rick would discourage other employees from stealing. He had Larry assemble the shop employees right before he handed out the payroll checks. They took the news in silence, all except Billy Jasper who walked out of the meeting. After the meeting, Larry posted notices on the bulletin boards reminding employees of Rick's "attempted theft of company property" and alerted all employees that the random tool box checks would continue indefinitely.

About three weeks later, Alex got a call from Rick Samsom's lawyer, who said he was giving the company a chance to settle before he sued for defamation. When Alex tried to tell the lawyer that they caught his client red-handed with the power screwdriver, he said, "Maybe you ought to talk to one of your employees, Charley Lawson. He'll tell you what really happened." The lawyer then explained that Charley had seen Larry Simpson put the screwdriver in Rick's tool box.

When Alex met with Larry, he denied putting the screwdriver in Rick's tool box, calling Charley Lawson a liar. "I don't know why he's helping out that kid," said Larry, "but I didn't set nobody up." Alex could always tell when Larry was lying, but he didn't let on. When Larry had left, Alex called Rick's lawyer and asked him what he would want to settle the whole thing. The lawyer said he would not take "a penny less than $100,000."

The defamatory communication

In today's litigious society, an employer is vulnerable to numerous legal challenges for a variety of communications that arise during the employment relationship. In particular, an incorrect or untrue communication regarding an employee may give rise to a cause of action for defamation. A defamatory statement is usually described as an untrue communication that exposes the individual to "public scorn, hatred, contempt, or ridicule" and thus injures his reputation. In order to bring a successful defamation action, the plaintiff must, at a minimum, establish that the alleged defamatory publication was communicated to a third person who recognized the communication to be defamatory. The plaintiff should also be prepared to show that he was damaged by the defamatory publication. In many jurisdictions, however, statements that injure an employee in his or her trade, business, or profession are considered libel *per se*, resulting in a presumption of damages. Special damages need not be pleaded or proved to sustain the claim.

Defamation by conduct

As explained above, defamation usually requires a defamatory "communication" to a third party. One issue that sometimes arises in discharge cases is whether conduct that implies that another person engaged in some kind of misconduct or violation of policy is sufficient as a defamatory communication. For example, in a case decided by the Maryland Court of Appeals, an employee was accused of stealing inventory from an automotive plant and was forcibly detained by four security guards as he left the plant. The plaintiff had to be grabbed by the guards and "assisted" to the guard shack while the plaintiff continued "screaming and shouting." He was questioned inside a glass-enclosed guard shack for 25 to 30 minutes, in full view of approximately 5,000 employees who were in the process of changing shifts. The employee traffic slowed as it passed the guard shack because the incident was unusual. Also, there was testimony that it was well-known that anyone who was detained by security guards was probably suspected of theft. The court held that the conduct of the guards was defamatory publication by conduct.

In a subsequent decision by another Maryland court, an employee who was escorted to her locker by three supervisors and then out of the nursing home was held not to be a defamatory publication by conduct. The court said that there was no testimony that "being accompanied to her locker and then from the building was in any way unusual or even that it was so perceived by other employees and residents of the nursing home." The court said that it did not believe that the mere act of an employer escorting an employee from the building after termination of employment constitutes a defamatory publication.

The cases that have found conduct to be a defamatory communication have usually involved facts that describe a fairly dramatic interplay of both words and conduct. For example, in the case of the employee detained at the automotive plant, the conduct of the guards in grabbing and detaining the employee resulted in an award of damages for assault and false imprisonment. In contrast, "escorting" discharged employees as they exit an employer's facility has not been construed to be so unusual (or perhaps not so egregious) as to give rise to a defamation by conduct claim.

As explained in Chapter 5, employers should take reasonable actions to protect other employees and even company property from the potential violence that can occur when an employee is discharged. Escorting an employee from the premises may be a necessary precaution. As defamation by conduct cases are the exception, rather than the rule, employers should not refrain from using an escort after termination because there exists a remote potential for a defamation suit.

The qualified privilege

Communications arising out of the employment relationship normally enjoy a qualified privilege. A false communication remains privileged when both the communicating party and the recipient have a mutual interest in the subject matter of the communication or some duty with respect to the communication. The privilege applies as long as the defendant acts in good faith and without malice. For example, communications from a former employer to a prospective employer are conditionally privileged. Similarly, in-house publications of defamatory communications in order to facilitate personnel administration are normally within the qualified privilege. As the privilege is qualified, however, it can be lost if the communication is made with "express or actual malice" or with excessive publication.

Express or actual malice means that the employer either had "knowledge of falsity or reckless disregard for the truth." Reckless disregard for the truth requires a showing that the employer had a high degree of awareness of the probable falsity of the communication. Accordingly, an employer may not "cover its eyes to the truth" or avoid conducting a routine investigation of a matter that would have uncovered the truth. For example, in one case, an employer's failure to conduct a routine inventory check prior to accusing an employee of theft was evidence of the employer's reckless disregard of the truth. Similarly, in another case, the failure of a supervisor to ask a long-term employee about an alleged breach of security was held to be reckless where the supervisor doubted that the employee's conduct breached security but nevertheless stated that it did.

Excessive publication occurs when individuals who do not have a legitimate job-related interest in a communication are nevertheless allowed to hear or read the published material. Thus, it would not be considered excessive publication to have a secretary type a letter that notifies an employee of his or her termination and explains the reasons for the termination, nor would it be inappropriate to show this letter to the employee's immediate supervisors. Each of these individuals has a legitimate job-related interest in the discharge letters. On the other hand, a general company-wide announcement about the reasons for the termination may be considered excessive publication because all employees at the facility do not have a legitimate job-related interest in the termination decision.

Defamation during the employment relationship

There are situations that arise during the employment relationship that can be fertile ground for defamation claims. For example, many employers require employees to undergo medical examinations at the start of employment. Medical information gathered during the examination must be kept in strict confidence. In addition to statutory liability for failing to safeguard the confidentiality of employee medical records, employers may also face defamation claims for communicating incorrect information regarding the medical condition of employees.

An employer who falsely characterizes an employee's mental condition can be potentially liable for defamation. For example, in a Massachusetts case, an employee sued his employer for libel and invasion of privacy after the director of personnel programs described his mental condition in a memorandum to an undetermined number of managers at the company. The employee had complained to his supervisor that he was suffering from "bad nerves, headaches, and an inability to sleep." At the suggestion of the supervisor, the employee went to see a general practitioner retained by the company. After the visit, the doctor called the employee's supervisor, telling him that the employee was paranoid and should see a psychiatrist immediately.

At a subsequent grievance meeting with his supervisor, the employee was distraught and crying. The supervisor made an appointment for the employee with a psychiatrist. The director of personnel programs summarized the events in a memorandum that stated his opinion that the latest episode between the employee and the supervisor indicated that the employee appeared to have a mental problem that went beyond the company's ability to handle. The employee alleged in his complaint that approximately 16 people learned about his medical condition.

Although the plaintiff's complaint was dismissed by a federal district court, the Supreme Judicial Court of Massachusetts ruled, on certification from the federal court of appeals, that an employer could lose its conditional privilege to disclose defamatory medical information if the information was "recklessly disseminated." The court also noted that an unambiguous publication that an employee had a specified mental disorder that makes him unfit for his job would be a publication defamatory on its face. Although the court of appeals ultimately affirmed the dismissal of the libel claims because the factual record did not establish a "reckless dissemination" (in fact, the court concluded that only two managers received the alleged defamatory memorandum), this case points out the potential danger in publishing medical information regarding employees, even to other managers within the corporation.

Another dangerous area of investigation for employers occurs when employees are requested to undergo drug testing. In order to be confident that its investigation into employee drug use is not reckless with regard to the truth or falsity of the test results, the employer must make sure that the testing is done at a certified laboratory that follows all federal guidelines for the collection and testing of urine specimens. In particular, the laboratory must use a confirming test that maximizes the accuracy of the test results. An employer must also maintain strict confidentiality standards with regard to the reporting and use of the results of drug tests. If an employer discloses that an employee has tested positive for the use of drugs and this information is later discovered to be incorrect, the employer may find itself facing defamation charges. Therefore, an employer can minimize the potential for a charge of defamation if confidentiality procedures are developed or strictly enforced. Even if the results of the tests are incorrect, the publication of the erroneous test results will not be actionable if it was not communicated to anyone other than those individuals who have a business need to know the results.

In a case out of Texas, an employee was tested for drugs after an on-the-job injury. The company doctor reported to the personnel office that the test was positive for methadone but added it was only a trace amount. The personnel office sent an internal memo to seven managers telling them that methadone was found in the employee's urine and that methadone is used by heroin addicts. The memo did not mention that only a trace amount was found in the urine specimen. The employee was fired for a safety violation and sued the company for libel. A jury awarded the plaintiff $100,000 in damages.

Finally, in a real "rock and a hard place" scenario, employers who falsely accuse an individual of engaging in sexual harassment of another employee may face a defamation claim unless the employer has conducted a thorough and deliberate investigation of the harassment charge in a confidential manner. Employers who move too quickly to discipline or discharge a manager accused of sexual harassment may be left with a plaintiff who wants to strike back at the employer by asserting that his reputation has been ruined by the sexual harassment allegations.

Employers must not arbitrarily discipline employees accused of harassment or fail to give hearing to the alleged harasser's side of the story simply because they are afraid of sexual harassment litigation. Instead, an employer must weigh all the facts, make credibility determinations as to who is telling the truth and give careful consideration as to the proper penalty in any particular case. If employers do investigate claims of sexual harassment in a thorough and deliberate manner, they are not likely to be vulnerable to defamation claims.

Can performance evaluations be defamatory?

Most employers use performance evaluations to appraise the relative performance levels of their employees. These evaluations are a useful tool in improving the overall performance of employees. Many evaluations are used as the basis for assigning salary levels. Thus, accurate and honest appraisals of performance are essential.

A case out of New Jersey, however, raises serious concerns over the continued utility of performance evaluations. A New Jersey jury found that both the company and one of its managers were guilty of defamation for negative statements set forth in a performance evaluation that ultimately cost an employee her job. The jury awarded the employee $465,000 in compensatory and punitive damages. The employee had lost her job during a reduction in force. Under the company's downsizing plan, employees were grouped into various categories on the basis of recent performance appraisals. Because the plaintiff's evaluation did not place her in the top echelon of the company's top performers as rated by the performance evaluations, she was laid off.

The decision is significant because, in most jurisdictions, critical statements included in performance evaluations are privileged and not subject to an action for defamation. In other words, in order to have an actionable claim for defamation, employees would have to demonstrate that their supervisor included the defamatory statement in the evaluation maliciously or with knowledge that the statement was untrue. If the reasoning of the New Jersey decision is applied in other states, employers are likely to be unsuccessful in urging their supervisors to be vigilant in pointing out the performance deficiencies of employees whom they supervise. A manager faced with potential liability for defamation will be predisposed to give a "watered-down" appraisal that would defeat the entire purpose of the performance evaluation process.

There are a number of states that hold that the circulation of documents within a corporation cannot satisfy the requirement of "publication" for defamation purposes because the corporation is merely communicating with itself. Other states disagree and hold that communications within a corporation can be defamatory. For example, in a decision by the Indiana Supreme Court, the court ruled that the distribution of an employee evaluation through several levels of management was a sufficient publication for purposes of bringing a defamation suit. The court said, "When intra-company communications injure an employee's occupational reputation, the result may be among the most injurious of defamation. We cannot deprive access to the courts for an employee who suffers very real and significant injuries as a result of intra-company defamatory falsehoods that would otherwise be actionable."

The tort of defamation can be brought against both the company and its individual supervisors. Potential liability is substantial as discharged employees can seek back pay, reinstatement, compensatory damages for pain and suffering, and punitive damages. The jury in the New Jersey case, for example, awarded the plaintiff $60,000 in back pay, $50,000 in front pay, $75,000 for emotional distress, $30,000 for damage to her reputation, and $250,000 in punitive damages. A change in defamation law that does not protect good faith criticism of employee performance from potential defamation claims would have a chilling effect on the performance appraisal process.

Legislation has been introduced in several states to remedy the potential harm that could result from any judicial trend making employment documents subject to defamation liability. These proposals would eliminate internal communications within business organizations relating to the assessment of performance of employees from the definition of "publication" under defamation law. As mentioned, the law varies from state to state as to whether statements made on an evaluation form are considered communications that can constitute a necessary publication for purposes of a defamation action. The proposed legislation would exclude statements in performance appraisals from the definition of publication and thus create absolute immunity from defamation for such statements. Therefore, regardless of the truth or falsity of statements made in evaluation forms, employees would not be able to bring defamation claims.

By eliminating the potential for defamation based on statements in evaluations, supervisors would be free to honestly evaluate all employees without fear of liability if they should make a mistake and place untrue statements on the evaluation form. It could be argued, however, that such proposals go too far in protecting employers from liability during the evaluation process. A supervisor who deliberately lies about an employee in a performance evaluation with resulting damage to the reputation of the employee would not be subject to liability and the injured employee would have no remedy despite the deliberate falsity of the comments within the appraisal form. This type of legislation is usually directed only at intra-company communications, however, and thus employees injured by publication of defamatory performance appraisals to persons outside the corporation would apparently still have a remedy. Ultimately, state legislatures must make a policy decision as to the necessity for giving greater protection to statements in evaluations so that the process of evaluating employees can be done honestly and effectively.

Defamation and discharge announcements

It seems that regardless of how much advice employers are given regarding the risk of a defamation suit if they over-publicize statements concerning employee misconduct, million-dollar verdicts continue to occur. Some employers either do not completely understand the full extent of liability to which they may be exposed in a defamation suit, or simply choose to "make an example" of the rule-violating employee in the hope that the discipline imposed on that individual will discourage other employees from engaging in similar conduct.

Employers that are contemplating the discharge of one of their employees must resist the temptation to broadcast the reasons for the discharge to the assembled work force. In light of the willingness of juries to "punish" offending employers by awarding employees both compensatory damages and punitive damages, any decision to publicize "facts" about employee discipline to the general work force is extremely risky behavior.

Although announcements about the discipline imposed for rule violations may effectively discourage other employees from engaging in similar conduct, such statements are fertile ground for defamation charges if they are later proven to be untrue and were published to employees who had no need to know the details.

The potential liability for employers because of defamation actions underscores the absolute necessity of performing a thorough investigation prior to discharging or disciplining an employee as well as the need for confidentiality in conducting personnel matters. A recent case out of Pennsylvania dramatically demonstrates the dangers of not following the rule of confidentiality.

In a case involving the discharge of a long-term employee of a large department store chain, the Superior Court of Pennsylvania ruled that a jury's award of $1.4 million in punitive damages was not excessive where the employee had been defamed by management's decision to tell other employees that she had stolen a bag of potato chips on the job. The plaintiff in this case was a 12-year employee with no history of discipline or misconduct with the company. She worked at the company's distribution center, which handled all of the company's products, including potato chips.

After news of the termination had spread throughout the workplace, the company's managers called a meeting of the plaintiff's co-workers and told them that she had been fired for eating a bag of potato chips. The plaintiff applied for unemployment benefits, and an unemployment compensation referee ruled that she did not steal the potato chips and awarded her unemployment compensation. The plaintiff then sued her former employer for defamation.

At trial, the jury heard evidence that the security officer's identification was not based on his own personal recognition of the plaintiff. Also, there was evidence that the company did not follow its own guidelines in investigating the incident. The trial court refused to allow the company to present evidence on the alleged theft, however, ruling that the unemployment hearing had given both parties a "full and fair opportunity" to litigate the issue of the truthfulness of the charge of theft. After the jury awarded $1.4 million in punitive damages, the company appealed.

On appeal, the Superior Court rejected the corporation's argument that it should not have been found liable for defamation because it was privileged to communicate the news of the discharge to co-workers because of their "anxiety" in the workplace after the plaintiff's discharge. The company argued that its statement to employees was within the qualified privilege because it reasonably relied on a report from its security department. The Pennsylvania court ruled, however, that there was sufficient evidence for the jury to conclude that management had failed to exercise due care in verifying the truth of the report before talking to the co-workers.

Other decisions underscore the danger in overpublicizing misconduct by discharged employees. In a case out of Texas, a discharged employee was awarded $15.5 million in actual and punitive damages on a libel claim. The employee's boss asked the plaintiff to purchase some items that were needed for the plant. Although the employee was reimbursed for these items, he was not repaid for a $35 telephone because he had lost the receipt. A few months later, while the employee was leaving the plant, he was stopped by a security guard. The telephone was found in his belongings and reported to the company as stolen. The company conducted a brief investigation and fired the employee. Subsequently, the company posted a notice on a bulletin board that the employee had committed a theft.

The employee sued the company for libel. According to the plaintiff, the company's internal documents indicated that he had not committed a theft. The plaintiff claimed that the company's action stemmed from its fear that employees were going to "walk away with the plant" in anticipation of a permanent shutdown. The plaintiff alleged that the company was looking to make an example of him.

The jury agreed with the plaintiff and found that his employer had falsely accused him of stealing a $35 telephone that he had purchased with his own money. Of the $15.5 million awarded to the plaintiff by the jury, $14 million of the total award was for punitive damages, whereas $1.5 million was for actual damage to the plaintiff's reputation and for mental anguish and physical injuries.

Although there are cases that have held that a "good faith" communication of the reasons for termination to a select group of employees would not be outside the qualified privilege, there are very few decisions that have found the employer's desire to discourage other employees from engaging in similar practices to be a good faith reason for communicating the reasons for discharge to other employees. There have even been cases where the qualified privilege has been destroyed by the decision of a supervisor to bring another employee into a discharge meeting to act as a witness.

In light of the significant value afforded employers by the qualified privilege and the substantial damages that can result from an overbroad publication of a defamatory remark, employers must be careful to keep all disciplinary and discharge decisions confidential. If a witness is brought into a discharge meeting, it should be another supervisor who has some operational connection with the personnel decision at issue or a representative from the human resources department.

Employment references—a dangerous practice?

One of the most frustrating dilemmas for an employer occurs when another employer calls for a reference on a former employee who was either a very poor performer or engaged in serious misconduct resulting in discharge. The employer may feel an obligation to reveal the poor work record to the prospective employer so that the prospective employer will not get stuck with an employee who is likely to repeat the poor performance.

A simple and common-place request for references regarding a former employee may not be as innocuous as it seems. If the employer provides a negative reference, that employer may have invited a lawsuit for defamation. Should an employer risk getting involved in litigation just to help out another employer?

A recent decision out of the District of Columbia demonstrates the dangers of providing a negative reference regarding a former employee based on information that is less than accurate. In this case, the District of Columbia Court of Appeals upheld a $250,000 award to a man who claimed that his former employer defamed him.

The plaintiff worked as a project manager for a construction company. He sued the company alleging that a project executive of the company slandered him while giving an employment reference to another construction firm after the company terminated him. The project executive described the plaintiff during a telephone conversation as "detail-oriented to the point of losing sight of the big picture." The company project executive also stated that the plaintiff "had a lot of knowledge and experience on big jobs," that "with a large staff he might be a very competent project manager," and concluded by saying, "Obviously, he no longer works for us and that might say enough." However, the project executive had no actual knowledge of the plaintiff's performance.

The plaintiff claimed that the defamatory statements damaged his professional reputation and standing and subjected him to humiliation and mental anguish. The company contended that the allegedly defamatory statements were protected as opinions and by a qualified privilege.

The District of Columbia Court of Appeals rejected the company's argument, finding that, given the context, the statements were expressions of fact giving rise to actionable defamation. The court of appeals held that the project executive's statements were made with gross indifference or recklessness and constituted abuse of any qualified privilege that may have existed. The court explained that the project executive had never supervised, worked with, evaluated, or read an evaluation of plaintiff, and that, moreover, the project executive testified that he had not received information from anyone in particular, let alone anyone who had a work-related relationship with the plaintiff. The court further found that the project executive admitted that he had no facts to support any of his statements to the prospective employer and that he had never sought to verify the information before giving his evaluation.

This decision illustrates the potential danger in providing references without accurately checking the facts. The decision also demonstrates the necessity for designating one management official to be responsible for all employment references. Obviously, the designated manager must have access to the former employee's personnel file and the authority to fully investigate the employee's work record before providing a reference.

The safest course for employers is to provide only a "neutral reference," that is, verifying dates of employment, position, and salary. Obviously, that will allow poor employees to continue to circulate from employer to employer, but the former employer will avoid the potential liability of defamation suits. Even where an employer is quite certain of the truth of his statements about the former employee and chooses to give more than a neutral reference, substantial financial risks still exist. The employer must be aware that although it ultimately may win a lawsuit, it will incur large legal fees to do so. Therefore, before an employer decides to institute a policy of providing more than neutral references, it must weigh the potential liability against the benefit that any prospective employer would obtain.

It is also imperative that the employer obtain a written release from the former employee before providing a reference. The release should have language by which the former employee agrees to hold the employer harmless for any statements it gives to prospective employers. However, even a release may not fully safeguard the employer from liability because the former employee may argue that he did not understand that he was waiving his right to sue for damages caused by defamatory statements. Thus, to be effective, the release must be very specific and unambiguous as to the waiver of rights.

Some states have passed legislation to address the tension between the need for comprehensive references and the potential for defamation claims arising from inaccurate negative references. For example, in October 1996, a statute went into effect in Maryland that gave employers reason to feel more secure about providing employment references to other employers regarding the job performance of former employees.

The Disclosure of Information Regarding Employees or Former Employee Act provides that any employer "acting in good faith may not be held liable for disclosing any information about the job performance or the reason for termination of employment of an employee or former employee...to a prospective employer at the request of the prospective employer...." The state legislature included an express presumption in this law that the employer providing the reference is acting in good faith "unless it is shown by clear and convincing evidence that the employer acted with actual malice toward the employee or former employee or intentionally or recklessly disclosed false information about the employee or former employee."

As a consequence of the "good faith" presumption incorporated into this statute, Maryland employers will at least be able to provide factually accurate references to prospective employers with little apprehension about facing protracted defamation litigation. Even if the information in the file was in error, as long as the employer had no knowledge that the information was false or the employer was not reckless with regard to the truth or falsity of the information (that is, the employer had done a thorough investigation before disciplining or discharging the employee), the increased burden on employees to prove "malice" on the part of the employer will in most cases prevent the employee from being successful in a defamation suit.

Compelled self-publication of defamation

One of the most frustrating developments in this area of the law is the decision by a few states to allow discharged employees to sue former employers for defamation, even though the employer did not publish the reasons for discharge to a third party. In other words, only the discharged employee had knowledge of the alleged defamatory communication and he or she alone made the decision to disclose such information to prospective employers.

In these cases, discharged employees convey the reasons for discharge to prospective employers and, when not hired, sue the former employer for defamation claiming that they were "compelled" to communicate the alleged defamatory statement. For example, in *Lewis v. Equitable Life Insurance Society*, the Minnesota Supreme Court recognized the doctrine of "compelled self-publication" and held that liability would be imposed for self-publication of defamatory statements "where the plaintiff was in some significant way compelled to repeat the defamatory statement and such compulsion was, or should have been, foreseeable to the defendant." The court affirmed an award of compensatory damages to the plaintiff.

If appears to be a fairly simple matter for a discharged employee to establish that his former employer should have known he would be compelled to disclose the reasons for his discharge when he applied for other employment. The plaintiff need only argue his "honest and forthright character" in explaining the "compulsion" to disclose the reasons for discharge to a prospective employer.

Fortunately, many states have not adopted the self-publication exception. For example, the Pennsylvania Superior Court has held that compelled self-publication of a defamation statement does not give rise to a cause of action for defamation. The plaintiff in this case was notified in a letter by his immediate supervisor that he was discharged because of his "very poor employment record [which] includes engaging in incidents of poor work performance, failing to give conscientious effort to your position, harassing and coercing another employee, maligning the company and demonstrating a poor attitude, among other things." The plaintiff sued for defamation under Pennsylvania law, claiming that he was compelled to publish the defamatory matter to prospective employers in job interviews and to family members and relatives.

The Pennsylvania Superior Court held that publication of a defamatory statement to the defamed party, followed by compelled publication by the defamed person to a third party, fails to state a claim for defamation under Pennsylvania law. The court explained: "Where the defamation action rests on the publication of an employee termination letter by the employer to the employee only, the requirement that the defamatory matter be published by the defendant is not met through proof of compelled self-publication."

Employer defenses

Potential defendants in a defamation action are apt to quote the old "saw" that "truth is an absolute defense." While it is true that a plaintiff cannot succeed in a defamation claim without establishing the falsity of a published statement, no plaintiff alleging defamation is ever going to admit that the statement he claims is defamatory is actually true. Therefore, the truth or falsity of a published statement will almost always be an issue for resolution at trial. A jury will determine whether an employer's statement that disparages an employee's reputation is true or false. The odds do not favor the employer in such a scenario.

Another defense that defendants are apt to seize upon in a defamation case is the argument that the published statement was intended as an opinion and not fact. While it is true that a statement that is purely an opinion will usually not be defamatory, liability may attach if the opinion implies an assertion of undisclosed facts or where the opinion is primarily an assertion of facts even though it is framed in "opinion-like" language. Thus, statements that a co-worker was a "fluffy," "bitch," or "flirtatious" were held to be "too imprecise" to be defamatory by a Minnesota appellate court. The court said that the "social context" of the statements (that they were made as part of "office gossip or banter"), would not lead a listener to believe they were statements of fact. In contrast, however, a supervisor's statement that he "had reason to believe an employee had sabotaged a corporation's computers" was ruled not to be pure opinion and thus actionable by the Supreme Judicial Court of Maine. The court said that a jury might reasonably conclude that the supervisor's expressed "suspicion" implied the existence of undisclosed defamatory facts. These cases demonstrate that the line between fact and opinion is not always clear.

A better defense for employers is to make sure that any statements about employees, whether made orally or as part of written evaluations or discharge notices, come within the qualified privilege that exists for statements made without malice, that is, where the employer is unaware of the falsity of the statement or is not reckless with regard to the truth or falsity of the statement. A North Carolina Court of Appeals decision demonstrates the applicability of this defense to a defamation claim brought by a terminated employee. The employee, a mental health worker, was alleged to have had sexual relations with a minor female patient at the hospital. The incident was discovered when a fellow employee reported that he had heard allegations of such misconduct from a third employee. The plaintiff sued both the employee who reported the incident and the employer alleging slander and intentional infliction of emotional distress. The trial court granted summary judgment to the hospital and the plaintiff appealed.

The court discussed the qualified privilege argument. The court noted that the reporting employee was directly responsible for patient care and had an ethical if not employment-based duty to report any allegations of abuse to the hospital. The allegations were made only to the employee's immediate supervisor and to other employees of the hospital who were directly involved in investigating the misconduct. The court noted that the hospital had a duty to investigate the charges of patient abuse and to report them to the state protective services agency. Thus, the scope of privilege was not exceeded by excessive publication of the statement to individuals who had no need to know.

This decision demonstrates that the courts will respect the right of an employer to communicate allegations of misconduct internally and to investigate those allegations when the employer does so in a reasonable and conscientious manner. The key to defending such cases is to ensure that the defamatory communication is treated as confidential and is not communicated to the general public or to other employees who are not directly involved in the investigation. Reports to outside agencies or to the police will not necessarily destroy the privilege, particularly if they are required by law or if there is reasonable suspicion that a crime has been committed.

How to avoid defamation liability

An employer should take the following steps to avoid liability for defamation claims.

♦ Investigate all disciplinary and discharge decisions thoroughly.

♦ Personnel documents regarding an individual employee (evaluations, disciplinary notices, or discharge letters) should only be circulated among individuals with a demonstrated need to review such documents as justified by business necessity.

♦ Do not broadcast the reasons for termination to the assembled work force or even to members of the discharged employee's department. Do not post a notice regarding a discharge on a bulletin board.

- Do not respond to questions from employees who were not involved in the incident or conduct that led to a termination decision. These employees should be told that it is a confidential personnel matter. Do not respond to questions from nonemployees.
- Provide only a "neutral reference" to other employers, verifying dates of employment, position, and salary.
- Do not provide additional information beyond a neutral reference unless the ex-employee provides you with a written waiver of all possible claims relating to the release of information. Even then, be very cautious; courts have ruled that ex-employees cannot consent to the publication of defamatory information.
- Develop a written policy for providing references that designates a specific managerial official as the response person for such inquiries. Supervisors should be instructed by the policy to refer all requests for references to the designated official.
- Keep all medical information confidential. Again, release of such information to designated persons should be authorized in a written consent-for-release form signed by the employee/patient.
- Do not communicate any drug test results to persons without a business-related need to know the results.

Chapter 9

Employee Privacy Is Not an Inalienable Right

Rhonda Fleming decided she needed some extra money while she finished her senior year at college. Although she was majoring in law enforcement, she applied for a waitress job at the local Burger and Beer Barn. Her roommate told her that the manager there always hired college girls to wait tables and she heard they made terrific tips.

When she got to the restaurant, Rhonda couldn't help noticing that all the waitresses were young and attractive with extremely full figures. After she filled out the application form, she was ushered into the manager's office. The manager was not in the office but Rhonda was instructed to wait. As she waited, Rhonda looked over all the awards the manager, Jerry Satts, had received from the company. Mr. Satts had been awarded "Manager of the Year" twice. There were plaques all over one wall of the office.

When Mr. Satts entered the office, he asked her to take a seat. Before they could start talking, however, a young man burst in the office, waving a piece of paper. Rhonda recognized him as a graduate student at the college. Ignoring Rhonda, he directed his comments at Mr. Satts, "You can't do this!" he said firmly, waving the announcement regarding drug testing in Mr. Satts' face. Mr. Satts did not respond, but turned to Rhonda and said, "If you would wait outside for a minute, Ms. Fleming, this won't take very long." Rhonda left the room but she had no problem overhearing what was said.

"Now, just what is your problem, Pete?" asked Mr. Satts. He knew Pete Johnson was upset about the drug testing policy that the corporation had decided to implement. All employees handling money, including bartenders like Pete, were subject to random drug testing. "I don't know why you're getting so excited. You don't use drugs, do you?" asked Mr. Satts.

"That's not the point!" Pete said in a loud voice. "You're trying to look into my private affairs. What I do on my day off is none of your business. Hasn't this company heard about the U.S. Constitution? The Fourth Amendment protects against unreasonable searches and seizures, you know. This drug testing violates every employee's constitutional rights!"

Mr. Satts sighed, he could tell Pete was a prelaw major. He cut Pete off, saying: "Look, Pete. I don't have time for this. The corporate lawyers have okayed this. Either you sign the consent form or you're gone. It's that simple."

"I'm not signing!" exclaimed Pete. "Well, then you can't work, Pete." said Mr. Satts. "You can pick up your last check on Friday; as of right now, you are fired." Pete Johnson stormed out of the office, almost knocking Rhonda over. Mr. Satts apologized and asked her to come in and sit down. He said, "Don't worry about this drug testing thing. Waitresses don't handle money, so the policy doesn't apply to you."

Mr. Satts did not sit behind his desk, however, but instead sat down next to Rhonda in the other chair in front of his desk. He turned his chair to face her and asked her a few questions about her reasons for wanting to work at the restaurant. Rhonda thought it was strange that he did not even look at her application. He did not care that she had no waitressing experience and told her she would work out fine.

As Rhonda was ready to start work right away, Mr. Satts gave her a uniform from a credenza drawer behind his desk. He told her to put it on and come back to his office before starting work. "The women's locker room is just down the hall to your left." said Mr. Satts. "I do an initial inspection of everyone's appearance before they start work. This company is very concerned with its public image and I want to make sure everyone is dressed appropriately."

Rhonda was a little surprised that the restaurant manager would be in charge of handing out waitress uniforms, but she hurried down the hall to get changed. She didn't want to miss too much of the dinner shift crowd—she was anxious to start earning those tips. The locker room had two rows of lockers with a long bench down each row. At the end of the row, floor length mirrors were fixed to the walls. Rhonda looked at the uniform; it was pretty standard. The skirt was a little short but the top was not overly revealing. Rhonda tried to check the size of her uniform before putting it on but she noticed the tag appeared to have been torn off.

She quickly slipped out of her street clothes and into the uniform. "I don't know why we have to change here; it's too cold in this locker room." She thought to herself. She had difficulty zipping up the back of the uniform, however, because it was about two sizes too small for her. In fact, the uniform was so snug, it was embarrassing. She checked the uniform in the mirror and realized she would never get it zipped up. Rhonda didn't even want to leave the locker room dressed in the uniform so she decided to change back into her street clothes before asking for another uniform.

Back in his office, Mr. Satts had taken one of the plaques off the wall and stood peering though a hole that had been drilled through his office wall into the locker room. Rhonda's decision to take off the undersized uniform was an unexpected bonus and he smiled broadly as he looked through the one-way mirror that he had bought for the locker room.

Unfortunately for Mr. Satts, Pete Johnson chose that moment to return to Mr. Satts' office to show him a law journal article on random drug testing as a potential invasion of privacy. Pete immediately understood what was going on. "You pervert," Pete said. "Get the hell away from that peep-hole."

Mr. Satts, although temporarily flustered, recovered quickly and said, "I don't know what you're talking about—this plaque just fell off the wall. Anyway, who do you think you are—bursting into my office unannounced. Get out! You don't even work here anymore."

"You are not going to get away with this," Pete promised as he exited Mr. Satts' office. He waited for Rhonda to come out of the women's' locker room. When Rhonda heard what had happened, she immediately left the restaurant and accompanied Pete to an appointment he had made with a local attorney. To Pete's dismay, however, the lawyer told Pete that a challenge to the restaurant's drug testing program would probably be unsuccessful. Nevertheless, the lawyer was very interested in representing Rhonda and the other female employees in an invasion of privacy action against Mr. Satts and the restaurant. Rhonda agreed to give the lawyer her full cooperation, because she was outraged by Mr. Satts' conduct. The lawyer promised immediate action to preserve the evidence of Mr. Satts' wrongdoing.

The expectation of privacy

There is a general misconception among employees that the U.S. Constitution places limitations on a private employer's right to engage in surveillance or conduct searches in the workplace. Private employers, however, are not subject to the restrictions of the constitution unless government action is clearly involved, that is, if the private employer is acting as a conduit or agent of the government or is being forced to act in a certain way by the government. Thus, employees do not normally have a constitutional right of privacy that would protect them from employer monitoring or prevent searches of personal belongings kept in their lockers or desks.

In some states, courts have protected the privacy rights of employees by allowing employees to sue for a tortious invasion of privacy based on a common law right "to be left alone." This privacy tort, commonly known as the tort of intrusion, protects employees from unreasonable or highly offensive invasions into their "solitude." This tort has not been widely used in employment situations, because it requires an unreasonable intrusion into a private place—a location where the individual has a "reasonable expectation of privacy." Nevertheless, in situations where the intrusion is outrageous and clearly without business justification, as with Mr. Satts' voyeurism in the introductory narrative, the employees will have a remedy.

Employees also have other protections against employer surveillance or searches. As will be discussed below, there are both federal and state statutes that regulate electronic "eavesdropping" by employers. Also, the National Labor Relations Act (NLRA) prohibits any surveillance of employees that "chills" the right of employees to engage in concerted activities (e.g., picketing) or to seek representation by a union. Many states have passed laws regulating drug testing in the workplace, even though such testing would not otherwise violate the employee's "right of privacy." Finally, a federal statute governing the use of polygraph or lie detector tests by employers has virtually eliminated the privacy concerns of employees relative to this information-gathering technique.

Individual privacy concerns usually arise because an employer wants to gain more definitive information about an employee or an applicant for employment. In most situations, the employer's questions are justified. For example, where there has been a workplace accident that caused serious bodily injury to one or more employees, few would argue with an employer's desire to conduct post-accident testing to rule out drug or alcohol impairment as a cause for the accident. Similarly, most applicants for employment do not have privacy concerns relating to reference checks or even criminal background checks by their prospective employers. As explained in Chapter 5, criminal background checks may not only be advisable but actually mandated by statute for certain positions. It is only where the employer overreaches and attempts to explore personal behavior having no possible relationship to workplace performance that the issue of privacy takes center stage as a litigation issue.

Sources of privacy protection

Concerns regarding employee privacy may also arise in the context of searches of employees or of employee lockers, desks, briefcases, automobiles, or purses. The need for such searches may arise in the context of suspected drug abuse or drug dealing, suspected use of alcohol, or during an investigation of theft from the company or from co-employees. The validity of claims of invasion of privacy in this situation generally turns on whether the employee involved had a reasonable expectation of privacy with regard to the area searched. Employee lockers and desks, although used exclusively by an employee, are in fact generally company property. On the other hand, briefcases, purses, and automobiles are generally the property of the employee, and as such, there may be a greater expectation of privacy with regard to these items.

Constitutional protection

Employees tend to overestimate their privacy rights in the workplace. For example, the U.S. Constitution does not protect the privacy of most employees. In *Skinner v. Railway Labor Executives Association*, the Supreme Court made it clear that the Fourth Amendment does not apply to searches by private parties. Similarly, many state constitutions and the protections afforded to privacy in those documents are designed only as a restraint on governmental conduct. Even in states where the state constitution does afford private sector employees protection against invasions of privacy, courts are reluctant to restrict the business activities of employers unless the employees can demonstrate that they had a reasonable expectation of privacy in the area that was allegedly subject to the employer's intrusion.

For example, the California constitution protects against invasions of privacy by private employers. Nevertheless, a judicial decision out of that state illustrates that an employee's right of privacy in the workplace still has limitations. A department store employee claimed an invasion of privacy when she learned that store management had installed a hidden camera in a "saferoom" off the fine jewelry department. The room was in fact a large storeroom that contained a large safe, a sink, counters for wrapping packages, and a phone. The employee asserted that employees assumed it was a private area where they could attend to personal needs. She claimed the room was used for confidential conversations between employees, changing clothes, applying make-up, as well as for personal hygiene.

Although the department store denied that there was any camera in the room, the California court ruled that even if there was a camera in the room, the employees would not have a reasonable expectation of privacy in a safe room that was used to store fine jewelry and had no inside lock on the door. The court dismissed the employee's constitutional privacy claim.

Common law protections

Because of the limitations of constitutional protections, employees have resorted to suing for a tortious invasion of privacy based on a common law right "to be left alone." This privacy tort protects employees from unreasonable or "offensive" invasions into their "solitude." As defined in the Restatement of Torts, "one who intentionally intrudes, physically or otherwise, upon the solitude or seclusion of another or his private affairs or concerns, is subject to liability to the other for invasion of his privacy, if the intrusion would be highly offensive to a reasonable person."

This tort has not been widely successful in employment situations because it requires an unreasonable intrusion into a private place. The "highly offensive to a reasonable person" element of this tort has also restricted its effectiveness as a remedy for employees.

There are cases dealing with workplace searches that have allowed recovery on invasion of privacy claims. For example, a Texas court found that a company had invaded the privacy of an employee when it searched his locker by cutting the employee's personal lock off the locker without his authorization. The employee had been permitted to use his own lock on the locker and the company's policy was silent as to the company's right of access to the locker. The employee was awarded $100,000 in damages.

In another case out of Oregon, a court ruled that a department store was liable for a tortious invasion of privacy after it subjected one of its cashiers to a strip search after a customer accused her of theft. In a case decided by the U.S. Court of Appeals for the Third Circuit, the court ruled that the plaintiff had stated an actionable claim for invasion of privacy under Pennsylvania law where it was alleged that a corporate officer had opened and read personal mail addressed to other employees.

These cases demonstrate that the common law tort for invasion of privacy has successful application only where the employer acts without business justification or conducts searches in a manner that is truly offensive. Employers have limited the application of the tort by putting employees on notice of the employer's right to make workplace searches, thus preventing a reasonable expectation of privacy from arising in employees' minds. For example, if the employer notifies employees that it reserves the right to conduct searches of lockers and informs employees that consent for such searches is a condition of employment, and further allows locks on the lockers only where employees share the combination for such locks with management, the employees will not have a reasonable expectation of privacy in their lockers. Similarly, employers should also notify employees that desks remain the property of the employer and are subject to searches. Employees should also not be given keys to their desks. If these precautions are followed, employees should not be able to argue that they thought the desks were a private area into which the employer could not intrude.

Public policy protections for privacy

As explained in Chapter 1, some courts have begun to circumvent the limitation imposed by the "state action" requirement for constitutional protection by using the "public policy" exception to the employment-at-will rule to impose privacy restrictions on employers. For example, the West Virginia Supreme Court of Appeals has held that drug testing by private employers is in violation of public policy unless the employer has an individualized suspicion of drug usage or unless the employee's duties affect the safety of others.

In *Twigg v. Hercules Corp.*, an employee claiming a right to privacy refused to submit to random drug testing being administered by his employer. The employee was discharged and he sued for wrongful discharge claiming that his termination from employment contravened a substantial public policy. The parties agreed that there was no basis for believing that the plaintiff had used any drugs.

In finding that the discharge violated public policy, the Supreme Court of Appeals held that a legally protected interest in privacy is recognized in West Virginia. There was no West Virginia statute prohibiting drug testing, yet the court decided to limit private employers' rights to conduct drug testing by finding a public policy in favor of an individual's interest in privacy based on state and federal constitutional prohibitions against unreasonable searches and seizures.

A similar use of the public policy exception to protect privacy rights occurred in *Kessler v. Equity Management, Inc.*, a case decided by the Court of Special Appeals of Maryland. In this case, the court held that a real estate management company that fired an apartment manager for refusing to enter the tenants' apartments and "snoop through" their private papers, had wrongfully discharged the manager and could be liable for damages.

The resident manager was allegedly instructed to enter the apartments of tenants by an agent of Equity Management, Inc., a private actor. There was no involvement by the government in the "snooping." Thus, even though the court acknowledged in its opinion that the constitution protects personal privacy from "forms of governmental invasion," it concluded that constitutional rights are implicated by the actions of a private employer. In effect, the court's decision burdens a private employer with the constitutional right of privacy by shielding the manager from discharge with a public policy created from a constitutional amendment. Even if the court's decision can be reconciled with those cases finding liability for discharging employees who refuse to commit an illegal act, a supervisor should not be allowed to disobey an order or instruction simply because the supervisor believes an employee's "privacy" might be invaded by a search of a desk or surveillance of workplace activities.

To avoid these "public policy" arguments grounded in constitutional rights, employers should find ways to reduce their employees' expectation of privacy, such as reserving the right to do workplace searches in company handbooks and personnel policies. Employees should be asked to acknowledge in writing that they understand the employer's policy provisions dealing with searches. Such statements on searches should specifically reserve the employer's right to discharge or discipline employees who refuse to cooperate with a workplace search. In other words, workplace privacy issues can be "managed" by employers so as to minimize any potential privacy claims.

Drug testing as an invasion of privacy

Preventing illegal drug use has become a national concern and no segment of society has escaped. Studies have shown that drug usage is widespread in the population as a whole and this has had a definite impact on the workplace. Employees with drug problems are absent more often, have more accidents, use more sickness benefits, and file more worker's compensation claims than the average worker.

Many private employers have turned to drug testing to identify employees and applicants who are using drugs illegally. As testing of employees becomes more prevalent, however, the number of legal challenges to testing programs has increased. As mentioned above, constitutional limitations on unreasonable searches and seizures normally apply solely to employment testing implemented in the public sector. Even though testing is clearly a "search," the Fourth Amendment right to privacy does not apply to testing done by private employers who have voluntarily initiated drug testing without compulsion from a government agency. Most courts have been satisfied to allow state legislatures to regulate drug testing by employers.

Courts have intervened in situations where it has been alleged that the drug testing procedures implemented by the employer are unreasonable or offensive and violate the common law right of privacy. The privacy tort of intrusion may implicate both the reasonableness of collection procedures that accompany drug testing programs and the employer's reason for implementing testing. For example, in *Borse v. Piece Goods Shop, Inc.*, a federal court of appeals in Pennsylvania said that an employer's drug testing program might intrude upon an employee's "seclusion" in at least two ways. First, the court concluded the manner of collecting the urine sample would implicate the employee's expectation of privacy, saying: "If the method used to collect the urine sample fails to give due regard to the employee's privacy, it could constitute a substantial and highly offensive intrusion upon seclusion." In particular, the court suggested that monitoring the collection of the urine sample to avoid adulteration could fall within the definition of an "intrusion upon seclusion" because it "involves the use of one's senses to oversee the private activities of another."

The court said that drug testing might also intrude upon an employee's privacy, because it can reveal a "host of medical facts about an employee, including whether she is epileptic, pregnant, or diabetic." The court concluded, therefore, that if an employer does not do a search in a "discrete manner" or if it reveals personal matters about the employee that are unrelated to the workplace, the search might be a tortious invasion of the employee's privacy. Finally, the court suggested that the proper standard for analyzing the legality of the drug testing program is to "balance the employee's privacy interest against the employer's business justification for the policy. Although the court said that it was not adopting a Fourth Amendment standard for assessing the reasonableness of the employer's search, but rather would require the invasion of privacy to be "substantial and highly offensive to the reasonable person," the balancing test proposed by the court of appeals was very similar to the standard that is applied in public sector cases.

....

237

A more appropriate standard for determining whether a testing program is tortious would require the court to focus on the issue of offensiveness and not simply weigh the employee's privacy interest against the employer's business justification. Because drug testing only reveals that an employee has recently used drugs and not whether he is impaired or "under the influence" of drugs, employees will often claim that the testing is an unreasonable or offensive invasion of privacy because it is an intrusion into their off-duty private affairs. Additionally, an employer who zealously tries to prevent contamination of the urine specimen by using direct observation of urination during collection could also be liable for an invasion of privacy.

There are very few courts that have addressed the dual issues of whether the purpose of drug testing and the observation of urination during the collection process would amount to a tortious intrusion into an individual's right of privacy. In one case out of Michigan, certain security guards of the employer were discharged after their urinalysis proved positive for the use of marijuana. The security guards claimed that the testing was an invasion of privacy, because they had the right to keep their off-duty illegal drug use a private matter, unless the employer could show that it affected their work performance. A federal court disagreed and found that the right to be free from intrusion is not absolute. The court said that the company had a significant interest in ensuring that their security officers were free from drug use. The court also found no merit to the employees' allegations that the method used by the company to secure the test results was objectionable to the reasonable person. The court said, "Each plaintiff admitted in deposition testimony that the urine sample was extracted in private with two male managers from the security department outside the bathroom stall to maintain the chain of custody of each sample." The court thus found no intrusion into the privacy rights of the employees from a testing program that did not include direct observation of urination.

The legitimacy of observed collection of urine samples under a common law right of privacy analysis may depend on the employer's reasons for requiring direct observation. Where a particular employee has previously presented an adulterated urine sample, direct observation by an employer representative may be justified. It appears clear, however, that collection procedures that do not require observation of urination will withstand an invasion of privacy challenge. In general, drug testing by private employers will likely be found to be reasonable business conduct and not offensive to a reasonable person. This is especially true where the employer is doing applicant screening or is testing employees only when there is an objective individualized suspicion that a specific employee is using drugs. Random testing is more problematic and may require a business justification to withstand an invasion of privacy challenge. Random testing programs have been upheld, however, where the employees being tested have duties implicating safety concerns or when the employees hold security-sensitive positions involving the property of the employer or the confidentiality of the employer's business operations.

Surveillance of employees in the workplace

Employers can have valid reasons for wanting to monitor their employees' behavior. For example, a retail employer who is experiencing an unexplained inventory shortage may decide to install closed circuit television in his warehouse to determine whether an employee theft problem exists. Video surveillance rooted in such business justification will undoubtedly be upheld as a legal exercise of an employer's rights. Similarly, closed circuit television monitoring to increase efficiency on a production line would probably also be legal regardless of any detrimental effect the monitoring may have on employee morale.

There may, however, be instances when electronic surveillance will violate federal law. For example, an employer experiencing union organizing may not use a video camera to see which employees show up at a union meeting. Also, a unionized employer may have a duty to bargain with the employees' collective bargaining representative before implementing closed circuit television monitoring in the workplace.

Television monitoring in the workplace can also be a tortious invasion of privacy. As explained previously, liability usually turns on the issue of whether the employees have a reasonable expectation of privacy in any particular areas in the workplace. If they have no reasonable expectation of privacy, surveillance by the employer will not be offensive to a reasonable person. There are actually very few areas in the workplace that can be deemed to be such a private place for the employees that monitoring would be forbidden. An obvious example, however, would be employee restrooms. Under most circumstances, an employer would have little business justification for installing cameras in the bathrooms.

Telephone monitoring

Some employers may have a need to monitor employee telephone calls, either to investigate misconduct or criminal activity, or to ascertain the quality of customer service being provided by their employees. Telephone monitoring is subject to much tighter legislative restrictions than video surveillance, however, and an employer can face federal or state penalties if the telephone monitoring system is not implemented properly. A decision by the Federal Court of Appeals for the Eighth Circuit illustrates the danger in conducting unrestricted telephone monitoring.

The court of appeals affirmed a district court's award of $40,000 to two employees of an Arkansas liquor store because the owners of the store had intercepted and taped their personal telephone calls in violation of the Omnibus Crime Control and Safe Streets Act of 1968. Title III of the Omnibus Crime Control Act (also known as the Electronic Communications Privacy Act) makes it unlawful for any person to willfully intercept, use, or disclose any "wire, oral, or electronic communications." The interception of telephone conversations is prohibited activity under the Act, unless such conduct comes within one of the exceptions to the statutory prohibitions.

For example, no violation of federal law exists if the employee consents to the telephone monitoring. Further, an exception exists that allows employers to intercept telephone calls made "in the ordinary course of business." This exception does not require the consent of the participants to the intercepted conversation, but the employer is obligated to cease listening to the conversation as soon as it is determined that the nature of the call is personal.

In the Arkansas case, the employer began secretly taping telephone calls to and from the liquor store after a break-in at the store resulted in the loss of $16,000. The owners suspected that one of the employees had been involved in the theft. The taping was continuous, however, and a series of personal calls between the employee and a man with whom she was having an extramarital affair were intercepted. Many of the conversations were sexually provocative in nature and included discussions of the couple's sex life and other personal matters between the two lovers. The court held that the vast majority of the phone calls were not business-related and awarded damages to the plaintiffs.

Because of the civil and criminal penalties that can be assessed for illegal eavesdropping on employee conversations and the privacy concerns that are raised by video taping employee conduct, employers are advised to proceed very carefully before implementing an employee monitoring program. Employers should check their monitoring and surveillance programs against the prohibitions set forth in the federal statute and any state laws that may be applicable.

....

Lie detector tests

One technique which, until recently, was used quite frequently by employers but which also gave rise to invasion of privacy claims is the polygraph or lie detector test. The test was viewed by employers as a useful tool for gathering information about prospective employees or for investigating misconduct by incumbent employees. Applicants for employment were not successful in bringing invasion of privacy claims to prohibit polygraphs. Courts almost uniformly held that an individual who was seeking to initiate an employment relationship with an employer did not possess a sufficient expectation of privacy to outweigh the employer's business justification for gathering information about the prospective employee.

Employees with some tenure with their employer have been more successful in raising privacy concerns regarding a polygraph, especially when the questions posed to them during a lie detector test strayed into unacceptable personal areas. For example, in one case, an employer was held liable for defamation and invasion of privacy. During a polygraph test prior to discharge, the employer asked the employee about drug use outside of work, among other questions. The employee was then fired for drug abuse. The employer told other employees that the plaintiff's use of drugs was the cause for the discharge, without explaining that there were other reasons contributing to the decision. A jury awarded the plaintiff $448,000 in damages.

The polygraph test is now used infrequently by employers. This is primarily because of the passage of the Employee Polygraph Protection Act of 1988. This law prohibits the use of the polygraph in the workplace with several limited exceptions. Although the title of the law refers to the polygraph, the law also restricts the use of voice stress analyzers or any other mechanical or electrical device that is used for the purpose of rendering a diagnostic opinion regarding the honesty of an individual.

In performing a test under the federal statute, the employer must strictly follow several detailed procedures. Initially, the employee must be provided with a written statement from the employer identifying the specific economic loss or injury that is the subject of the investigation, indicating that the employee had access to the property, and describing the basis of the employer's reasonable suspicion that the employee was involved in the incident. The employee must also receive written notice of the employee's right to consult with legal counsel or a union representative prior to taking the examination. Prior to the test, the employee must sign a form acknowledging that he or she understands that he or she cannot be required to take the test, and that any statements made during the test may constitute evidence upon which an adverse employment decision may be made. In addition to the above notices, the employee must receive all questions to be asked during the examination in advance. The examiner may not ask questions other than those shown to the employee in advance. The federal Act also prohibits the examiner from asking degrading or intrusive questions or inquiring into the religious beliefs, racial bias, political views, sexual behavior, or union activities of the employee. The employee retains the right to terminate the test without prejudice at any time.

In addition to federal law, many states have passed additional restrictions on the use of polygraph tests. Even in those states where polygraph testing is still not completely prohibited, the statutory procedure that now must be followed under federal law in giving a lie detector test is so complex and time-consuming that the effort may not be worthwhile.

Privacy in the computer age

The issue of when an employer's conduct interferes with an employee's right to privacy is one that may arise with increasing frequency in the years to come, because of the increase in personal computer use and the advent of the "personal work station." Although employers can to some extent sympathize with employee concerns regarding privacy, legislative policy makers need to be aware of the legitimate functions served by management programs such as electronic monitoring and surveillance. In the current climate of global business competition, American businesses should not be prohibited from using these legitimate management techniques because of irrational or overblown concerns about employee privacy. Rather, concerns regarding the employee's right to privacy must be balanced against the employer's legitimate need to operate its business as efficiently and productively as possible.

Technology in today's workplace is rapidly changing. The privacy concerns of employees are increasingly coming in conflict with their employer's desire to have access to electronic communications between employees as well as communications by employees that may be directed outside the workplace. This is a rapidly developing area of the law— employers can expect many changes in the next few years, both statutory and judicial. Nevertheless, understanding privacy rights in the computer age is still just a matter of applying traditional legal theory to modern problems.

As has been explained previously, some searches during employment have been ruled to be so intrusive as to be a violation of the common law right of privacy. Clearly, an audit of an employee's computer files would qualify as a search. Employers can avoid liability for such a search, however, by not promoting an expectation of privacy for employees in the information they store on the computer. They should give employees written notice of the employer's right to access computer files and should tell employees that their consent for such a search is a condition of employment.

In other words, traditional employer techniques aimed at dispelling an expectation of privacy can be applied to the paperless workplace. For example, the monitoring of electronic conversations between employees should not be considered intrusive if they are put on notice that the employer expects the e-mail system to be used only for business purposes and that all information stored on the computer remains the property of the employer. Similarly, the monitoring of voice mail messages will also not be an invasion of privacy if the employees have notice that the employer has the right to monitor such messages and the employer explains the business purpose for such monitoring. For example, the employer's reason for such monitoring could be to track response time to client inquiries or to guard against the release of proprietary information to competitors. In the case of either e-mail or voice mail, an expectation of privacy can also be diminished by prohibiting the use of passwords.

There are statutes that might be used by employees to protect their e-mail or voice mail communications. As explained previously, the federal Electronic Communications Privacy Act prohibits the interception, use, or disclosure of protected wire, oral, or electronic communications. Monitoring of conversations should be allowed under the federal statute when consent for such monitoring can be implied from the employer's announcement of its intention to monitor phone conversations, voice mail, and e-mail. When employers get employees to "sign off" on the policy, the consent issue under the federal statute should be resolved. The "ordinary course of business" exception to the statutory prohibition can also be used by employers as long as the monitoring of voice mail is limited to legitimate business goals, such as improving customer service. However, the employer cannot monitor these communications continuously. Once the employer ascertains that certain messages are personal, the monitoring should cease. Obviously, however, an employee could be disciplined if the employer's policy clearly prohibits personal phone calls or the personal use of voice mail or e-mail.

There are state privacy statutes that make interception illegal unless all parties give prior consent. Again, however, consent can be implied if all employees acknowledge in writing that they have been told that e-mail is not to be used for private purposes and understand that the employer will monitor such electronic conversations. A business justification for such monitoring should be relatively easy to establish when employers have been sued because their employees circulated sexually degrading or racially offensive material on the computer network. Also, an employer can be liable for defamation if it allows slanderous or libelous material to be published through the e-mail system.

A written policy dealing with electronic communications is the best way to prevent problems from arising. Some of the more important elements of such a policy are as follows:

+ Prohibit the personal use of e-mail or voice mail systems.

+ The policy should authorize employer access to voice mail, e-mail, or computer files. Employees acknowledge this by signing the policy.

+ The policy should provide that contents of computer and e-mail communications are the property of the employer.

+ State the business reasons for the policy, for example, preventing excessive personal use of company's systems, monitoring customer service, or assuring compliance with company policies.

+ Tell employees that the privacy of e-mail and voice mail is not guaranteed; that passwords are prohibited and that you will override them if they are used.

+ Prohibit offensive, slanderous, vulgar, obscene, harassing, or threatening messages through e-mail.

+ Prohibit communication of sexually oriented messages or images, or downloading of similar material from the Internet.

+ Prohibit the exchange of trade secrets, proprietary information or other confidential information via e-mail or the Internet.

+ Prohibit solicitation using e-mail. If the computer is limited to business use, those using it will be on work time. No solicitation should be allowed.

♦ Prohibit the use of unauthorized screensavers. Screensavers can be miniature billboards for messages in the workplace. Employers are entitled to control the work environment to avoid inappropriate messages even though the degree of communication to others is limited in scope.

Publicity of private facts

There is another branch of the privacy tort that can sometimes have application in the workplace. The Restatement of Torts labels this privacy tort as "Publicity Given to Private Life" and defines it as follows: "One who gives publicity to a matter concerning the private life of another is subject to liability...for invasion of privacy." The disclosure must be offensive to a reasonable person. To be actionable, many courts have required that the private facts actually be communicated to the public at large. There are several decisions, however, that have allowed the plaintiff to go forward with a claim even though the publicity giving rise to the tort was communicated to a more limited group of people.

For example, the Supreme Judicial Court of Massachusetts has ruled that disclosure of private facts to employees within the same corporation would be sufficient publication to create an invasion of privacy. This case involved an employee who complained that a manager had circulated a memorandum about him to approximately 15 other people in the company. This memorandum described the plaintiff's behavior in a grievance meeting where plaintiff became distraught and started crying. The memorandum also suggested that the plaintiff had a mental problem that was beyond the company's treatment expertise.

In making its decision, the court suggested that not every disclosure of private facts would constitute an invasion of privacy. The court said that the disclosure must amount to an "unreasonable interference with the employee's right of privacy." In making that determination, the court said that the employer's legitimate business interest in obtaining and publishing the information to others had to be balanced against the "substantiality of the intrusion."

The plaintiff also claimed that the treating physician, hired by his employer, had also violated his privacy by discussing his mental condition with other managers. In allowing this communication by the doctor, the plaintiff claimed the company was also liable. The Massachusetts court said that when the medical information is reasonably necessary to serve a valid interest of the employer, it would not be an invasion of privacy for the physician to disclose the information to the employer. The court stated a different balancing test for determining the unreasonableness of the interference with privacy when a physician-patient relationship is involved: "The test...involves a balancing of the degree of intrusion on privacy and the public interest in preserving the confidentiality of a physician-patient relationship...against the employer's need for the medical information."

Private information regarding employees, especially medical information, should be kept confidential. In addition to potential tort liability for disclosure of this information, there are state and federal statutes that protect the confidentiality of medical records. Only those managers with a demonstrated "need to know" should be informed of the employee's medical condition. Obviously, employee health personnel and plaintiff's immediate supervisor might need to be aware of a medical condition that could have an effect on his performance. Publicity of private medical facts beyond those individuals could be an invasion of privacy.

Avoiding invasion of privacy claims

Here are some steps employers should take to avoid invasion of privacy claims.

- ♦ An employer's drug-testing policy should be in writing. Employees would sign a statement acknowledging that they have read the policy and understand that their consent for testing is a condition of employment.

- ♦ In company handbooks and personnel policies, employers should reserve the right to do workplace searches. Employees should acknowledge in writing their understanding that consent for such searches is a condition of continued employment.

- ♦ Employees should be given written notice that items like desks or lockers remain company property despite possession by employees. Employees should not be given keys to their desks or be allowed to put personal locks (locks where management does not know the combination or does not have a key) on their lockers.

- ♦ All medical information, drug testing results, or other private, personal information about the employee should be kept confidential. Only those individuals who have a solid business justification to support their need to know such information should be allowed access to the information.

- Keep employee medical information in a confidential file that is separate from the personnel file. Employees should be asked to sign consent forms that allow disclosure of medical information to designated individuals in specific situations.
- Develop a written policy to address electronic communications in the workplace.
- Instruct supervisors as to the liability that can arise from unreasonable publicity of private facts regarding employees' personal matters. Train supervisors about "need to know" principles and ask them to restrict publication of private information regarding employees to only those individuals whose "need to know" is supported by a clear business justification.

Chapter 10

It's Never Too Late for Union Avoidance

Jim Faraday sat across the bargaining table listening to his labor lawyer argue with the union business agent about whether the foreman, Butch Ringer, would be allowed to do bargaining unit work under the terms of the new contract. The Teamsters had recently been elected as the collective bargaining representative for the company's 11 machine shop employees. The vote was eight to three in favor of the Union. Now, the company and the union were trying to negotiate a first contract. Things were not going too well.

"Look, this is a small shop," said Fred Harraman, the company's lawyer. "It has always had a working foreman. We need Butch to be able to pitch in and help out sometimes."

"Fine," answered Terry Cooper, the union business agent, "we'll give you a working foreman provision. But he has to join the union and pay dues like everybody else. Also, we need to have the union shop clause and dues check-off."

"That's unacceptable," said Harraman, "Butch is going to be evaluating employee performance and making discipline and discharge recommendations. If he joins the union, I see a real conflict of interest there."

"He doesn't pay, he doesn't work," said Cooper with a shrug.

"We've been down this road before," Jim Faraday thought to himself. This was the 13th bargaining session with the union, and they did not seem to be getting any closer to a contract. In fact, the union had given the company a deadline for reaching an agreement or it was taking the men out on strike. Some of the guys even brought picket signs with them to the negotiating session.

Jim wondered how they ever got to this point. He remembered how it all started. Terry Cooper came waltzing into his office with eight of the employees—they were all wearing Teamsters jackets. "I represent a majority of your shop employees," Cooper had said. "Let's talk."

Fred Harraman wrote the union a letter telling Cooper the issue of representation had to be settled by a National Labor Relations Board (NLRB) election and eventually, after some wrangling at a hearing about whether the foreman and the company's blueprint draftsman should be allowed to vote, an election was scheduled. The scheduled date allowed the company to hold meetings with the shop employees for about six weeks.

"A lot of good it did us," thought Jim. "Not that it was Fred's fault. We made some good arguments against unionism and Fred was very helpful by providing resource materials to us." Jim had thought his employees were much too independent to want to join a union like the Teamsters. Jim could not understand where he had gone wrong. The employees knew that the company's wages were competitive and they already had a good health insurance plan and a 401(k) plan. "It just doesn't make sense," thought Jim.

Jim's attention was drawn back to the negotiations when two employees started talking about why they didn't want Butch Ringer doing their work. Jim always listened more attentively when the union business agent stopped talking and let the employees get a word in edgewise.

"I don't want Butch doing our work," said Pete Harper. "He'll just screw it up; either that, or he'll sit on his fat ass and get in the way!"

Jim spoke up in defense of Butch Ringer, "Pete, you're not being fair. Butch has always worked hand-in-hand with you guys."

"Yeah, he worked 'hand-in-hand' all right—my hand twisted behind my back," said Pete. The other guys on the negotiating team laughed.

"What are you guys talking about?" asked Jim Faraday.

"Look, Mr. Faraday, you don't know what's been going on," said Harry Fogle, another mechanic. "If you try to cross Ringer, he'll get you. He nearly twisted my thumb clean off one day upstairs behind the crane."

"That's right," said Sam Smiley. "He pushed me around pretty good a couple of months ago. He warned me that if I said anything, he would come get me!"

Pete spoke for the group, "Mr. Faraday, Butch really should be fired. All these guys have had run-ins with him. If you want to keep him on—fine. But don't expect us to work side by side with him."

Jim Faraday looked at Fred Harraman in amazement. He truly did not know this was going on. "Do all of you feel this way?" Jim asked, directing his question to the six mechanics who were present at the negotiating table.

They all nodded, and then Harry Fogle spoke up again. "Mr. Faraday, that Butch Ringer is bad news. He's why you got this union in here. We needed protection."

Jim Faraday said, "You guys should have come to me. I would have helped."

"I think it's too late for that now," said Terry Cooper, the Teamsters business agent.

Jim Faraday sat back in his chair while Fred Harraman asked for time to caucus. Jim Faraday thought to himself, "Now, I understand... too late, but at least all this makes sense now."

Where have all the unions gone?

Most employers are aware of the general decline in union membership over the last two decades and some may have begun to believe that their company will never be organized by a union. The decline in membership may be attributed to union complacency after the prosperity of the 1960s, the switch from a manufacturing to a service-based economy, the failure by unions to accommodate women and minorities into their ranks, and concerted efforts by business to remain union-free. To a large extent, unions have failed to respond to a changing and more competitive environment.

Employers, however, must not be complacent and assume that third party representation of their employees is not a possibility. When employers fail to practice good employee relations and ignore the signs of employee dissatisfaction, opportunity knocks for the union organizer. In the opening sketch, Jim Faraday failed to stay in touch with his workers; he was too busy. He left the day-to-day supervision of his employees to his foreman. Little did he know, his foreman was abusing the shop employees and no amount of wages and benefits could keep the union out.

In general, however, the continued reluctance of employees to pay their hard-earned money to a third party representative and organized labor's refusal to change its traditional organizing tactics has created an atmosphere for continued success by employers in remaining nonunion. Although certain industries remain strongholds of union activism, most employers can stay union-free by maintaining a policy of positive employee relations and open lines of communication with their employees. Employers who practice good employee relations will not be targeted by unions because normally their company will have the reputation of being a good place to work and employees will take pride in their company and pride in their work. They will also perceive that they will receive fair treatment and recognition for a job well done. In such an atmosphere, the union's message falls on deaf ears.

In this chapter, we will review the steps employers should take to keep unions from organizing their employees. This chapter includes a summary a of typical campaign strategy for defeating a union when an employer is faced with a representation election before the National Labor Relations Board (NLRB or "the Board"). Unions know about such strategies but often fail to successfully counter management's campaign to stay union-free. That is why it is usually "never too late for union avoidance."

Most employees say "no" to unions

A 1995 study conducted by Harvard University and the University of Wisconsin found that an overwhelming majority of the nation's employees prefer cooperative employee-management committees in their workplaces to union representation. According to the employees polled in the study, they no longer see unions as a "solution" to the problems facing them and their families in a rapidly changing world. One of the primary reasons given in the study for the decline of unionism in the United States is that unions have not protected their members and their jobs. In addition, employees report that they do not believe that unions are making an important contribution in the American workplace today.

The conclusions drawn from this study appear to be corroborated by data gathered by the Department of Labor's Bureau of Labor Statistics. In 1995, membership in labor unions nationwide fell to 16.4 million workers. This figure represents only 14.9 percent of all employed workers in the United States. These figures are somewhat distorted by union success in organizing government employees. In the private sector, unions represent only 9.4 million workers, which constitutes only 10.4 percent of private nonagricultural workers.

Union leaders have vowed to reverse the trend of declining membership by employing new techniques for attracting employees to their membership. Organizers are beginning to appeal to the specific interests of women in the workplace by using such issues as child care, pensions, or pay equity. Organizing tactics such as media campaigns and corporate campaigns have recently been effective in increasing union membership in limited sectors of the economy, such as ladies garment industry and certain sectors of the retail industry. Some unions have joined together in consolidated campaigns against large employers, pooling their resources and efforts rather than competing for the votes of nonunion employees.

Employee-management committees

Employers recognize that changes in the American workplace require new and innovative programs to address workplace issues, such as productivity and quality of service, and they understand that they do not face these challenges alone. Consequently, employers have begun to include employees in the decision-making process. Employee participation committees, known as quality circles, quality groups, and total quality management, have been introduced in many businesses and industries. By emphasizing teamwork and cooperation between employees and management, these committees not only have led to improvements in productivity and quality of service, but have also enhanced employee morale by assuring employees that they are valuable members of the organization.

Naturally, unions have strongly opposed the establishment of such committees, claiming that employers introduced such programs to discourage union organizing. Unions often attempt to thwart employee-management cooperation by filing unfair labor practice charges against employers that have employee participation committees. Unions argue that such cooperative committees violate the National Labor Relations Act (NLRA) because they constitute employer-dominated "company unions."

Often, the NLRB has agreed with this union argument. The NLRB interprets the definition of labor organization in the NLRA very broadly, and virtually any collaborative employee-management committee that concerns itself with an issue that can be construed to be a "term or condition of employment" may be found to be a labor organization. As a result, the NLRB has found many such committees unlawful and has ordered them to be dissolved.

A 1992 decision by the NLRB, *Electromation, Inc.*, brought the issue of employee committees to the forefront again. Despite the increasing desire of employees to become involved in the decision-making process, the Board made it clear in *Electromation* that employee-involvement committees run the risk of violating the NLRA unless they are strictly limited with regard to their scope and operation. In light of the Board's antiquated view of labor-management relations, some employers have discontinued their plans to implement innovative operational structures that emphasize employee participation.

In an effort to eliminate the uncertainty over the legality of employee involvement programs, members of both houses of Congress have introduced bills to lift the ban on certain types of company-sponsored employee committees. The objective of this legislation is to eliminate the barriers to workplace cooperation and to give workers the "opportunity to share their views on working conditions and their ideas on improving plant productivity."

Although the legislation leaves the prohibition against company-dominated unions intact, and in no way reduces the right of employees to form a union, organized labor continues to lobby vigorously against the proposal. Unfortunately, despite the fact that labor laws drafted in the 1930s are in dire need of positive revisions to meet the needs of today's workplace, employers can expect any attempt to change these labor laws to meet with concentrated resistance by unions.

Unions look to reinvigorate organizing

Facing decreasing membership in the private sector, the new leadership of the labor movement has announced ambitious new programs to organize nonunion employers across the country. John J. Sweeney, president of the AFL-CIO, labor's umbrella organization, has placed organizing at the top of labor's agenda. Mr. Sweeney comes from the Service Employees International Union (SEIU), one of the few unions that has had recent success with organizing and membership growth. It was predicted that he would bring the SEIU's aggressive and often confrontational style with him to the AFL-CIO.

The new AFL-CIO leadership was elected to reverse the long-term decline in union membership. So far, the announced goal of organizing more workers has been mostly rhetoric. There was a flurry of union organizing initiatives in 1996, including the creation of a separate organizing department in the AFL-CIO and the allocation of $20 million to organizing efforts.

One key to the union's new organizing approach will be to target specific companies, rather than to merely respond to inquiries from employees. The service industries have experienced the greatest growth in number of jobs in recent years and will be a prime target. White collar employees could also be targets of this new organizing approach. Financial institutions are frequently mentioned as potential targets for union organizing. Reorganization and job insecurity in the health care industry make those employees likely targets also.

Mr. Sweeney has acknowledged that it will take time before unions actually see a resurgence in union membership. He has asked every affiliated international and local union of the AFL-CIO to "shift resources and staff into organizing on a massive scale" for 1997. In fact, the AFL-CIO allocated $30 million to organizing in 1997. The unions will continue to use corporate campaigns and pressure tactics, and if a company cannot be organized, the end result of such campaigns may be to put the company out of business.

In addition, the AFL-CIO's Executive Council unveiled two new programs in 1997 that were aimed at changing the image of organized labor. Both of those programs, a multimillion-dollar media campaign and a program to encourage more activity by the central labor councils, focus on grassroots efforts and demonstrate the shift in organizing tactics to the local level.

Time will tell whether the AFL-CIO's new initiative will prove successful. However, employers who have not given much thought to a union organizing drive should begin preparing now. Many employers held supervisory training sessions on union avoidance in the distant past, but have had significant turnover in their supervisory staff since that time. Other employers may have disregarded their no-solicitation/no-distribution policies or even eliminated them from their employee handbook. Many businesses have no contingency plan in place for how to respond if union organizers pay a visit to their facility. Now is the time to perform a union vulnerability audit and to take the steps necessary to place the company in the best possible position to avoid union organizing.

Some signs of union organizing

If employees do become interested in union representation, they are not likely to announce their intentions to management. Instead, the organizing campaign will proceed covertly until the union supporters have enough support to file a representation petition with the NLRB. Any Regional Office of the NLRB can accept a petition if it is supported by at least 30 percent of the employees in the proposed voting unit. Normally, however, unions will not file a representation petition with the Board unless they have the support of at least 50 percent of the employees in the voting unit.

Support for the union is usually shown by authorization cards signed by individual employees. These cards are not simply requests for an election or "interest cards," but a signed statement from an employee that the employee wants the union to be his or her "collective bargaining" agent. In other words, the card represents a legal commitment that the employee wants the union to be his exclusive representative in bargaining with the company about wages and conditions of employment. For example, most union cards state, "I, (the undersigned employee)...hereby authorize the union, or its chartered local union to represent me for the purpose of collective bargaining." If the union receives cards signed by a majority of the employees in a potential bargaining unit, it may send the employer a letter asking management to "bargain" without any vote by the employees whatsoever. (It may enclose with that letter copies of the signed cards in its possession.) Generally, an employer is permitted to insist that a union win an NLRB secret ballot election before recognizing it as the representative of employees.

During a union organizing campaign, an employer should communicate with its employees in an attempt to educate them about union representation prior to the representation election itself. Under normal circumstances, an employer will have only about six to eight weeks between the petition and the election to get its message across to employees. That is why it is extremely beneficial to get advance notice of an organizing effort prior to receiving an election petition from the NLRB. There are some traditional signs of union organizing that may or may not be present in a work force as a precursor to the filing of a representation petition with the NLRB. Management must learn the signals that organizing is occurring and respond accordingly. Some of these include:

♦ An employee writes down the names of the other employees in the department by copying them from the time cards, or someone asks for sensitive personnel information without good reason, or personnel records or documents "disappear."

♦ Employees abruptly stop talking when supervisors approach.

♦ Employees begin gathering in unusual places outside of work.

♦ Employees from separate departments or different job levels begin meeting and talking together. Some employees circulate from department to department.

♦ New groups of employees are formed, with new informal leaders.

♦ Non-union people begin meeting and talking with known union supporters.

♦ There is unusually intense conversation or activity during breaks or lunch periods.

- Employees start leaving the premises for lunch or are absent from customary social "get-togethers."
- Employees who are normally friendly and talkative become quiet and uncommunicative.
- Employees avoid being seen with management.
- A former employee shows up before or after regular working hours to talk with former friends and employees. (This is particularly suspect behavior if the former employee left on bad terms.)
- Strangers appear in the company parking lot or in work areas.
- The "rumor grapevine" shuts down completely.
- The nature of employee complaints changes, or the frequency of complaints increases.
- Complaints begin to be made by a delegation, not by single employees.
- Some employees become much more militant and start "demanding" their rights.
- There is a noticeable increase in questions raised about company rules, policies, practices, benefits, etc.; employees begin showing unusual and critical curiosity about the company's affairs and policies.
- A surge of anti-company or anti-supervisor graffiti appears on the walls of restrooms, locker rooms, cafeteria, etc.
- Easygoing employees suddenly become "activists" or begin using buzz words associated with union activity, such as "seniority," "grievance," or "concerted activity."
- A previously popular employee suddenly becomes unpopular and is needled by co-workers.
- New employees (who are actually union "plants") may excessively boast of their interest in their job, their approval of the company and its policies, their respect for the boss, etc.
- Good workers begin doing poor work, or poor workers begin doing good work. An employee becomes "too" cooperative.
- Organizing activity at a nearby business or at a competitor's business is discussed by the employees.
- Contact with employees by a union representative.

- An employee tells a supervisor that there is organizing, even if the employee claims the union doesn't have a chance.
- Authorization cards, handbills, or leaflets appear on the premises and parking lot.

You can keep union organizers out

Many employers, unfamiliar with their own property rights and perhaps more wary of union "rights" than they need to be, do not realize that they can keep nonemployee union organizers off company property. A 1992 decision of the U.S. Supreme Court has upheld the right of employers to bar nonemployee union organizers from entering an employer's private property for the purpose of attempting to organize its employees. Under the Court's ruling, only in very limited circumstances will employers now be required to permit unions onto their property.

In *Lechmere Inc. v. NLRB*, the Supreme Court addressed the relationship between the rights of employees to organize under Section 7 of the NLRA and the property rights of their employers. The case arose in the context of the United Food and Commercial Workers Union's attempt to organize the employees of a retail store owned and operated by Lechmere. Lechmere's store was located in a shopping plaza in Newington, Connecticut. After Lechmere denied the nonemployee union organizers access to the parking lot to place handbills on employee cars, the union filed unfair labor practice charges with the NLRB.

The Supreme Court found that Lechmere had not violated the Act. The Court stated that "Section 7 simply does not protect nonemployee union organizers *except* in the rare case where 'the inaccessibility of employees makes ineffective the reasonable attempts by nonemployees to communicate with them through the usual channels.' " The Court explained that a balancing of Section 7 rights versus private property rights should be considered only after it is clear that reasonable access to the employees is "infeasible." The Court further noted that reasonable access is infeasible only when the "location of a plant and the living quarters for the employees place the employees beyond the reach of reasonable union efforts to communicate with them," such as at logging camps, mining camps, and mountain resort hotels.

In applying these principles in *Lechmere*, the Court found that the employees were accessible to the union. Specifically, the record showed that the union had been successful in contacting a substantial percentage of the employees by mail, telephone, and home visits. The Court further explained that direct contact is not a necessary element of reasonable access and that signs or advertising also may suffice.

Employers can prohibit nonemployee organizers from entering their property to solicit their employees. Employers may ordinarily refuse to allow outside union organizers access to their plant, parking lot, or to any other part of their premises, provided that there is adequate opportunity for union organizers to contact employees without entering company property. Also, the company may not discriminate against the union by allowing other solicitations or distributions on its property, such as by charitable organizations, by vendors, or by rival unions. Employers should implement and uniformly enforce a no-access rule for nonemployees that can be used effectively during union organizing campaigns.

Decisions like *Lechmere* dictate that unions must rely on employee organizers to win representation rights. Indeed, an organizing campaign almost always starts with a small group of employees who work secretly to increase support for a union. These employees may seek out the assistance of a union on their own initiative or the union may have fomented the employee unrest by sending a union employee to ostensibly work for the employer while he organizes the employees from the inside. These "plants" or "salts," as they are called, care little about the employer's product or their own job duties—their goal is to organize the employee work force for the union. Unfortunately, this "salting" tactic has been legitimized by the Board and the courts and these union "plants" have the full protection of the National Labor Relations Act.

Employers should implement no-solicitation, no-distribution rules to regulate employee organizing. This kind of rule, if enforced uniformly, will prevent employees from engaging in oral solicitation of union membership or distribution of union materials during "working time." The rule should also forbid the distribution or circulation of literature by employees in work areas during both working and nonworking times. A sample No Solicitation, No Distribution rule, with a nonemployee no-access provision, is included in the Appendix on page 274.

The importance of front-line supervision in union avoidance

Supervisors who communicate effectively with the employees working for them—that is, they *talk* and *listen* to employees—and who administer the company's policies in a fair and uniform manner are essential to union avoidance. If employees don't trust the front-line supervisors in the company, the employer will most likely lose the representation election.

The primary step supervisors must take is to practice positive employee relations—open, honest communication with employees and fairness in the application and enforcement of policies. In addition, they must be committed to a union-free workplace.

What supervisors can expect with a union

Here are a few points all supervisors should think about if they have even the slightest notion that working in a union shop would not be burdensome to them.

- ♦ Supervisors will have someone second guessing them; a shop steward will police their decisions.
- ♦ Supervisors will work more hours and longer workweeks because of grievance meetings, negotiations, and arbitrations.
- ♦ Shop stewards may file numerous grievances against the supervisor to get him or her to relax standards or may pressure management to remove the supervisor from his or her position.
- ♦ The supervisor's job may be more dangerous, such as in a situation when he or she has to cross picket lines during strikes.
- ♦ Loss of peace of mind caused by threats to the supervisor and family members during labor strife.
- ♦ Tension and an up-tight working atmosphere.
- ♦ Rigid union seniority restricting work assignments.
- ♦ Employee dissension, suspicion, and poor discipline caused by union interference.
- ♦ Performing an employee's job during strikes and work stoppages.
- ♦ Union gets all the credit for wage and benefit increases.
- ♦ Employee morale breakdown.
- ♦ An "us versus them" attitude develops.

Supervisory steps in preserving nonunion status

Supervisors who are committed to a union-free workplace will take a number of steps to ensure that employees working for them are happy, or at least secure in the belief that they will get a fair shake from the supervisor. Here is what a good supervisor will do to promote union avoidance:

....

- Opens lines of communication.
- Realizes that a supervisor can promote a motivated group of employees or create an atmosphere that invites union intervention.
- Participates in "two-way" communications.
- Recognizes there are problems in every group of employees, but believes such problems can be solved.
- Solves problems either by explaining the policy to the employees or taking steps to correct the situation.
- Learns what employees think of the company.
- "Sells" the many benefits provided by the company.
- Establishes an atmosphere that makes employees comfortable in talking about matters of concern to them.
- Knows the employees' background and relationships.
- Looks for opportunities to suggest promotion of qualified employees. A supervisor should tactfully point out weaknesses of employees so that they can advance with the company.
- Disciplines evenhandedly; avoids favoritism in scheduling assignments, overtime, etc. The supervisor should know what discipline has been imposed in the past and put past practice to use.
- Recognizes and responds to evidence of employee discontent.
- Cultivates leadership among the employees.
- Supervises people, not a file.

The supervisor should solve small problems daily; neglecting the concerns and needs of employees indicates a lack of interest in employee welfare. A good supervisor does the following:

- Gives a pat on the back for a job well-done.
- Shows an interest in employee suggestions about operations.
- Gives a sincere "Hello, how are you?" to employees every day.
- Interprets all policies regarding overtime, shifts, etc., only after he or she is sure the interpretation is correct.
- Is sensitive to and anticipates employee concerns; does not sit back and wait for employee complaints.

What type of campaign works best?

When faced with an impending representation election, many employers initially lean toward a neutral or low-key campaign in the weeks preceding an election. This is a mistake. If the employer stays neutral, it will lose the election. There are many employees who sign an authorization card because they are fooled by the union's promises and don't know the real facts about unions. There are others who are just trying to get management's attention and who realize that they don't have to vote for the union in the election. Still others sign cards because of peer pressure. All these employees, even though they have signed cards, want to hear the company's message. If the employer stays neutral or does not adamantly oppose the union, these employees will think that the company does not care whether it is organized or that it has, in effect, "surrendered" to the desire for union representation.

Although there is no evidence that a less vigorous campaign wins significant points with employees, some employers adopt such an approach apparently in a mistaken belief that a more neutral stance is required by the representation process itself. This is just not true. Simply because a substantial number of employees may have instigated the organizing drive and eventually supported the filing of the petition with the NLRB, an employer need not sit on the sidelines and let opposing employee factions fight it out. An employer should stay engaged during an organizing campaign by stressing the positive qualities of a nonunion workplace and the company in general and by providing comprehensive information to employees about NLRB election procedures and their right to participate in the election process.

Employers must communicate their views to employees during a representation campaign. The message should be positive and factually accurate. In this way, employees will never resent hearing the employer's side of the story. There are many ways to communicate the company's message, including direct contact and conversation between supervisors and employees, letters to employees' homes; bulletin board postings, handouts, paycheck enclosures, video presentations, and group speeches. The most effective method for gaining the support of employees in opposition to the union is one-on-one conversations between supervisors and employees.

Possible campaign themes

A number of themes can be used by an employer in confronting a union-organizing campaign. Some are as follows:

"Most employees are nonunion." With all the statutory protections available to employees, unions have become irrelevant. Unions maintain power only in the legislative arena where PAC dollars are available for lobbying. Union activity in this arena, however, can be portrayed as defensive and obstructionist. As mentioned, eight out of every nine employees have chosen to be nonunion for good reasons. A modern work force is a flexible work force without artificial barriers to improvements in skills, transfer, or promotion.

"Union finances are funded by members." Many employees who are enticed into becoming union members do so because of inflated promises of higher salaries and greater benefits. These employees fail to consider, however, the financial burdens that often accompany union membership, especially the obligation to pay dues, fees, and assessments. Unions must file financial reports with the federal government and often these documents contain useful information for the employer's campaign. Unions can be shown to be a big business with enormous budgets dedicated to the salaries and benefits of union leaders. Employees should be reminded that it is union dues, paid out of their weekly salaries, that will pay for the salaries and benefits of union leaders. It should also be explained that much of the money they will have to pay in dues will not come back to assist them but will be used for organizing activities elsewhere or lobbying and political campaigns.

In response to this theme, management must be prepared for a challenge from union supporters as to why the company does not reveal its own financial report. One answer is that the union's financial report is relevant because the employees' dues payments will be funding the union's expenditures whereas the opposite is true with company revenues: they are used to pay the employees' salaries and benefits.

"Union corruption is a legitimate concern." Certain unions have a particularly sordid past that is well-documented in newspaper articles and case summaries of judicial decisions. Although this theme should be used only in the early stages of the campaign and should not be overdone, this information may be an eye-opener for employees who have only been exposed to a local union organizer. Corruption at the International Union level can be made relevant by showing the control exercised over local unions by the International Union.

"Retain your independence." This theme appeals to employee desires to speak for themselves. It works well where individual supervisors already have a good relationship with employees in their department. It is a very basic message: union representation means that management can no longer deal directly with employees to solve workplace problems. A "No" vote means no union, and the freedom for employees to speak for themselves without a union "go-between." Union dominance and control over the individual employee can be emphasized in this theme. Also, the "collective" nature of the union as an institution makes it very vulnerable to an argument that the desires and opinions of individual employees will be ignored.

Union control can be illustrated by the fact that the union's primary goal in negotiations is to obtain a union shop clause (forcing the employee to pay dues as a condition of employment) and a dues check-off clause (dues deducted automatically from the employees' checks). The local union's bylaws should also be a fertile source of information for demonstrating the union's control over the individual, including its system for disciplining (trial, fines, expulsion) members for speaking out against the union.

"Don't let them push you around." Employers who want to communicate their views regarding the merits of staying union-free to employees but who do not want to run the risk of alienating the employees by being too heavy-handed about the union sometimes choose a "don't let them push you around" or "you have rights" theme for the campaign. This theme can be used when unions are too aggressive in trying to win certification. Issues like preservation of employee privacy (too many phone calls or union visits to the home) and stopping harassment or threats by overzealous union supporters can be emphasized. The employer is viewed as the "good guy" in this scenario by trying to preserve a "zone of neutrality" for those employees who don't want to get involved in the debate.

"There are no guarantees in the collective bargaining process." This theme allows the employer to point out that, although the union, like all unions, is making lavish promises to employees to obtain their vote, none of these promises can be fulfilled except with the voluntary agreement of the company. In other words, the union cannot provide any guarantees as to the outcome of negotiations. During negotiations, wages and benefits may go up but they can also go down. The employer is also allowed to point out that in a substantial number of cases, negotiations for a first-time contract never result in an agreement. This latter message should be accompanied by a disclaimer that "the company would always bargain in good faith."

"Striking employees face heavy financial burden." There is no
more important campaign theme than the dangers of a union strike and
the burden employees and their families will face (*not* the union leadership) if they are forced to go out on strike. In addition to the obligation to
pay union dues and fees, union members face the severe financial consequences of strikes.

Many employees who are encouraged by their union leaders to walk
off their jobs are simply not prepared for the economic consequences that
result from a decision to strike. In most cases, employees have not been
informed of the economic realities of a strike by their union leadership.
An employee who goes out on strike for economic reasons will lose all
wages while on strike. Where positions are available, but the striking
employee still refuses to go back to work, that individual will also not be
entitled to unemployment compensation. Striking employees also lose
their fringe benefits such as medical insurance and life insurance that
can be discontinued at the commencement of a strike. The employee who
chooses to walk off a job and strike is not even entitled to food stamps.

Another important issue to emphasize about strikes is the employer's
right to hire replacement workers to keep operations going during a
strike. Striking employees can be permanently replaced while they are
out on an economic strike. When the strike ends, they may no longer
have a job. Although their names must be placed on a preferential hiring
list, the employer is not required to bump employees who may have been
hired to work during the strike. Also, because strikes inevitably result in
a loss of production and sales, the employer is not likely to be in a hiring
mode for some time after the strike.

Employers who are faced with union organizing drives should make
their employees aware of the problems that can arise during union
strikes. The union's strike record should be highlighted if it is particularly egregious. Employees should be made aware that they will receive
no financial assistance from the state or federal government when the
union strike fund is found to be insufficient to provide for their basic
needs during a strike.

Finally, unions are attempting to respond to the shift in the American economy from manufacturing to service-based businesses by changing
their image from that of bastions for predominately white, male, blue-collar
workers to that of organizations attuned to the values and concerns of
minorities and women. In fact, in their attempt to make themselves more
palatable to the traditional professions, such as those involved in health

care, some unions are portraying themselves as "professional associations" rather than labor unions. Regardless of the rhetoric, old habits are hard to break. When faced with any type of dissonance among its ranks, unions resort to their old tried-and-true methods of conflict resolution—threats, intimidation, and violence. There is always a recent strike story that can be used to highlight the potential for violence during strikes.

"You're doing fine without a union." A frequent theme in representation campaigns is to stress how well employees are doing without a union. In such campaigns, managers discuss how well the company's employees are treated and how costly union dues are for union members. Despite the frequency with which companies use this theme, results can be mixed. Managers have to be careful that they don't promise things will be even better if the employees vote against the union. Rather, management must be able to document the benefits already afforded employees. Highlighting the benefits already provided to employees has its advantages because a campaign that over-emphasizes the negatives of the union is usually not as effective as one that stresses the positives of the company. Obviously, however, an employer who does not provide competitive wages and benefits for its employees will have trouble with this theme.

"You're in good hands." This theme stresses the employees' importance to management, the fairness with which employees will always be treated, and management's desire to "work together" with employees. In other words, management must let the employees know that the company will not let them down. There are ways to assure employees that things will be "okay" after the union is defeated without promising specific increases in wages and benefits. The often-used phrase "We have heard your concerns" or "You don't need a union to achieve your personal and professional goals" sends a message to employees despite its ambiguity.

The basic message is that employees do not need union representation to be treated fairly by the company; that there will be no retaliation, regardless of the outcome of the election; that management can solve all problems without outside third party representation; and that the company will always pay the best wages and have the best benefits it can afford to pay.

Union avoidance "do's" and "don'ts"

During a union organizing campaign, it is important to keep in mind three basic rules: 1) a company is not permitted to discriminate against employees because of their union sympathies or activities in order to discourage such activity; 2) a company is not permitted to interfere with union organizing by making threats or promises in order to discourage such activity; and 3) the employer may express its opinions against the union and give examples of problems encountered by other employees because they got mixed up with a union—as long as it does not violate the first two rules in the process.

The NLRB will strictly scrutinize an employer's conduct (including that of its supervisors) during a union-organizing campaign. An employer's conduct or statements may be considered unlawful and serve as grounds for setting aside an election. How far the NLRB will go in enforcing its election conduct rules is largely unpredictable. Nevertheless, the employer's primary goal must be to win the election; it cannot let a fear of post-election objections filed with the NLRB dilute or weaken its message to employees. Remember, if the margin of victory is great enough, most unions will not bother filing objections.

Company representatives may freely express the company's position and attempt to enlist employee support for that position. It is permissible to:

♦ State that the company is opposed to the unionization of its employees.

♦ State the company's reasons why it considers it unnecessary for its employees to be represented by a union.

♦ Question whether the union has any real interest in the welfare of the employees, or whether the union merely wishes to obtain revenues through dues, initiation fees, assessments, and fines.

♦ Point out that the union cannot keep the promises it is making to employees to obtain their vote.

♦ Emphasize the possibility of strikes and the loss of earnings and hardships caused by strikes. In this regard, the company may point out that employees on strike may not be entitled to unemployment compensation and that union strike benefits, if any, are meager. Nonstriking employees may also be fined by the union for crossing picket lines. The terrible strike record of the particular union involved should also be discussed.

♦ Bring any unfavorable factual publicity that the union or its representatives have received as a result of Senate committee hearings, court proceedings, newspapers reports of picket line violence, corruption, theft, etc., to employees' attention.

- Emphasize the wage rates and benefit programs that the company's employees currently enjoy without the necessity of paying dues.

- Point out that the union, if it were successful in organizing, would probably make every effort to obtain a "union shop" clause, whereby employees would have to pay dues and initiation fees to the union just to keep their jobs or, failing such payments, they could be discharged at the request of the union. This would mean that no matter how much an employee disagreed with the goals of the union, he or she would have to finance the union as a condition of continued employment.

- Emphasize that an election pending before the NLRB will be conducted by secret ballot, and that even those employees who signed union membership or authorization cards are free to vote against the union.

- The company may point out that the union cannot provide any guarantees. During negotiations wages and benefits may go up but they can also go down.

- The company may point out that federal law forbids a union or its agents from restraining or coercing employees in the exercise of their rights, including the right not to support a union.

- In making speeches to employees, the company may assemble the employees on company premises, during working hours, and may pay the employees for the time spent in attending meetings. (The company is not obligated to give the union a similar opportunity to address the employees.) The only restriction is that this may not be done within the 24-hour period immediately preceding the starting time of voting in a NLRB election.

During a union organizational campaign, company representatives may not make any statement, whether by direct conversation, letter, bulletin board posting, or speech, that contains a promise of benefit or threat of reprisal that is tied to the issue of union representation. Thus, for example, it is *not* permissible for the company to:

- Promise or imply that employees will get a wage increase, a better job, or any other similar benefit if they keep the union out. (But you can give examples of where nonunion employees have done considerably better than unionized employees.)

....

267

- Threaten or hint that employees will receive a wage cut, smaller wage increases, a less desirable job, or any other loss of benefits if the employees support the union or if the union organizes the plant.

- Threaten or hint that employees will be discharged, demoted, laid off or otherwise discriminated against if the union succeeds in organizing the plant.

- State or hint that the company will close down its operations if the union succeeds in organizing the plant. (But the employer can show where unions have failed to keep their members' jobs secure, i.e., plant closings.)

- State or hint that the company will refuse to bargain with the union if the union is successful in organizing the plant. (But management can state that the company can say "NO" to union demands that it does not consider to be in the best interest of the company or its employees.)

- Have managers interrogate employees at any time, including during hiring, regarding their union sympathies or activities—or that of other employees. (An employee can always volunteer to share his or her knowledge and thoughts with a supervisor, however.)

- Forbid employees to discuss union matters on the company premises during nonworking time. (Rules prohibiting solicitation during "working time" are proper.)

- Prohibit employees from passing out union literature during "nonworking time" except in work areas or certain public areas.

- Have company representatives and supervisors call employees into their private offices, individually or in small groups, for the purpose of making statements in opposition to the union or to inquire about the union. (An employee-initiated discussion is another matter.)

- Permit loyal employees to engage in antiunion activities and distribute antiunion literature on company time and premises, while denying prounion employees similar rights to engage in prounion activities.

- In general, a company may not forbid its employees from wearing union buttons or other union insignia while at work. (Occasionally the message can be disallowed if it is beyond all bounds of decency or interferes with business relations, e.g., a department store sales clerk or a nurse in a patient room.)

- Keep union meetings under surveillance for any purpose nor create the impression of surveillance. (However, a supervisor may continue to legally observe activities occurring at or about work during the ordinary course of his activities.)

- Have management or supervisory personnel visit employees in their homes for the purpose of discussing matters relating to union organizational activities.

- During a union organizing campaign, and particularly following the period when a union has demanded recognition by the company or filed a petition with the NLRB, the employer should not institute wage increases or other employee benefits, unless it can be clearly demonstrated that such benefits were within serious contemplation prior to the time the union demanded recognition and that such benefits were instituted in the normal course of business, and not for the purpose of influencing the employees in their choice of a bargaining representative.

"T-I-P-S"

There is an acronym used by all management labor attorneys and union avoidance consultants to help supervisors avoid unfair labor practices during a union organizing campaign. Think of the word "TIPS" when dealing with employees during any organizing activity and it will cover most of the pitfalls a supervisor can run into.

Threaten. Management cannot threaten individuals participating in union activities with reprisals such as reducing employee benefits, firing the employee, or threatening retaliation in any way.

Interrogate. Management cannot interrogate employees as to whether or not they signed any card or whether they are supporting the organization activity, how they intend to vote, or what they think about union representation—or about anyone else's activities. (An employee can voluntarily tell a supervisor anything he or she cares to, however, and the supervisor can discuss union issues with the employee.)

Promise. Management cannot promise wage or benefit increases, promotion, or any other future benefit.

Surveillance. Management cannot "spy" on union activities to determine who is attending union meetings. This applies to both worktime and nonworktime, on and off the company premises. (Observing employee behavior at work is a routine part of the job and is not "spying.")

The definition of unlawful "threats," "interrogation," "promises," and/or "surveillance" is subject to complex rules and decisions. All "circumstances" surrounding the exchange or activity will be considered in making a determination as to whether the employer's conduct was permissible or impermissible. The most innocent question can constitute "interrogation," particularly if it is construed as coercive. The most logical discussion of anticipated changes in wages or benefits can be held to be "promises." What a supervisor intends as a prediction of the result of unionization can be misconstrued as a "threat." The most important thing for employers to remember, however, is that they have a legal right to express opinions and should encourage their supervisors to speak out in favor of the company.

How to stay union-free

Union avoidance can be achieved only through diligence along with attention to the desires and sentiments of employees. Employers should periodically audit their work force to determine whether management's relationship with its employees remains strong or whether problems exist that may make the employees receptive to union organizing. Management must take a very critical look at employment conditions to see whether there are areas that can be improved so that they can blunt any possible chance of a union organizing drive. The following list of factors can be used as a guide to determine whether employment conditions are conducive to union avoidance or union acceptance:

- ◆ Do employees feel ignored? Have they received only a minimum amount of information about the company's business health, its goals and achievements?

- ◆ Have management's rules and policies been consistently enforced?

- ◆ Are employee gripes, complaints, and grievances being discussed and cleared up promptly by management? Is there a grievance procedure in place for dealing with employee complaints?

♦ Have there been recent incidents of discipline or discharge that may have been implemented without a thorough and impartial investigation?

♦ Do employees believe their wages and other benefits are competitive with industry standards?

♦ Are there any unsatisfactory working conditions that might be improved by management? For example, are employees working long hours without sufficient breaks?

♦ Do employees feel stymied with regard to their future opportunities with the company?

♦ Can management be perceived in any manner as having played favorites with respect to promotions and increases in wages?

♦ Are there any employees who have been demoted or for some other reason may be bitter against the company and thus likely to promote the union to other employees?

♦ Have there been increases in employee contribution payments for group insurance or pension benefits?

♦ Have jobs been combined or functions added to various positions so that employees are now doing more work for the same rate of pay?

♦ Have changes in work policies or procedures been introduced without advance notice or explanation to employees?

♦ Are any procedures in place, whether informal or formal, that facilitate the communication of employee sentiments to management?

♦ Are there any supervisors who are using pressure tactics rather than leadership to secure productivity?

♦ Have there been any unkept promises on important issues such as raises, bonuses, extra holidays, increased vacation, or other benefits?

The foregoing factors may be used as a device to gauge an employer's vulnerability to union organizing. In general, employee attitudes toward job security, fair pay, opportunity for advancement, ability to talk to management, fairness by management in administering policies, and pride in the company are the best indicators for gauging union vulnerability.

Summary of union avoidance strategies

While no one can guarantee that a particular company will not become the target of an organizing effort, there are some basic strategies that employers should follow to minimize the likelihood that union representation will be viewed as an attractive option by employees.

Consistency in the application of policies. A frequent tactic used by union organizers to foment employee interest is to cite instances where employment policies were applied in an inconsistent or arbitrary manner. Therefore, it is important that personnel policies and procedures be consistently and uniformly enforced by all supervisory personnel.

Communication. Open and clear lines of communication between management and employees need to exist. An employer's stated "Open Door" policy is meaningless if an employer fails to respond to employee questions and fails to elicit employee input and suggestions. Even if the response to a question or suggestion is "No," the employees are at least kept in the loop.

Because of a lack of communication, employers often fail to comprehend the real reasons behind a union organizing campaign. For example, a desire for increased wages is seldom the reason that employees seek union representation. One way for employers to assess employee concerns is through the use of employee attitude surveys. These surveys reveal employees' sentiment about their jobs, their supervisors, and the company. The surveys allow employers to recognize potential problem areas that could become a source of discontent among employees. By addressing or correcting problems, the employer will demonstrate responsiveness to employees' concerns and can possibly forestall a potential organizing drive.

Finally, employers are often reluctant to communicate to employees their desire for a union-free workplace. That is a mistake. Instead, employers should clearly articulate their beliefs regarding the negative effect that unions have in the workplace. A statement clearly explaining the employer's position on unions should be included in employee handbooks. A copy of a sample handbook statement regarding unions is included in the Appendix on page 274.

Supervisory training. The earlier stages of a union organizing effort are usually conducted covertly. During this time, a union organizer will try to gather support among employees by meeting privately with small groups of employees after work hours or by telephoning individual employees at home. Although unions naturally want to keep their organizing activities secret for as long as possible, supervisory personnel need to be aware of the early signs of union organizing so that pro-active, counter-union steps can be quickly initiated by management. In addition, supervisory personnel need to be familiar with the legal parameters within which they can operate and still avoid unfair labor practice charges and objections filed by disgruntled union organizers.

Policies and Procedures to Keep Your Business Out of Court

Certain policies and procedures are used quite frequently by employers, but these need to be updated and kept current to reflect changes in employment law. This appendix contains samples of some of the more common employment policies as well as disclaimer language for use in handbooks and application forms. Each of the sample policies should be modified to conform to the requirements of local law and/or the particular facts of the employer's business.

Problem Resolution - Complaint Procedure

The Company is committed to providing the best possible working conditions for its employees. Part of this commitment means encouraging an open and frank atmosphere in which any problem, complaint, suggestion, or question will receive a timely response from supervisors and management.

The Company strives to ensure fair and honest treatment of all employees. Supervisors, managers, and employees are expected to treat each other with mutual respect. Employees are encouraged to offer positive and constructive criticism.

If employees disagree with established rules of conduct, policies, or practices, they can express their concern through the problem resolution procedure. No employee will be penalized, for voicing a complaint with Company management in a reasonable and business-like manner, or for using the problem resolution procedure.

If a situation occurs that causes employees to believe that a condition of employment or a decision affecting them is unjust or inequitable, they are encouraged to make use of the following steps. The employee may discontinue the procedure at any step. NOTE: If the complaint involves harassment by an immediate supervisor, the employee may proceed immediately to step 2.

- ♦ **Step 1:** Discuss the problem with your immediate supervisor.

- ♦ **Step 2:** If your supervisor cannot resolve the problem to your satisfaction, you should put your complaint in writing and submit it to the Department Manager. You can stop by the Human Resources office to obtain a complaint form. A Human Resources Specialist can help you prepare your complaint if you desire assistance. The Department Manager will discuss the complaint with you and with your supervisor, if appropriate.

- ♦ **Step 3:** If you are still not satisfied that your problem has been resolved, you may submit it in writing to the Vice President , Operations for final resolution. The Department Manager will prepare a written summation of management's response to the complaint through the first two stages of the process.

Not every problem can be resolved to everyone's total satisfaction, but only through understanding and discussion of mutual problems can employees and management develop confidence in each other. This confidence is important to the operation of an efficient and harmonious work environment, and helps to ensure everyone's job security.

Special procedure: Discharge

Appeals of discharge decisions should be submitted in writing to the Vice President, Human Resources. The Vice President, Human Resources will implement the discharge hearing procedure and arrange a date for the hearing before the Joint Employee-Management Appeals Panel. A copy of the hearing procedures and decision-making rules can be obtained from the Human Resources Department.

∽ ∽

Application Form Disclaimer

I understand that nothing contained in this employment application is intended to create an employment contract between the Company and myself for either employment or the providing of any benefit. No promises of any kind regarding employment with the Company have been made to me. If an employment relationship is established, I understand that my employment will be at-will and that I or the Company have the right to terminate my employment at any time for any reason. Further, I understand that no officer, agent, representative, or employee of the Company has any authority to enter into any agreement for employment for any specified period of time or to make any agreement for specific wages, benefits, or other conditions of employment, unless such agreement is committed to writing and signed by the Chief Executive Officer of the Company. Finally, I understand that any representations made by officers, agents, or employees of the Company during the interview process are only their own personal expectation of the requirements and conditions of employment should I be hired and it is entirely possible that the actual requirements and conditions of employment will be entirely different and contrary to any representations made to me.

_____

Employee Signature

Employee Handbook Acknowledgment

This Employee Handbook is intended as a general guide to the policies, procedures, and benefits of the Company. It is not intended to set forth either expressed or implied contractual obligations of the Company. The Company retains the right to change the provisions of this Handbook as circumstances warrant.

I understand that as an employee, I have the right to terminate employment at any time and for any reason. Likewise, I acknowledge that the Company has the right to terminate my employment at any time and for any reason.

I have read the foregoing information and comprehend its meaning. I acknowledge receipt of the Employee Handbook. I understand that I am responsible for reading and becoming familiar with the contents of the Handbook. I also understand that this acknowledgment will be placed in my personnel file for permanent reference.

_____

Employee Signature

_____

Employee Name (Please Print)

_____

Witness

_____

Date

Nondiscrimination Policy

It is the Company's policy to provide equal employment opportunity to all employees and qualified applicants without regard to race, color, religion, sex, sexual orientation, age, national origin, marital status, Vietnam Era Veterans status, or physical or mental disability, to the extent required by law. This policy applies to all personnel actions, benefits, and terms and conditions of employment including, but not limited to, hiring, placement, training, compensation, transfer, promotion, leave-of-absence, termination, layoff, and recall. It is the Company's policy to prohibit any kind of harassment of co-employees, supervisors, or subordinates because of their race, color, religion, sex, sexual orientation, age, national origin, marital status, Vietnam Era Veterans status, or physical or mental disability, to the extent required by law. Violations of this non-discrimination policy should be brought to the attention of your supervisor or a department manager if your supervisor is the subject of the complaint. Additionally, a violation of this policy may be made the subject of a complaint under the Company's problem-solving procedure.

The Company considers the implementation and monitoring of this policy to be an important part of each supervisor's responsibility. Supervisors will inform all employees of our policy and shall take positive steps in an effort to seek adherence to the policy by all employees within the realm of their responsibility.

The failure of any employee or supervisor to fully comply with this policy will be grounds for disciplinary action up to and including discharge.

Prohibition Against Harassment

The Company expects all employees to work in a manner that respects the feelings of their co-workers. It is the policy of the Company that all employees have the right to work in an environment free from harassment based upon race, sex, sexual orientation, national origin, religion, age, or any physical or mental condition or disability. Any harassment of employees by their co-workers, supervisors, or third parties will not be tolerated.

Unlawful harassment can include physical contact or verbal abuse or kidding which is directed at another individual because of that individual's sex, sexual orientation, race, national origin, religion, age, or disability and which is considered unacceptable or unwelcome by another individual. This includes comments and compliments that extend beyond mere courtesy, jokes that are clearly unwanted or considered offensive, and other comments, innuendo, or action that offends others.

Impermissible sexual harassment includes (1) sexual advances and other verbal or physical conduct where submission to the conduct is made a term or condition of employment or is used as the basis for employment decisions and (2) unwelcome verbal or physical conduct of a sexual nature that unreasonably interferes with an employee's work or creates a hostile or abusive work environment.

An employee who believes that he or she is being harassed in violation of this policy should bring the matter to the attention of his or her supervisor, any other manager, or the Director of Human Resources. There will be no retaliation for bringing a complaint. All complaints and follow-up investigations will be handled in a confidential manner.

Nonaggression Policy

Policy statement

1. It is the policy of the company to insure that the workplace is free from intimidation, belligerence, harassment, aggressive or violent behavior, and other types of antisocial behavior by employees, visitors, or others. Threats, aggressive behavior, verbal abuse, or violence on the part of any employee, visitor, or others will not be tolerated.

2. It is the purpose of this policy to identify those behaviors which are viewed as not acceptable in the workplace and to explain the procedures that will be followed when such behavior or conduct occurs. The listing of unacceptable conduct or behaviors is not intended to be exhaustive.

Employee responsibilities

1. Employees are expected to treat co-employees, supervisors, visitors and others with respect and dignity at all times while on-duty at the company or while present on company property.

2. Employees are to refrain from the use of loud or profane language when dealing with co-employees, supervisors, visitors, and others while on-duty. Employees are not to engage in horseplay with any other individual while present on company property.

3. Employees are not to use aggressive or intimidating behaviors when dealing with other employees, supervisors, visitors, or others. Threats of any kind are prohibited.

Violation of this policy

1. Conduct in violation of this policy is considered a major offense. Any employee who is found to be in violation of the policy will be subject to immediate disciplinary action, up to and including termination.

Employee assistance program

1. The company provides access to an Employee Assistance Program (EAP) for all employees. The initial consultation is at no charge to the employee. Employees who are experiencing difficulties in their personal lives or work-related problems are advised to avail themselves of EAP services.

2. The company reserves the right to mandate referral to EAP for any employee and make satisfactory completion of the EAP service a condition of continued employment at the company.

3. The fact that an employee has sought the services of the EAP, however, does not mean that an employee will not be subject to disciplinary action for violation of this policy.

Complaint procedure

1. Any employee who believes that he/she is being subjected to aggressive or hostile behavior should advise his/her immediate supervisor of the situation. If the immediate supervisor is not available or if it is not practicable to contact the immediate supervisor, the employee should contact the Vice President/Human Resources.

2. Complaints of this nature will be treated with confidentiality and promptly investigated. Based on the results of the investigation, appropriate disciplinary action will be taken, including discharge.

Supervisor responsibilities

1. Each supervisor is expected to monitor his or her work area to ensure conformity with this policy.

2. If situations arise which represent violations of this policy, supervisory personnel are expected to intervene, if reasonable and practicable, to halt any aggressive or hostile behavior and then take necessary and appropriate disciplinary action.

3. No supervisor is expected to put his or her personal safety in jeopardy. If necessary, security personnel should be notified and assistance should be obtained before a supervisor intervenes in any situation which may put the supervisor's safety in jeopardy.

Notification of violation of this policy

1. Any violation of this policy must be immediately reported to Human Resources and Security. If individuals wish to remain anonymous, they may wish to report aggressive conduct on the "hotline" number: 888-555-5555. This number should not be used for an emergency situation, however. If a violation of this policy occurs during the evening or night shift or during the weekend, the manager in charge must be immediately informed.

No weapons provision

1. Weapons of any kind (knives, hunting knives, rifles, guns, etc.) are strictly prohibited everywhere on company property including the inside of any buildings, outside areas adjacent to any building or parking lots where company employees park their vehicles. The fact that an employee may possess a lawful registration to own or to carry a weapon does not modify the express ban on the possession or carrying of all weapons on company property.

Solicitation and Distribution Policy

In an effort to ensure a productive and harmonious work environment, persons not employed by the Company may not solicit or distribute literature in the workplace at any time for any purpose. The Company recognizes that employees may have interests in events and organizations outside the workplace. However, employees may not solicit for any purpose during working time. Employees may not distribute literature for any purpose during working time or in working areas.

"Working time" includes the working time of both the employee doing the solicitation or distribution and the employee to whom it is directed. "Working time" means the period scheduled for the performance of job duties, not including mealtimes or break times or other periods when employees are properly not engaged in performing their work tasks.

∽ ∽

The Company's Position on Unions

It is the Company's position that labor unions are not in the best interest of employees or our Company. We strongly believe that by being honest with each other and working together we can build a mutually successful future. Our experience has shown that when employees deal openly and directly with supervisors, the work environment can be excellent, communications can be clear, and attitudes can be positive. We believe that our managers amply demonstrate their commitment to employees by responding effectively to employee concerns.

No organization is free from occasional problems; but, when difficulties do arise, all of our employees are free to speak out. If employees have concerns about working conditions or compensation, they are strongly encouraged to voice these concerns openly and directly to their supervisors. We also have a very effective complaint procedure which provides an objective review of any dispute.

In an effort to protect and maintain direct employer/employee communications, we will resist organization, within applicable legal limits, and protect the right of employees to speak for themselves. If a union representative asks you to sign a union authorization card, we suggest you use caution and refuse to sign. Instead, contact your supervisor or a Human Resources representative for the true facts about unions. When employees carefully examine the option of union representation, including such issues as regular deductions from paychecks for union dues, union dominance and control at the expense of individual freedoms and strikes, they almost always decide to reject union representation.

Index